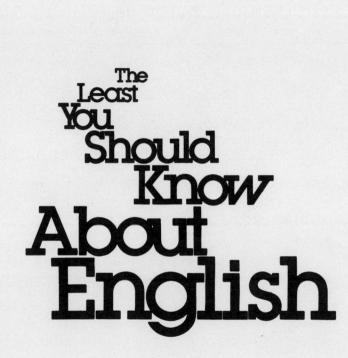

The
Least
You
Should
Know
About
English

FORM A
Second Edition

The Least You Should Know About English

Basic Writing Skills

TERESA FERSTER GLAZIER
Western Illinois University

HOLT, RINEHART AND WINSTON

New York   Chicago   San Francisco   Philadelphia
Montreal   Toronto   London   Sydney
Tokyo   Mexico City   Rio de Janeiro   Madrid

This text is available in Form A, Second Edition; Form B; and Form C so that a different form may be used in various semesters. The three forms are essentially the same except that they have different exercises and writing assignments.

Library of Congress Cataloging in Publication Data

Glazier, Teresa Ferster.
   The least you should know about English.
    1. English language—Rhetoric.   2. English language—
Grammar—1950–   . I. Title.
PE1408.G5592   1982   808'.042   81–4239
                                          AACR2

ISBN 0–03–059781–1

CBS COLLEGE PUBLISHING
Holt, Rinehart and Winston
The Dryden Press
Saunders College Publishing

To the Instructor

This book is for students who have resisted the rules of English composition for twelve years and who may profit from a simplified approach. The main features of the book are these:

1. It's truly basic. Only the indisputable essentials of spelling, grammar, sentence structure, and punctuation are included because research has shown that putting too much emphasis on mechanics is not the way to help students learn to write.
2. It stresses writing. Although at first glance it may appear to be merely a workbook, writing is emphasized. Besides doing the exercises, the students are asked to write their own sentences to practice the rules. And the small but important section beginning on page 186 presents simple writing assignments progressing from free writing and personal writing to persuasive writing with a thesis, summary writing, and finally the letter of application. Ideally, some writing is done in preparation for each class period—original sentences, a complete thesis statement, a rough draft, a final draft, or a revision. Students learn to write by writing.
3. It uses little linguistic terminology. A conjunction is a connecting word; gerunds and present participles are *ing* words; a parenthetical constituent is an interrupter. Students work with words they know instead of learning a vocabulary they'll never use again.
4. It has abundant practice sentences as well as a number of practice paragraphs—enough so that students learn to use the rules automatically.
5. It includes thematically related, informative sentences about astronomy, architecture, botany, current events, geography, space, zoology . . . thus making the task of doing the exercises at least somewhat interesting.
6. It provides perforated answer sheets at the back of the book so that the students can correct their own work, thus teaching themselves as they go.
7. It takes modern usage into account. Accepted forms (as reported by Robert G. Pooley in *The Teaching of English Usage*) such as *It is me* and *Everybody . . . they* are recognized.
8. It includes four essays for improving the students' reading through

learning to spot main ideas and their writing through learning to write concise summaries.

9. It provides for the instructor a packet of 28 ditto master tests (two for each section) *ready to run*. These tests are free upon adoption of the text and may be obtained through the local Holt representative or by writing to the English Editor, Holt, Rinehart and Winston, 383 Madison Avenue, New York, NY 10017.

Along with the ditto master tests, a daily test is valuable. A single sentence (such as *They're going there with their son* for the "Words Often Confused" chapter) dictated at the beginning of each class hour and corrected on the spot will provide an incentive for doing each day's exercises.

Students who have heretofore been overwhelmed and discouraged by the complexities of English should, through mastering simple rules and through writing and rewriting simple compositions, gain enough competence and confidence to cope with a regular composition course.

T.F.G.

Macomb, Illinois

Contents

WHAT IS THE LEAST YOU SHOULD KNOW?

3. PUNCTUATION AND CAPITAL LETTERS

4. WRITING

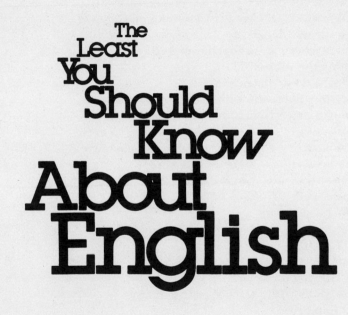

The
Least
You
Should
Know
About
English

**What Is
the Least
You Should
Know?**

What **Is** the Least You Should Know?

Most English workbooks try to teach you as much as they can. This one will teach you the least it can—and still help you get by in college English courses. You won't have to bother with predicate nouns and subordinating conjunctions and participial phrases and demonstrative pronouns and all those terms you've been hearing about for years. You can get along without them if you will learn thoroughly a few basic rules. You *do* have to know how to spell common words; you *do* have to recognize subjects and verbs to avoid writing fragments and run-together sentences; you *do* have to know a few rules of punctuation—but rules will be kept to a minimum.

Unless you know these few rules, though, you will have difficulty communicating in writing. Take this sentence for example:

Let's eat grandfather before we go.

We assume the writer isn't a cannibal but merely failed to capitalize and put commas around the name of a person spoken to. If the sentence had read

Let's eat, Grandfather, before we go.

then no one would misunderstand. Or take this sentence:

The instructor flunked Mac and Chris and Ken passed.

Did Chris flunk or pass? There's no way of knowing unless the writer puts a comma either after *Mac* or after *Chris*. If the sentence reads

The instructor flunked Mac and Chris, and Ken passed.

we know Chris flunked, but if the sentence reads

The instructor flunked Mac, and Chris and Ken passed.

then we know Chris passed. What you will learn in this course is simply to make your writing so clear that no one will misunderstand it.

The English you'll learn to write in this course is called Standard English, and it may differ slightly from the English spoken in your community. All over the country, various dialects of English are spoken. In northern New England, for example, people leave the *r* off certain words and put an *r* on others. President Kennedy said *dollah* for *dollar*, *idear* for *idea*, and *Cubar* for *Cuba*. In black communities many people leave the *s* off some verbs and put an *s* on others, saying *he walk* and *they walks* instead of *he walks* and *they walk*.

But no matter what English dialect people *speak*, they all must write the same dialect—Standard English. You can say, "Whacha doin? Cmon," and everybody will understand, but you can't write that way. If you want your readers to understand what you write without having to decipher it like a foreign language, you will have to write the way English-speaking people all over the world write—in Standard English. Being able to write Standard English is essential in college, and it probably will be an asset in your career.

It is important to learn every rule in this book as you come to it because many rules depend on the ones before. For example, unless you learn to pick out subjects and verbs, you'll have trouble with run-together sentences, with fragments, with subject-verb agreement, and with punctuation. The rules are brief and clear, and it should not be difficult to master all of them . . . *if you want to*. But you do have to want to!

Here is the way to master the least you should know:

1. Study the explanation carefully.
2. Do the first exercise (ten sentences). Then tear out the perforated answer sheet at the back of the book and correct your answers from it. If you miss even one answer, study the explanatory page again to find out why.
3. Do the second exercise and correct it. If you miss a single answer, go back once more and study the explanatory page. You must have missed something. Be tough on yourself. Don't just think, "Maybe I'll hit it right next time." Go back and master the rules, and *then* try the next exercise. It is important to correct each group of ten sentences before going on. That way you'll discover your mistakes while you still have sentences to practice on.
4. You may be tempted to quit when you get several exercises perfect, but don't do it. Make yourself finish every exercise. It's not enough to *understand* a rule; you have to practice it. Just as understanding the strokes in swimming won't help unless you actually get into the pool and swim, so understanding a rule about writing isn't going to help unless you practice using it until it becomes automatic.

But rules and exercises are not the most important part of this book. The most important part begins on page 186—when you begin to write. The writing assignments, grouped together for convenience, are to be used along with the exercises. We all have ideas we'd like to express, and the writing assignments will help you get started. You learn to write by writing, and the more you write, the better your writing will be.

Mastering these essentials will take time. Generally, college students are expected to spend two hours outside of class for each hour in class. You may need more. Undoubtedly, the more time you spend, the more your writing will improve.

At the end of a semester, when one class was asked how the course could be improved, the almost unanimous recommendation was, "Tell the students the first day that the course isn't a breeze. The stuff looks simple, but it's not. You have to work. If you slide through the first weeks, you're sunk. But if you do all the exercises and write all the papers, you'll learn a lot."

Spelling

1   Spelling

Anyone can learn to spell. You can get rid of most of your spelling errors by the time you finish this book if you want to. It's just a matter of deciding you're going to do it. If you really intend to learn to spell, master seven parts of this section. They are

YOUR OWN LIST OF MISSPELLED WORDS
WORDS OFTEN CONFUSED
CONTRACTIONS
POSSESSIVES
WORDS THAT CAN BE BROKEN INTO PARTS
RULE FOR DOUBLING A FINAL CONSONANT
A LIST OF FREQUENTLY MISSPELLED WORDS

Master these seven parts, and you'll be a good speller.

YOUR OWN LIST OF MISSPELLED WORDS

On the inside back cover of this book write correctly every misspelled word in the papers handed back to you. Review them until you are sure of them. That will take care of most of your errors.

WORDS OFTEN CONFUSED

a, an

Use *an* before a word that begins with a vowel sound (*a, e, i, o,* and *u* when the sound is *uh*).

> an orange, an essay, an heir (silent *h*), an honest man (silent *h*), an umbrella, an umpire, an uncle, an ulcer (all the *u*'s sound like *uh*).

Use *a* before a word that begins with a consonant sound (all the sounds except the vowels) plus *u* or *eu* when the sound is *yu*.

> a pencil, a hotel, a history book, a university, a uniform, a union, a unit (all the *u*'s sound like *yu*), a European trip (*Eu* sounds like *yu*).

accept, except

Accept is a verb and means "to receive willingly." (Verbs are explained on p. 50.)
Except means "excluding" or "but."

> I *accept* your gift (receive it willingly).
> Everyone came *except* him (but him).

One way to distinguish between *accept* and *except* and between *affect* and *effect* (below) is to remember that the ones that begin with *a* (*accept* and *affect*) are always verbs. (*Effect* may occasionally be a verb meaning "to bring about," but it isn't used in these exercises.)

advice, advise

Advise is a verb. Use *advice* when it's not a verb. Pronounce these words correctly, remembering that the *s* sounds like *z*, and you won't confuse them.

> I *advise* you to go.
> I don't need any *advice*.

affect, effect

Affect is a verb and means "to influence." *Effect* means "result." If *a, an,* or *the* is in front of the word, then you'll know it isn't a verb and will use *effect*.

> The lack of rain *affected* the crops.
> The lack of rain had an *effect* on the crops.

all ready, already

If you can leave out the *all* and the sentence still makes sense, then *all ready* is the form to use. (In that form, *all* is a separate word and could be left out.)

> I'm all ready to go. (*I'm ready to go* makes sense.)
> Dinner is all ready. (*Dinner is ready* makes sense.)

But if you can't leave out the *all* and still have the sentence make sense, then use *already* (the form in which the *al* has to stay in the word).

> I'm already late. (*I'm ready late* wouldn't make sense.)

are, or, our	*Are* is a verb. *Or* is used between two possibilities, as in "tea *or* coffee." *Our* shows we possess something. We *are* studying English. Take it *or* leave it. *Our* class meets at eight.
brake, break	*Brake* means "to slow or stop motion." It's also the name of the device that slows or stops motion. *Break* means "to shatter" or "to split." It's also the name of an interruption, as "a coffee break." You *brake* to avoid an accident. You slam on your *brakes*. You *break* a dish or an engagement or a track record. You enjoy your Thanksgiving *break*.
choose, chose	I will *choose* a partner right now. I *chose* a partner yesterday.
clothes, cloths	Her *clothes* were attractive. We used soft *cloths* to polish the car.
coarse, course	*Coarse* describes texture, as *coarse* cloth. *Course* is used for all other meanings. Remember this sentence: Of *course you* are taking this *course*. Find the three *u*'s in that sentence and then remember that those words are always spelled with *u*. Her suit was made of *coarse* material. Of *course* I enjoyed that *course*.
complement, compliment	A *complement* completes something. *Compliment* means "praise." Remember "*I* like compliments," and you will remember to use the *i* spelling. A 30-degree angle is the *complement* of a 60-degree angle. She gave him a *compliment*.
conscience, conscious	The extra *n* in *conscience* should remind you of NO, which is what your conscience often says to you. The other word *conscious* simply means "aware." My *conscience* bothers me because I didn't vote. I was not *conscious* that it was raining.
desert, dessert	*Dessert* is the sweet one, the one you like two helpings of. So give it two helpings of *s*. The other one, *desert*, is used for all other meanings. We had apple pie for *dessert*. Don't *desert* me. The camel moved slowly across the *desert*.

pre - post

do, due	You *do* something. But a payment or an assignment is *due*; it is scheduled for a certain time.
	   I *do* the best I can.
	   My paper is *due* tomorrow.

does, dose	*Does* is a verb. A *dose* is an amount of medicine.
	   He *does* his work well.
	   She *doesn't* care about cars.
	   He took a *dose* of medicine.

forth, fourth	The number *fourth* has *four* in it, but note that *forty* does not. Remember the word *forty-fourth*. When you don't mean a number, use *forth*.
	   This is our *fourth* game.
	   That was our *forty-fourth* point.
	   She walked back and *forth*.

have, of	*Have* is a verb. When you say *could have*, the *have* sounds like *of*, but it must not be written that way. Always write *could have, would have, should have, might have*. Use *of* only in a prepositional phrase (see p. 56).
	   I should *have* finished my work sooner.
	   Then I could *have* gone home.
	   I often think *of* him.

hear, here	The last three letters of *hear* spell "ear." You *hear* with your ear. The other spelling *here* tells "where." Note that the three words that indicate a place or point out something all have *here* in them: *here, there, where*.
	   I can't *hear* you.
	   Where are you? I'm right *here*.

it's, its	*It's* is a contraction and always means "it is" or "it has." *Its* is a possessive pronoun. (Possessive pronouns such as *its, yours, hers, ours, theirs* are already possessive and never take apostrophes. See p. 28.)
	   It's too late now. (It is too late now.)
	   It's been a long time. (It has been a long time.)
	   The committee gave *its* report.

knew, new	*Knew* has to do with knowing (both start with *k*). *New* means "not old." I *knew* that I wanted a *new* job.
know, no	*Know* has to do with knowing (both start with *k*). *No* means "not any." I *know* she has *no* money left.

EXERCISES

Underline the correct word, referring to the explanatory pages if necessary. When you've finished ten sentences, tear out the perforated answer sheet at the back of the book and correct your answers. Correct each group of ten sentences before continuing so that you'll catch your mistakes while you still have sentences to practice on.

☐ EXERCISE 1

1. We're looking for a (knew new) house and (all ready already) have seen several we like.
2. The house (doesn't dosen't) have to be large so long as (it's its) in a good location.
3. I (know no) the initial (affect effect) of a house is important.
4. We told the realtor we trust her (advice advise), and she liked the (complement compliment).
5. We're not looking anywhere (accept except) in this area, for we like it (hear here).
6. We intend to (choose chose) a house not far from where we (are our) living now.
7. Of (coarse course) we (know no) there may be problems.
8. We're (conscience conscious) that (are our) old house may not sell quickly.
9. That might (affect effect) our ability to raise (a an) adequate down payment.
10. Perhaps we should (have of) sold the old house first (are or) at least tried to.

☐ EXERCISE 2

1. I'm writing (a an) economics paper that's (do due) Monday.
2. I (choose chose) a subject that I (know no) something about.
3. (It's Its) the (affect effect) of property tax on the schools.
4. I (know no) I should (have of) finished the paper yesterday.
5. But at least (it's its) (all ready already) to type now.
6. Our instructor (does dose) not (accept except) late papers.
7. But of (coarse course) I have (a an) entire weekend to type it.
8. I think (it's its) going to have a good (affect effect) on my grade.
9. (Are Our) grades (are our) a combination of the paper and the final exam.
10. I (hear here) the final (doesn't dosen't) count as much as the paper.

□EXERCISE 3

1. I put on my work (clothes cloths) and went out to spend (a an) after-noon in the garden.
2. (Hear Here) I am with a big garden and no one to (advice advise) me about it.
3. I'm (conscience conscious) that I (know no) little about gardening.
4. I want a pleasing (affect effect) without putting (forth fourth) too much effort.
5. There's (all ready already) a nice background of bushes, but I must (choose chose) what flowers to plant.
6. I don't (know no) whether (it's its) better to plant annuals (are or) perennials.
7. Of (coarse course) I (know no) perennials take less work in the long run.
8. Since I've had (know no) experience, I need (advice advise).
9. I should (have of) realized (it's its) going to be a big job.
10. And I should get (a an) estimate of what it will cost.

□EXERCISE 4

1. (Hear Here) (are our) the plans we've made for (are our) vacation.
2. We want to see some (knew new) country and are heading for the (desert dessert) in Arizona.
3. I (know no) (it's its) better to explore it in the winter.
4. But we had (know no) time then, and we (do due) have time now.
5. We've (all ready already) planned (are our) route.
6. We decided to (accept except) the (advice advise) of a friend who's been there.
7. He suggested we take (a an) hour's (brake break) in the middle of each day to rest.
8. We (choose chose) a route that will take us to the Grand Canyon the (forth fourth) day of our trip.
9. Of (coarse course) we'll spend time there to get the full (affect effect) of (it's its) grandeur.
10. I (know no) (it's its) going to be (a an) exceptionally good trip.

□EXERCISE 5

1. She's taking a (coarse course) in tailoring and makes a lot of (clothes cloths).
2. I (know no) she gets lots of (complements compliments) on her work.

3. She (doesn't dosen't) (choose chose) any but the best fabrics.
4. She's (conscience conscious) that (it's its) quality that counts.
5. (Knew New) styles (or our) fabrics always interest her.
6. She's (all ready already) finished (a an) entire wardrobe for herself.
7. This is the (forth fourth) season she's been designing (clothes cloths).
8. All of her friends (are our) asking her to (do due) sewing for them.
9. I (hear here) she has more requests than (it's its) possible for her to (accept except).
10. She should (have of) taken the (advice advise) of her instructor and made a career of designing.

☐EXERCISE 6

1. What (are our) you going to (choose chose) for (desert dessert)?
2. I'd (advice advise) you to (choose chose) fruit (are or) something light.
3. I (know no) (it's its) hard to refuse cake (are or) pie.
4. I took a (coarse course) in nutrition (hear here) at the college.
5. Now I'm (conscience conscious) of the (affect effect) of good nutrition.
6. Of (coarse course) your (conscience conscious) must be your guide.
7. Everyone's going to (accept except) our invitation (accept except) Cleo.
8. Most of them have (all ready already) phoned us.
9. I (knew new) it was good to plan a party for the semester (brake break).
10. (A An) end-of-the-semester party (does dose) have advantages.

☐EXERCISE 7

1. (It's Its) hot in (hear here) (all ready already) this morning.
2. Of (coarse course) we should (have of) left the windows open last night.
3. I (knew new) this morning that I should wear my coolest (clothes cloths).
4. But (know no) matter how I dress, I (know no) I'll be hot.
5. I (hear here) we won't get a (brake break) from the heat wave for a week.
6. It (doesn't dosen't) (do due) any good to talk about it though.
7. One thing we can't (choose chose) is (are our) weather.
8. We have to (accept except) what comes.
9. The best (advice advise) is not to dwell upon it, and it won't have such (a an) (affect effect).
10. But naturally one is (conscience conscious) of it all the time.

☐EXERCISE 8

1. I'm taking (a an) honors (coarse course) and hope to get (a an) university degree.

2. (It's Its) my (forth fourth) year in college, and I'm (all ready already) looking forward to next year.
3. Would you (advice advise) me to (accept except) that position?
4. Your (advice advise) will have an (affect effect) on my decision.
5. The Sahara is the largest (desert dessert) in the world.
6. That (does dose) of bitter medicine had a good (affect effect).
7. She wasn't (conscience conscious) that he was giving her a (complement compliment).
8. They should (have of) let her (choose chose) her own (clothes cloths).
9. I (know no) you'll like it (hear here) in (are our) community.
10. (A An) occasional holiday (does dose) (brake break) the monotony.

□EXERCISE 9
1. We should (have of) won that (forth fourth) game.
2. The coach walked back and (forth fourth) trying to (choose chose) the best strategy.
3. The meal began with (a an) appetizer and ended with (desert dessert).
4. He should (have of) heeded his (conscience conscious).
5. (It's Its) difficult to (brake break) an old habit.
6. My father's (advice advise) had (know no) (affect effect) on me.
7. Of (coarse course) I had (all ready already) made up my mind.
8. The report for my psychology (coarse course) is (do due) tomorrow.
9. (Doesn't Dosen't) he ever give you a (complement compliment)?
10. They (are our) going to (accept except) (are our) offer.

□EXERCISE 10
1. I wasn't (conscience conscious) that it was time for (are our) coffee (brake break).
2. He refused to (accept except) any (advice advise).
3. A shack covered with (coarse course) palm leaves stood on the (desert dessert).
4. The team should (have of) been ready (a an) hour ago.
5. They're (all ready already) now, however, for (a an) exciting game.
6. She got many (complements compliments) on her (knew new) clothes.
7. He (choose chose) to (desert dessert) his post that summer.
8. (It's Its) hard to think of (a an) answer to such a question.
9. I (knew new) the gloomy house had an (affect effect) on his mood.
10. I (know no) I have (all ready already) wasted too much time.

WRITING YOUR OWN SENTENCES
Writing your own sentences is the best way to master the words you've been studying. On a separate sheet write five sentences using some of the words you may formerly have had trouble with.

Or you may wish to start a journal with your five sentences, adding each day the sentences you are asked to write at the end of each chapter. If you write about things that interest you, then you'll be inclined to reread your journal occasionally and review the rules you have learned.

WRITING ASSIGNMENT
Turn to page 186 for your writing assignment.

WORDS OFTEN CONFUSED (continued)

Here are more words that are often confused. Study them carefully, with their examples, before attempting the exercises. When you've mastered all 39 of the word groups in these two sections, you'll have taken care of many of your spelling problems.

lead, led	The past form is *led*. The present form is *lead*, which rhymes with *bead*. (Don't confuse it with the metal *lead*, which rhymes with *dead*.)
	I will *lead* the parade today.
	I *led* the parade yesterday.

not tight

loose, lose

Loose means "not tight." Note how *l o o s e* that word is. It has plenty of room for two *o*'s. The other one, *lose*, has room for only one *o*. Use it for all other meanings.
    My shoestring is *loose*.
    They are going to *lose* that game.
    Don't *lose* your cool.

right wrong

moral, morale

Moral has to do with right and wrong; *morale* means the spirit of a group or an individual. Pronounce them correctly, and you won't confuse them—*móral, moréle.*
    It was a *moral* question.
    The *morale* of the team was excellent.

passed, past

Passed is a verb. Use *past* when it's not a verb.
    He *passed* the house.
    He walked *past* the house. (It's the same as *He walked by the house*, so you know it isn't a verb.)
    He is living in the *past*.
    He was going on his *past* reputation.

# of something

peace, piece

Remember "piece of pie." The one meaning "a *piece* of something" always begins with *pie*. The other one, *peace*, is the opposite of war.
    I gave him a *piece* of my mind.
    They signed the *peace* treaty.

personal, personnel

people

Pronounce these two correctly, and you won't confuse them—*pérsonal, personnél. Personnel* means a group of workers.
    He had a *personal* interest in the election.
    She was in charge of *personnel* in the factory.

principal, *main*
principle *rule*

Principal means "main." Both words have *a* in them:
> princip**a**l
> m**a**in

The *principal* of the school spoke. (main teacher)
The *principal* difficulty is time. (main difficulty)
He lost both *principal* and interest. (main amount of money)
A *principle* is a "rule." Both words end in *le*:
> princip**le**
> ru**le**

He lived by his *principles*. (rules)
I object to the *principle* of the thing. (rule)

quiet, quite

Pronounce these two correctly, and you won't misspell them. *Quiet* rhymes with *diet*. *Quite* rhymes with *bite*.
Be *quiet*.
The book is *quite* interesting.

right, write

Right means "correct" or "proper." *Write* is what you do with a pen.
I got ten answers *right*.
It's not *right* to waste natural resources.
I'm going to *write* my paper now.

compare

than, then

Than compares two things. *Then* tells when (*then* and *when* rhyme, and both have *e* in them).
I'd rather have this *than* that.
The movie was better *than* I had expected.
Then he started home.

possessive *points out something*

their, there, they're

they are

Their is a possessive pronoun. *There* points out something and is spelled like *here*. (Remember the three words indicating a place or pointing out something all have *here* in them: *here, there, where*.) *They're* is a contraction and always means "they are."
Their house is painted pink.
There is where I left it.
There are several choices.
There were clouds in the sky.
They're planning to come. (They are planning . . . .)

threw, through   *Threw* means "to throw something" in past time. If you don't mean "to throw something," use *through*.
He *threw* the ball. I *threw* away my chance.
I walked *through* the door.
He *threw* the ball *through* the window.

[handwritten: to throw]

to, too, two   *Two* is a number. *Too* means "more than enough" or "also." Use *to* for all other meanings.
I have *two* brothers.
The lesson was *too* difficult and *too* long. (more than enough)
I found it boring *too*. (also)
It was *too* much for *two* people *to* eat.

[handwritten: also]

weather, whether   *Weather* refers to atmospheric conditions. *Whether* means "if."
This *weather* is too hot for me.
I don't know *whether* I'll go.
Whether I'll go depends on the *weather*.

[handwritten: if]

were, where   *Were* is a verb. *Where* refers to a place. (Remember the three words indicating a place or pointing out something all have *here* in them: *here, there, where*.)
Were you the winner?
Where is he? There he is.
Where are you? Here I am.

[handwritten: place]

who's, whose   *Who's* is a contraction and always means "who is" or "who has." *Whose* is a possessive pronoun. (Possessive pronouns such as *whose, its, yours, hers, ours, theirs* are already possessive and never take apostrophes. See p. 28.)
Who's there? (Who is there?)
Who's been using my tennis racket? (Who has been . . . .)
Whose book is this?

[handwritten: who is   possessive]

woman, women   Remember that the word is just *man* or *men* with *wo* in front of it.
wo man . . . woman . . . one woman
wo men . . . women . . . two women

[handwritten: plural]

you're, your   *You're* is a contraction and always means "you are." *Your* is a possessive pronoun.
You're very welcome. (You are very welcome.)
Your toast is ready.

[handwritten: you are   possessive]

EXERCISES

Underline the correct word. When you've finished ten sentences, tear out
the answer sheet at the back of the book and correct your answers. WATCH
OUT! Don't do more than ten sentences at a time, or you won't be teaching
yourself while you still have sentences to practice on.

☐ EXERCISE 1

1. That (peace piece) of pie is (quiet quite) small.
2. I should (have of) ordered more (than then) that.
3. (You're Your) not ready for (desert dessert), are you?
4. (Hear Here) is the menu for you to (choose chose) from.
5. I (know no) you don't need my (advice advise).
6. Of (coarse course) it (doesn't dosen't) matter what you order.
7. (It's Its) bound to have (to too) many calories.
8. Why not (brake break) (you're your) diet rules for once?
9. (Who's Whose) that (woman women) at the next table?
10. I think I (knew new) her sometime in the (passed past).

☐ EXERCISE 2

1. (Were Where) are those notes I (threw through) away?
2. I'm at (loose lose) ends and about ready to (loose lose) my mind.
3. (It's Its) (all ready already) past midnight.
4. I (knew new) I shouldn't have waited (quiet quite) so late to finish my
   paper.
5. I (know no) I've got to (right write) my final draft before morning.
6. It will be my (forth fourth) draft, and (it's its) got to be good.
7. (It's Its) true that rewriting (does dose) improve a paper.
8. My (principal principle) worry is that I'll have (to too) many misspelled
   words.
9. I should (have of) worked harder on spelling in the (passed past).
10. This (coarse course) is having a good (affect effect) on my writing.

☐ EXERCISE 3

1. (Their There They're) expecting a larger crowd (than then) last year.
2. This (weather whether) is (to too two) cold (to too two) suit me.
3. He walked (passed past) the garden, which was (all ready already) in
   bloom.
4. If (you're your) (threw through) with that book, I'd like to see it.
5. (Were Where) did those (woman women) go?

6. (Who's Whose) going to (right write) to the company?
7. I wonder (weather whether) they lost both the (principal principle) and the interest on their investment.
8. When the children are (quiet quite), I get a little (peace piece).
9. It was his (personal personnel) opinion rather (than then) that of the company.
10. I (knew new) he wouldn't (loose lose) his confidence.

EXERCISE 4
1. (You're Your) never (quiet quite) unless (you're your) asleep.
2. His (personal personnel) life (doesn't dosen't) concern me.
3. (You're Your) apt to (loose lose) your chance if you don't (right write) to them immediately.
4. The captain (lead led) the team to (it's its) victory.
5. He gave me (a an) inquiring glance as he (passed past) by.
6. She has high (moral morale) (principals principles).
7. (Were Where) did you (loose lose) your keys?
8. I wonder (weather whether) the (peace piece) between those countries will last.
9. The (woman women) on the platform was speaking about (Woman's Women's) Rights.
10. (Who's Whose) more worthy (than then) he is?

EXERCISE 5
1. I don't (know no) (quiet quite) what to think of his (advice advise).
2. The dog (lead led) (it's its) puppies out of the kennel.
3. A (peace piece) of (loose lose) gravel hit the windshield.
4. (You're Your) not (all ready already) to go, are you?
5. With a (loose lose) scarf tied around her head, she (lead led) the way.
6. (You're Your) (conscience conscious) will give you good (advice advise).
7. The (personal personnel) are encouraged to invest (their there they're) money in the firm.
8. The (principal principle) of the school (passed past) him in the hall.
9. The lecture was (quiet quite) interesting but much (to too two) long (to too two) suit me.
10. She gave me a (peace piece) of paper to (right write) on.

EXERCISE 6
1. Yesterday he (lead led) the protesters to the courthouse and (than then) back again.

2. Today he will (lead led) them on (their there they're) second march.
3. He gave me a (peace piece) of (advice advise).
4. I'm (threw through) with my assignment before (it's its) (do due).
5. (Who's Whose) name did you check on (you're your) ballot?
6. The (knew new) ruling has had (a an) (affect effect) on the (personal personnel) in that office.
7. The (moral morale) of the team is higher (than then) before.
8. (Does Dose) the coach think (their there they're) ready to play?
9. (Their There They're) is no time to waste if (their there they're) going to make the plane.
10. Which (peace piece) of cloth do you like—the (coarse course) one or the fine one?

□ EXERCISE 7

1. I wonder (weather whether) the (weather whether) kept him from going.
2. (Were Where) is (you're your) umbrella?
3. I think (their there they're) plans are better (than then) ours.
4. If I have a choice, I (choose chose) steak rather (than then) fish.
5. (Who's Whose) (advice advise) are you going to follow?
6. My (principal principle) objection to the speech was that it was (to too two) wordy.
7. He (threw through) the ball to the (right write) of the batter.
8. The (woman women) were hoping they could get the bill (passed past).
9. (Were Where) do you (right write) to get the information?
10. I suppose (you're your) (to too two) busy to come with me.

□ EXERCISE 8

1. The rhinoceros is threatened by extinction unless the (advice advise) of the authorities is followed.
2. Poachers kill the rhino just to get (it's its) horn, which sells for more (than then) silver.
3. (Were Where) (does dose) one find word derivations?
4. Derivations (are our) in square brackets before or after the definition in (you're your) dictionary.
5. (Right Write) me a postcard if (you're your) not (to too two) busy.
6. We're (all ready already) for our (desert dessert).
7. (Their There They're) planning to add to the (personal personnel) of the company.
8. I don't (know no) (weather whether) I (passed past) that (coarse course).
9. (Who's Whose) (principals principles) are you going to live by?
10. It (does dose) not matter if the sails are a little (loose lose).

☐ **EXERCISE 9**
1. (Their There They're) were (to too two) many people at (their there they're) party.
2. The (affect effect) of his (advice advise) was greater (than then) he expected.
3. You can never be (quiet quite) sure of the (weather whether) here.
4. I was (to too two) tired (to too two) listen to the lecture.
5. The (moral morale) of the (personal personnel) in that firm is high.
6. (Were Where) did you find that (peace piece) of cake?
7. I was (quiet quite) sure (their there they're) was none left.
8. (You're Your) (right write) that (it's its) time to go.
9. His (principal principle) concern (does dose) seem to be her happiness.
10. Do you (know no) that (woman women) who is waving to you?

☐ **EXERCISE 10**
1. (Who's Whose) going to (right write) that letter?
2. First we walked (passed past) the dam; (than then) we circled the lake.
3. It (does dose) not matter (weather whether) (you're your) on time.
4. (It's Its) not (to too two) clear (who's whose) to blame.
5. My (principal principle) difficulty (does dose) seem to be spelling.
6. Since taking this (coarse course), I spell better (than then) before.
7. I'm (quiet quite) sure (their there they're) coming tomorrow.
8. But I'm not sure (weather whether) it'll be morning (or our) afternoon.
9. They bought a (knew new) car for (their there they're) trip.
10. I'm (threw through) with this section now and (know no) all the words.

WRITING YOUR OWN SENTENCES
On a separate sheet, or in your journal, write five sentences using words you may formerly have had trouble with.

WRITING ASSIGNMENT
From now on you will be expected to continue with the writing assignments (which begin on p. 186) along with doing the exercises.

CONTRACTIONS

Two words condensed into one are called a contraction.

is not	isn't
you have	you've

The letter or letters that are left out are replaced with an apostrophe. For example, if the two words *do not* are condensed into one, an apostrophe is put where the *o* is left out.

do not	don't

Note how the apostrophe goes in the exact place where the letter or letters are left out in these contractions:

I am	I'm
I have	I've
I shall, I will	I'll
I would	I'd
you are	you're
you have	you've
you will	you'll
she is, she has	she's
he is, he has	he's
it is, it has	it's
we are	we're
we have	we've
we will, we shall	we'll
they are	they're
they have	they've
are not	aren't
cannot	can't
do not	don't
have not	haven't
let us	let's
who is, who has	who's
where is	where's

One contraction does not follow this rule:

will not	won't

In all other contractions that you're likely to use, the apostrophe goes exactly where the letters have been left out. Note especially *it's, they're, who's,* and *you're.* Use them when you mean two words. See page 28 for the possessive forms—*its, their, whose,* and *your*—which don't take apostrophes.

EXERCISES

Put an apostrophe in each contraction where a letter or letters have been left out. When you finish ten sentences, tear out the perforated answer sheet at the back of the book and correct your answers. Be sure to correct each group of ten sentences before going on so you'll catch your mistakes while you still have sentences to practice on.

☐ EXERCISE 1

1. I'm not sure why I didn't learn these rules earlier.
2. If I'd learned them in grade school, I'd be better off now.
3. I'm sorry I didn't at least learn them in high school.
4. I wish I'd mastered them when I didn't have so much else to do.
5. But since I didn't, I've got a big job ahead of me.
6. Its a demanding task, but it's not impossible.
7. It's important to learn Standard English now, or I'll have trouble later.
8. Anyone who can't write acceptably isn't going to make it in college.
9. One can't expect professors to correct errors in basics, for they've more to do than that.
10. But if I spend enough time, I'm sure I'll make up for what I've missed.

☐ EXERCISE 2

1. I'm probably going to lose the part-time job I've had for a month.
2. If a firm isn't getting business, naturally it's going to lay off workers.
3. In the firm where I've been working, there's a threat of layoffs.
4. The management hasn't made any statement, but we've heard rumors.
5. Of course anyone who's been hired recently can't expect to stay.
6. It's only fair that someone who's been with the firm a long time should stay.
7. Since I'm one who's been hired recently, I'll be the first to go.
8. I'm already looking for another job, but they're hard to find.
9. In fact I've decided there's not much use in continuing to look.
10. I've been thinking that spending all my time on my studies wouldn't be a bad idea.

☐ EXERCISE 3

1. I can't figure out why I didn't hear the alarm.
2. You'd be tired too if youd studied as late as I did.
3. I've been working hard but still haven't finished.
4. Don't you think it's time we took a break?
5. Let's listen to the news and see whats happening.
6. I'm doing more reading now, and I find that it's helping my writing.

7. I'd never before realized that it's important to read widely.
8. Just by reading I've improved my vocabulary.
9. And it's amazing that reading has had its effect on my spelling too.
10. I've found that reading can do a lot for me that TV can't.

□ EXERCISE 4

1. Didn't you know that she's running for representative in this district?
2. She's a friend of labor, and she's had lots of experience in government.
3. You've heard, of course, that she's against the gun lobby.
4. I couldn't have worked harder for that candidate if I'd been paid.
5. Of course she's expecting to win. Don't you think she will?
6. That referendum doesn't have enough support and isn't likely to pass.
7. I won't vote for it, and many of my friends don't intend to.
8. You're planning to vote, aren't you?
9. That's too bad that your brother isn't going to vote.
10. It's important for everyone to vote if were to have a government by the people.

□ EXERCISE 5

1. I've been reading about the data *Voyager I* sent back to Earth in 1980.
2. Scientists didn't know much about Saturn before, but they've learned a lot.
3. For example, they'd always thought Saturn had six rings, and now they've learned there are about 1,000.
4. They'd never before been able to get a good look at Saturn.
5. Isn't it amazing that a spacecraft no bigger than a compact car could discover so much that scientists didn't know?
6. One scientist said, "We've learned more about the Saturn system in the past week than in the entire span of recorded history."
7. It's impossible to imagine *Voyager I*'s speed of 91,000 km an hour, isn't it?
8. What's amazing is that the spacecraft completed all its maneuvers flawlessly in its two-day close encounter.
9. Scientists haven't begun to comprehend all the data that's been sent back.
10. It'll take years before they've made use of all the findings.

□ EXERCISE 6

1. Haven't you noticed how many people are riding bicycles these days?
2. I've just read that in 1972 bicycles outsold cars for the first time.

3. Today bicycles aren't merely for diversion; they're an important means of transportation.
4. And they aren't only energy savers; they're health givers as well.
5. There's nothing better for the cardiovascular system than a bicycle ride to work.
6. If you've had a bicycle ride in the morning, you'll feel better all day.
7. A few cities are aware of the trend; they're putting in bicycle lanes.
8. It's a problem, however, to make room for bicycle lanes in busy city streets.
9. It's going to take time to solve the conflict between bicycles and cars.
10. But it's certainly true that bicycles save fuel, provide healthful exercise, and leave the air clean; they're not to be taken lightly.

☐ EXERCISE 7

1. I've been reading that scientists are studying noise levels.
2. They're looking for ways to reduce noise levels near airports and other places where noise can't be eliminated.
3. They've found one way to muffle sound is to plant small forests.
4. The forest floor with its heavy layer of decaying leaves absorbs sound like a sponge.
5. Also it's been found that tree trunks deflect sound to the forest floor.
6. Forests not only muffle sound; they're also useful as visual screens.
7. If people can't see where sound comes from, they aren't so disturbed by it.
8. Thus city planners find it's worthwhile to plant small urban forests.
9. But the forests aren't only sound barriers.
10. They're pleasant recreation spots as well.

☐ EXERCISE 8

1. I've discovered it's not difficult to paint a room.
2. I'd always thought I'd have a painter do our living room.
3. But after learning the price, I decided I'd do it myself.
4. Even if you've never painted before, it's not hard.
5. First it's important to buy a good grade of paint.
6. Then you'll need to fill in nail holes and sand uneven places.
7. Then you're ready to paint a six-inch border around the woodwork so you'll be able to do the rest of the walls with a roller.
8. Next you're ready for the fastest part—rolling the paint on the walls.
9. It's almost always necessary to add a second coat, and you're lucky if you don't need a third.
10. Soon you'll be in a paint store again choosing colors for the next room.

☐ EXERCISE 9

1. It's time for him to be here, but there's no sign of him.
2. I can't imagine why he's late.
3. What's going to happen if he doesn't show up?
4. We can't go without him. I'm sure of that.
5. Don't forget that I'm going to St. Louis next week.
6. I'm hoping I won't be gone long.
7. I wouldn't go if I didn't have to.
8. I'd like to postpone the trip, but I can't.
9. It's an important meeting, and I'm expected to be there.
10. And next month I think I'm going to Pasadena, but it's not definite.

☐ EXERCISE 10

1. He doesn't get much done because he hasn't learned to say no.
2. She's learned to study no matter who's in the room.
3. It's true that they're working harder now.
4. He's the most conscientious person I've ever known.
5. He's mighty generous too, isn't he?
6. You're planning to travel this summer, aren't you?
7. I'm afraid you're too late for that tour though; it's all booked.
8. Two's company; three's a crowd.
9. We'd made all our preparations and then couldn't go.
10. We haven't decided what we're going to do.

WRITING YOUR OWN SENTENCES

Doing exercises helps one learn a rule, but even more helpful is using the rule in writing sentences. On a separate sheet, or in your journal, write three sentences using contractions, especially any you've had trouble with.

WRITING ASSIGNMENT

Turn to the section beginning on page 186 for your writing assignment.

POSSESSIVES

The trick in writing possessives is to ask yourself the question, "Who does it belong to?" (Modern usage has made *who* acceptable when it comes first in a sentence, but if you want to sound old-fashioned, you can say *"Whom* does it belong to?" or even *"To whom* does it belong?") If the answer to your question does not end in *s*, then add an apostrophe and *s*. If it does end in *s*, simply add an apostrophe.

one boys bike	Who does it belong to?	boy	Add *'s*	boy's bike
two boys bikes	Who do they belong to?	boys	Add *'*	boys' bikes
the mans hat	Who does it belong to?	man	Add *'s*	man's hat
the mens hats	Who do they belong to?	men	Add *'s*	men's hats
childrens game	Who does it belong to?	children	Add *'s*	children's game
one girls coat	Who does it belong to?	girl	Add *'s*	girl's coat
two girls coats	Who do they belong to?	girls	Add *'*	girls' coats

This trick will always work, but you must remember to ask the question every time. And remember that the key word is *belong*. Who does it *belong* to? If you ask the question some other way, you may get an answer that won't help you. Also, if you just look at a word without asking the question, you may think the name of the owner ends in an *s* when it really doesn't.

Cover the right-hand column and see if you can write the following possessives correctly. Ask the question each time.

the womans dress _____	woman's
the womens ideas _____	women's
Dicks apartment _____	Dick's
James apartment _____	James'
the Whites house _____	the Whites'
Mr. Whites house _____	Mr. White's

(Sometime you may see a variation of this rule. *James' book* may be written *James's book.* That is correct too, but the best way is to stick to the simple rule given above. You can't be wrong if you follow it.)

In such expressions as *a day's work* or *Saturday's game*, you may ask how the work can belong to the day or the game can belong to Saturday. Those are simply possessive forms that have been in our language for a long time. And when you think about it, the work really does belong to the day (not the night), and the game does belong to Saturday (not Friday).

A word of warning! Don't assume that because a word ends in *s* it is necessarily a possessive. Make sure the word actually possesses something before you put in an apostrophe.

Possessive pronouns are already possessive and don't need an apostrophe added to them.

my, mine	its
your, yours	our, ours
his	their, theirs
her, hers	whose

Note particularly *its*, *their*, *whose*, and *your*. They are already possessive and do not take apostrophes. (The contractions *it's*, *they're*, *who's*, and *you're* stand for two words and of course have to have apostrophes.)

As a practice exercise, cover the right-hand column below with a sheet of paper, and on it write the correct form (contraction or possessive). If you miss any, go back and review the instructions.

(It) raining.	It's
(You) car needs washing.	Your
(Who) to blame?	Who's
(They) planning to come.	They're
The cat drank (it) milk.	its
(Who) been sitting here?	Who's
The wind lost (it) force.	its
(Who) going with me?	Who's
My book has lost (it) cover.	its
(It) all I can do.	It's
(You) right.	You're
(They) garden has many trees.	Their
(It) sunny today.	It's
(Who) car shall we take?	Whose
The club lost (it) leader.	its
(Who) umbrella is that?	Whose
(You) too late now.	You're
I have lost (they) address.	their
Do you have (you) ticket?	your
(They) always late.	They're

Here's one more practice exercise. Cover the right-hand column with a sheet of paper, and on it write the possessives.

1. My cousins love their grandfather's house.

   grandfather's (You didn't add an apostrophe to *cousins*, did you? The cousins don't possess anything.)

2. Students grades depend on their tests.

   Students' (Who do the grades belong to?)

3. I invited James to my parents house.

   parents' (James doesn't possess anything in this sentence.)

4. My parents went to James house.

   James' (The parents don't possess anything in this sentence.)

5. Ann's job pays more than yours.

   Ann's (*Yours* is a possessive pronoun and doesn't take an apostrophe.)

6. Last years crop was the best yet.

   year's (The crop belonged to last year.)

7. The Browns cottage is spacious.

   Browns' (Who does the cottage belong to?)

8. The Browns went to their cottage.

   (No apostrophe in this sentence. *Their* is the possessive pronoun telling who the cottage belongs to. The sentence merely tells what the Browns did.)

9. Our cottage is bigger than theirs.

   (No apostrophe in this sentence because possessive pronouns *our* and *theirs* don't take apostrophes.)

10. The womens team played the girls team.

    women's, girls' (Did you ask who each team belongs to?)

11. The girls were proud of their team.

    (No apostrophe. *Their* is the possessive pronoun telling who the team belongs to, and the girls don't possess anything in this sentence.)

12. The three judges verdict was fair.

    judges' (Who did the verdict belong to?)

13. The three judges gave a verdict.

    (No apostrophe. The sentence merely tells what the judges did.)

14. The gardens are in need of rain.

    (No apostrophe. The gardens don't possess anything.)

EXERCISES

Put the apostrophe in each possessive. WATCH OUT! **First,** make sure the word really possesses something; not every word that ends in s is a possessive. **Second,** remember that a possessive pronoun doesn't take an apostrophe. **Third,** don't be confused because the word seems to end in s. You can't tell where the apostrophe goes until you ask the question, "Who (or what) does it belong to?" In the first sentence, for example, "Who does the watch belong to?" "Girl." Therefore you will write *girl's.*

☐ EXERCISE 1

1. I saw a girls watch on the table.
2. My husbands job has good fringe benefits.
3. Have you seen Neds new Corvette and Dennis new Mustang?
4. The store sells only mens and boys clothing.
5. I'm going to stay at my brother-in-laws camp.
6. The track teams trophy is displayed in the entrance hall.
7. Normas mother is head of the local League of Women Voters.
8. The audiences applause was tremendous.
9. The car in front of their house isn't theirs.
10. It's the Johnsons car.

☐ EXERCISE 2

1. The ladies enjoyed the chairpersons jokes.
2. I'm afraid Terrys studying is interfering with his social life.
3. We were all impressed with the senators speech.
4. Jeffreys ability in dramatics may carry him far.
5. Someones cat crawled in the window.
6. The bird didn't abandon its nest until its young were able to fly.
7. Yesterdays game was the best of the season.
8. The committee planned its publicity for the Bloodmobile.
9. They hid the photo that was on Georges study table.
10. Last nights party lasted until dawn.

☐ EXERCISE 3

1. Do you plan to join the Womens Club?
2. The worlds tallest known species of tree is the coast redwood.
3. Maybe I can get Moms car.
4. Have you read Haleys account of finding his relatives in Africa?
5. We spent Thanksgiving at Aunt Rebeccas cottage.
6. The visitors were impressed with Dads garden.

7. I don't like having to do someone else's job.
8. My brother's roommate is here for the weekend.
9. Tom's watch is invariably slow.
10. Charles' car was parked in the driveway.

☐ EXERCISE 4

1. The girls' voices were low and tense.
2. The gardens are all drying up.
3. He wasn't listening to his wife's explanation.
4. Whose book is this?
5. It's probably either Martha's or Sarah's.
6. I'm not asking for anyone's advice.
7. The Girls' Athletic Club held its meeting Tuesday.
8. My father's hobby is collecting rock and mineral specimens.
9. Most of Michael's time is spent in studying.
10. Gerald's motto seems to be to study hard—the night before exams.

☐ EXERCISE 5

1. Chicago's skyline isn't as impressive as New York's.
2. The club's first president served four years.
3. I like Bob Dylan's poems.
4. That college's chief claim to fame is its football team.
5. It was hard to accept that judge's decision.
6. Mr. Jones keeps his lawn in beautiful condition.
7. Mr. Jones' lawn is in beautiful condition.
8. Have you ever seen Niagara Falls in the winter?
9. I borrowed Diana's bicycle.
10. Everyone was pleased about Cheryl's summer job.

☐ EXERCISE 6

1. Children's symphonies are now being organized in many cities.
2. They didn't know what to do with Harry's guitar.
3. He had left his guitar in its case at the Student Union.
4. He refused to take anybody's word on the matter.
5. The library had its annual book sale Saturday.
6. The note invited him to the dean's office.
7. Each day's work should give one a sense of achievement.
8. We were tired after Saturday's workout.
9. Are you going to the governor's reception?
10. The car lost its grip on the road.

☐ EXERCISE 7

1. The presidents veto was a surprise.
2. Jerrys desk is always in order.
3. I was surprised at Pauls courage.
4. We were all invited to the twins party.
5. The young colt was standing by its mother.
6. My dads car is smaller than my mothers.
7. We stopped to see Peters puppet theater.
8. The childs disappointment was plain.
9. The car dealers have their reputation to think about.
10. Ralphs mind isn't exactly on his studies these days.

☐ EXERCISE 8

1. The settlers hard work and courage helped them through the hard winter.
2. What was Babe Ruths batting average?
3. The bartenders eyes widened with astonishment.
4. Beethovens Fifth Symphony is a masterful elaboration of the "fate motif."
5. This motif was one of the French peoples secret symbols during World War II.
6. Lincolns gaunt frame was a comforting sight to the North during the Civil War.
7. The mothers eyes showed her approval.
8. His grades show his determination to get ahead.
9. The chief asset of that house is its charming garden.
10. Hurrying out of the room, he grabbed someone elses books instead of his own.

☐ EXERCISE 9

1. Teds motor scooter is faster than Leroys.
2. Their sweaters were covered with snow.
3. As the plane descended, its wings became icy.
4. The students commencement gowns did not arrive in time.
5. Who will win the primary is anybodys guess.
6. The professor read everybodys paper in class.
7. The professors comments were interesting.
8. Someones paper had excellent specific details.
9. Another persons paper was amusing.
10. Two students papers were exceptionally well organized.

☐ EXERCISE 10

1. Chauffering is a big part of a days program for me.
2. My first trips are to Tonys grade school and to Sues morning kindergarten.
3. In the afternoon it'll probably be to Sues ballet or violin lesson.
4. After school I pick up Tony and take him somewhere—perhaps to his Cub Scouts meeting or to the orthodontists office.
5. One or two more trips in the evening will finish the days driving.
6. It's all part of a mothers day.
7. I've been listening to this weeks weather report.
8. Chicagos temperature is higher than Miamis.
9. She's proud of all her familys heirlooms.
10. There's a great difference in peoples tastes in antiques.

WRITING YOUR OWN SENTENCES

On a separate sheet, or in your journal, write five sentences using possessives.

Review of Contractions and Possessives

Put in the necessary apostrophes. Try to get these exercises perfect. Don't excuse an error by saying, "Oh, that was just a careless mistake." A mistake is a mistake. Be tough on yourself.

□ EXERCISE 1

1. Ive been reading about how bananas grow.
2. Id always thought they grew on trees, but they dont.
3. The banana plant doesnt have a trunk like a tree; its trunk is made of overlapping leaves like that of a celery stalk.
4. When the stalk is full grown, its from 8 to 16 inches thick but so soft it can be cut with a knife.
5. A banana plants leaves may be 12 feet long and more than 2 feet wide.
6. In some countries the leaves are torn into strips to make mats, and the fibers are used to make twine.
7. When a banana plants blossoms fall off, a cluster of tiny bananas pointing to the ground can be seen.
8. Thats the way Id always thought bananas grew, but they dont.
9. As they grow, they begin to point upward until when theyre fully grown, theyre all pointing to the sky.
10. Then theyre harvested and may travel as much as 4,000 miles to our grocery stores.

□ EXERCISE 2

1. Id been traveling with Doug for a week, and wed never thought of stopping for any sightseeing.
2. Dougs goal was to get to his home in Nevada as soon as possible.
3. Then as we approached the Colorado-Utah border, we saw signs advertising the Dinosaur National Monument.
4. We decided wed stop, and weve always been glad we did.
5. Wed never seen anything like it before; its one of our countrys most amazing sights.
6. It contains the worlds largest known deposits of petrified skeletons of dinosaurs, some the size of a chicken and others as long as 60 feet.
7. Its impressive to see them embedded there just as theyve been for millions of years.
8. And at the visitors center we saw how the excavators work.
9. We learned a lot wed never known before about dinosaurs.
10. It was like reading a chapter of the earths history.

□EXERCISE 3

1. One of my friends cant bear to throw anything away.
2. Now shes found a use for the familys old Christmas tree.
3. Shes decorated it with strings of raisins, apple bits, and popcorn and stuck it in a showdrift with its trunk firmly on the ground.
4. Shes also added ears of dried corn and pine cones stuffed with suet.
5. Already the birds and squirrels have found the feast, and most of its been eaten.
6. Some people say everythings good for something.
7. Ive just learned that even poisonous snake venom is good for something.
8. Doctors are now separating its enzymes to make various medicines.
9. Theyve made medicines that stop bleeding, that dissolve blood clots, and that kill pain.
10. So a poisonous snakes bad reputation is getting a second thought.

□EXERCISE 4

Its going to be a summer of traveling for my brothers. Theyre going to the West Coast in Marks car. They had thought of taking Miles van, but its a gas guzzler. Marks VW wont be so expensive to run. Theyve not planned their route yet, but theyll no doubt hit Idaho because Marks best friend lives there, and a few nights lodging and a few free meals wont be unwelcome. The boys will be gone a month or maybe longer if theyre lucky enough to find jobs. Their objective is to see whether theyd lIke to settle in the West and also simply to see some country theyve not seen before.

WORDS THAT CAN BE BROKEN INTO PARTS

Breaking words into their parts will often help you spell them correctly. Each of the following words is made up of two shorter words:

over run . . . overrun	room mate . . . roommate
over rate . . . overrate	with hold . . . withhold

Becoming aware of prefixes such as *dis, inter, mis,* and *un* is also helpful. Then when you add a word to the prefix, the spelling will be correct:

dis appear	disappear	mis spell	misspell
dis appoint	disappoint	mis step	misstep
dis approve	disapprove	un natural	unnatural
dis satisfied	dissatisfied	un necessary	unnecessary
dis service	disservice	un nerve	unnerve
inter racial	interracial	un noticed	unnoticed
inter related	interrelated		

Have someone read the above list for you to spell, and mark those you miss. Then memorize the correct spellings by noting how each word is made up of a prefix and a word.

RULE FOR DOUBLING A FINAL CONSONANT

Most spelling rules have so many exceptions that they aren't much help. But here's one that has almost no exceptions and is really worth learning.

Double a final consonant when adding an ending beginning with a vowel (such as <u>ing, ed, er</u>) if the word

   1. **ends in a single consonant,**
   2. **preceded by a single vowel (the vowels are <u>a, e, i, o, u</u>),**
   3. **and the accent is on the last syllable.**

We'll try the rule on a few words to which we'll add *ing, ed,* or *er.*

begin
   1. It ends in a single consonant—*n,*
   2. preceded by a single vowel—*i,*
   3. and the accent is on the last syllable—*be gin'.*
   Therefore we double the final consonant and write *beginning, beginner.*

stop
   1. It ends in a single consonant—*p,*
   2. preceded by a single vowel—*o,*
   3. and the accent is on the last syllable (there is only one).
   Therefore we double the final consonant and write *stopping, stopped, stopper.*

benefit
   1. It ends in a single consonant—*t,*
   2. preceded by a single vowel—*i,*
   3. but the accent is not on the last syllable; it is on the first—*ben' e fit.*
   Therefore we do not double the final consonant. We write *benefiting, benefited.*

sleep
   1. It ends in a single consonant—*p,*
   2. but it is not preceded by a single vowel; there are two *e*'s.
   Therefore we do not double the final consonant. We write *sleeping, sleeper.*

kick
   1. It doesn't end in a single consonant. There are two—*c* and *k.*
   Therefore we do not double the final consonant. We write *kicking, kicked.*

Note that *qu* is really a consonant because *q* is almost never written without *u.* Think of it as *kw.* In words like *equip* and *quit,* the *qu* acts as a consonant. Therefore *quit* does end in a single consonant preceded by a single vowel, and the final consonant is doubled—*quitting.*

Also note that *bus* may be written either *bussing* or *busing.* The latter is more common.

EXERCISES

Add *ing* to these words. Correct each group of ten by using the perforated answer sheet at the back of the book.

☐ EXERCISE 1

1. put
2. control
3. admit
4. mop
5. plan

6. hop
7. jump
8. knit
9. mark
10. creep

☐ EXERCISE 2

1. return
2. swim
3. sing
4. benefit
5. loaf

6. nail
7. omit
8. occur
9. shop
10. interrupt

☐ EXERCISE 3

1. begin
2. spell
3. prefer
4. fish
5. hunt

6. excel
7. wrap
8. stop
9. wed
10. scream

☐ EXERCISE 4

1. feel
2. motor
3. turn
4. add
5. subtract

6. stream
7. expel
8. miss
9. get
10. stress

☐ EXERCISE 5

1. forget
2. misspell
3. fit
4. plant
5. pln

6. trust
7. sip
8. flop
9. reap
10. cart

A LIST OF FREQUENTLY MISSPELLED WORDS

Have someone dictate this list of commonly misspelled words and mark the ones you miss. Then memorize the correct spellings, working on ten words each week.

Be sure to pronounce the following words correctly so that you won't misspell them: *athlete, athletics, environment, government, mathematics, nuclear, probably, sophomore, studying.* Also try to think up memory devices to help you remember correct spellings. For example, you *labor* in a *laboratory*; the two *l*'s in *parallel* are parallel; and the *r* separates the two *a*'s in *separate.*

1. absence	34. discipline	67. independent
2. across	35. discussed	68. intelligence
3. actually	36. disease	69. interest
4. all right	37. divide	70. interfere
5. a lot	38. dying	71. involved
6. amateur	39. eighth	72. knowledge
7. among	40. eligible	73. laboratory
8. analyze	41. eliminate	74. leisure
9. appreciate	42. embarrassed	75. length
10. argument	43. environment	76. library
11. athlete	44. especially	77. likely
12. athletics	45. etc.	78. lying
13. awkward	46. exaggerate	79. marriage
14. becoming	47. excellent	80. mathematics
15. beginning	48. exercise	81. meant
16. belief	49. existence	82. medicine
17. benefit	50. experience	83. necessary
18. buried	51. explanation	84. neither
19. business	52. extremely	85. ninety
20. certain	53. familiar	86. ninth
21. college	54. February	87. nuclear
22. coming	55. finally	88. occasionally
23. committee	56. foreign	89. opinion
24. competition	57. government	90. opportunity
25. complete	58. grammar	91. parallel
26. consider	59. grateful	92. particular
27. criticism	60. guarantee	93. persuade
28. decision	61. guard	94. physically
29. definitely	62. guidance	95. planned
30. dependent	63. height	96. pleasant
31. development	64. hoping	97. possible
32. difference	65. humorous	98. practical
33. disastrous	66. immediately	99. preferred

100. prejudice	117. safety	134. success
101. privilege	118. scene	135. suggest
102. probably	119. schedule	136. surprise
103. professor	120. secretary	137. thoroughly
104. prove	121. senior	138. though
105. psychology	122. sense	139. tragedy
106. pursue	123. separate	140. tried
107. receipt	124. severely	141. tries
108. receive	125. shining	142. truly
109. recommend	126. significant	143. unfortunately
110. reference	127. similar	144. until
111. relieve	128. sincerely	145. unusual
112. religious	129. sophomore	146. using
113. repetition	130. speech	147. usually
114. rhythm	131. straight	148. Wednesday
115. ridiculous	132. studying	149. writing
116. sacrifice	133. succeed	150. written

USING YOUR DICTIONARY

By working through the following twelve exercises, you will become familiar with what you can find in an up-to-date desk dictionary.

1. PRONUNCIATION

Look up the word *longevity* and copy the pronunciation here.

Now under each letter with a pronunciation mark over it, write the key word having the same mark. You will find the key words at the bottom of one of the two dictionary pages open before you. Note especially that the upside-down *e* (ə) always has the sound of *uh* like the *a* in *ago* or *about*. Remember that sound because it is found in many words.

Next, pronounce the key words you have written, and then slowly pronounce *longevity*, giving each syllable the same sound as its key word.

Finally note which syllable has the heavy accent mark. (In most dictionaries the accent mark points to the stressed syllable, but in one dictionary it is in front of the stressed syllable.) The stressed syllable is *jev*. Therefore you will say the word putting all the force possible into that syllable.

When two pronunciations are given, the first is the more common. If the complete pronunciation of a word is not given, look at the word above to find it.

Look up the pronunciation of these words, using the key words at the bottom of the page to help you pronounce each syllable. Then note the heavy accent mark and say the word aloud.

condolence   comparable   koala   mischievous

2. DEFINITIONS

A word may have a number of meanings. Read through all the meanings and then decide which one suits the material you are reading.

Look up the meaning of each italicized word and write a definition appropriate to the sentence.

1. When he didn't come to work, we suspected he was *malingering*. _____

_____

2. She felt *apathetic* about her new job. _____

_____

3. His *sedentary* occupation gave him no opportunity for exercise. _____

_____

4. Her lack of experience was an *insuperable* barrier to her promotion at

that time. _____

_____

3. SPELLING

By making yourself look up each word you aren't sure how to spell, you'll soon become a better speller. When two spellings are given in the dictionary, the first one (or the one with the definition) is the more common.

Underline the more common spelling of each of these words.

archaeology, archeology   dialog, dialogue

encyclopaedia, encyclopedia   gray, grey

4. COMPOUND WORDS

If you want to find out whether two words are written separately, written with a hyphen between them, or written as one word, consult your dictionary. For example:

half sister   is written as two words
brother-in-law .is hyphenated
stepson   is written as one word

Write each of the following correctly.

non conformity _____   short order _____

runner up _____   south paw _____

self contained _____   week end _____

5. CAPITALIZATION

If a word is capitalized in the dictionary, that means it should always be capitalized; if it is not capitalized in the dictionary, then it may or may not be capitalized, depending on its use. For example:

Indian   is always capitalized

college   is capitalized or not, according to use
            She is attending college.
            She is attending North Shore Community College.

Write these words as they are given in the dictionary (with or without a capital) to show whether they must always be capitalized or not.

Chickadee _____   Halloween _____

Democrat _____   Spanish _____

6. DERIVATIONS

The derivations or stories behind words will often help you remember the current meanings. For example, if you heard that a doctor had given a patient a placebo and you consulted your dictionary, you would find that *placebo* originally was a Latin word meaning "I shall please." Knowing the derivation is a help in remembering the present-day definition—"a harmless, unmedicated substance given merely to please the patient."

Look up the derivation of each of these words. You'll find it in square brackets either just before or just after the definition.

aster _____

metropolis _____

apathy _____

sandwich _____

euthanasia _____

7. USAGE

Because a word is in the dictionary is no indication that it is in standard use. The following designations indicate whether a word is used today and where and by whom.

obsolete	now gone out of use
archaic	not now used in ordinary language but retained in some Biblical, literary, and legal expressions
colloquial / informal	used in informal conversation but not in formal writing
dialectal / regional	used in some localities but not everywhere
slang	popular but nonstandard expression
nonstandard / substandard	not used by educated people

Look up each italicized expression and write the designation that indicates its usage.

1. Dolores and Phil got *hitched* last Sunday. _____

2. She didn't have many *boughten* dresses. _____

3. Why so pale and wan, fond lover?
   Prithee, why so pale? _____

4. She came to the party with a *far-out* hair do. _____

5. Add just a *smidgen* of salt to the recipe. _____

6. He had no worries because his parents were *well heeled*. _____

7. He did a *snow job* in convincing the boss. _____

8. We were told not to go but went *anyways*. _____

8. SYNONYMS

Sometimes at the end of a definition a group of synonyms is given. For example, at the end of the definition of *beautiful*, several synonyms for *beautiful* are defined. And if you look up *handsome* or *pretty*, you will be referred to the synonyms under *beautiful*.

List the synonyms for the following words.

new _____

acknowledge _____

condense _____

gaudy _____

9. ABBREVIATIONS

Find the meaning of the following abbreviations.

ibid. _____   km _____

i.e. _____   Ph.D. _____

10. NAMES OF PEOPLE

The names of people will be found either in the main part of your dictionary or in a separate biographical section at the back.

Identify the following.

Thoreau _____

Geronimo _____

Hippocrates _____

Beatrix Potter _____

11. NAMES OF PLACES

The names of places will be found either in the main part of your dictionary or in a separate gazetteer section at the back.

Identify the following.

Agra _____

Georgian Bay _____

Karnak _____

Mauna Loa _____

12. FOREIGN WORDS AND PHRASES

Give the language of these expressions and their meaning.

auf Wiedersehen _____

au courant _____

adios _____

e pluribus unum _____

REVIEW

As a review, find these miscellaneous bits of information in your dictionary.

1. When was Pompeii destroyed?
2. How long is the Suez Canal?
3. What is the capital of Portugal?
4. How many kilometers are in a mile?
5. What is the population of San Mateo?
6. When did Nebuchadnezzar die?
7. What is the plural of *cupful*?
8. What is the source of penicillin?
9. Near what country is the Great Barrier Reef?
10. What is the meaning of the British term *petrol*?

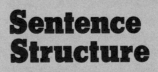

2

**Sentence
Structure**

2   Sentence Structure

The most common errors in freshman writing are fragments and run-together sentences. Here are some fragments:

Having given the best years of his life to his farm
Although we had food enough for only one day
The most that I possibly could do
Because I had tried very hard

They don't make complete statements. They leave the reader wanting something more.

Here are some run-together sentences:

We missed Nancy she is always the life of the party.
We had a wonderful time everyone was in a great mood.
I worked hard I should have got a better grade.
It was raining the pavement was slippery.

Unlike fragments, they make complete statements, but the trouble is they make *two* complete statements, which should not be run together into one sentence. The reader has to go back to see where there should have been a pause.

Both fragments and run-together sentences bother the reader. Not until you can get rid of them will your writing be clear and easy to read. Unfortunately there is no quick, easy way to learn to avoid them. You have to learn a little about sentence structure—mainly how to find the subject and the verb in a sentence so that you can tell whether it really is a sentence.

FINDING SUBJECTS AND VERBS

When you write a sentence, you write about *something* or *someone*. That is the subject. Then you write what the subject *does* or *is*. That is the verb.

Birds fly

The word *Birds* is the something you are writing about. It's the subject, and we'll underline it once. *Fly* tells what the subject does. It shows the action in the sentence. It's the verb, and we'll underline it twice. Because the verb often shows action, it is easier to spot than the subject. Therefore always look for it first. For example, in the sentence

Pat drives his car to the campus every day.

which word shows the action? <u>Drives</u>. It's the verb. Underline it twice. Now ask yourself who or what drives. <u>Pat</u>. It's the subject. Underline it once.

Study the following sentences until you understand how to pick out subjects and verbs.

Last night the rain flooded our basement. (Which word shows the action? <u>Flooded</u>. It's the verb. Underline it twice. Who or what flooded? <u>Rain</u>. It's the subject. Underline it once.)

Yesterday my brother ran five miles. (Which word shows the action? <u>Ran</u>. And who or what ran? <u>Brother</u>.)

This year my sister plays the clarinet in the college orchestra. (Which word shows the action? <u>Plays</u>. Who or what plays? <u>Sister</u>.)

Often the verb doesn't show action but merely tells what the subject *is* or *was*. You will need to learn to spot such verbs (*is, are, was, were, seems, appears* . . . .)

Dan is my friend. (First spot the verb <u>is</u>. Then ask who or what is. <u>Dan is</u>.)

That guy in the blue jeans and red shirt is our team captain. (First spot the verb <u>is</u>. Then ask who or what is. <u>Guy is</u>.)

Allison seems happy these days. (First spot the verb <u>seems</u>. Then ask who or what seems. <u>Allison seems</u>.)

That movie appears popular. (First spot the verb <u>appears</u>. Then ask who or what appears. <u>Movie appears</u>.)

Sometimes the subject comes after the verb.

In the stands were five thousand spectators. (Who or what were? <u>Spectators were</u>.)

Where is the fire? (Who or what is? <u>Fire is</u>.)

There was a large crowd at the party. (Who or what was? <u>Crowd</u> <u>was</u>.)
There were not nearly enough plates for everybody. (Who or what were? <u>Plates</u> <u>were</u>.)
Here was positive evidence. (Who or what was? <u>Evidence</u> <u>was</u>.)

Note that *there* and *here* (as in the last three sentences) are never subjects. They simply point out something.

In commands the subject often is not expressed. It is *you* (understood).

Open the door! (<u>You</u> <u>open</u> the door.)
Eat your spinach! (<u>You</u> <u>eat</u> your spinach.)

As you pick out subjects in the following exercises, you may wonder whether, for example, you should say the subject is *trees* or *redwood trees*. It makes no difference so long as you get the main subject, *trees*, right. In the answers at the back of the book, usually—but not always—the single word is used. Don't waste your time worrying about whether to include an extra word with the subject. Just make sure you get the main subject right.

EXERCISES

Underline the subject once and the verb twice. Find the verb first, and then ask **Who** or **What.** When you've finished ten sentences, compare your answers carefully with those on the perforated answer sheet.

☐ **EXERCISE 1**
1. Redwood <u>trees</u> <u>are</u> enormous.
2. <u>They</u> <u>grow</u> to over 300 feet.
3. <u>They</u> <u>are</u> the largest living things in the world today.
4. <u>Redwoods</u> <u>grow</u> in a limited area along the coast of California.
5. <u>They</u> <u>resist</u> decay.
6. And <u>their</u> bark <u>resists</u> fire.
7. Thus redwood <u>trees</u> <u>live</u> a long time.
8. <u>Many</u> <u>were</u> here at the time of Columbus.
9. Thus <u>many</u> <u>are</u> about 500 years old.
10. <u>Their</u> wood <u>varies</u> in color from light cherry to dark mahogany.

☐ EXERCISE 2

1. From the top of a small hill we saw the prairie fire.
2. The fire swept across the dry land.
3. First there was only smoke.
4. Then there were a few flames.
5. Higher and higher rose the flames.
6. Fortunately a motorist saw the fire.
7. Minutes later he alerted the fire department in a nearby town.
8. Fire fighters spread out across the prairie.
9. They soon had the fire under control.
10. Only a small cabin on the edge of the prairie burned.

☐ EXERCISE 3

1. My instructor stresses the importance of concentration.
2. One's attitude is important too.
3. I keep a study schedule these days.
4. I worked until midnight on my paper.
5. My paper now has a logical development.
6. Finally I typed my paper.
7. Typed papers make a good impression.
8. My paper satisfies me now.
9. I really enjoyed my work.
10. Hard work usually brings results.

☐ EXERCISE 4

1. The koala is popular in every zoo.
2. It is a native of Australia.
3. The koala looks a bit like a teddy bear.
4. No other plant-eating animal has such a restricted diet.
5. Its food consists almost exclusively of leaves of the eucalyptus tree.
6. And it eats only from certain types of eucalyptus trees.
7. Leaves from other types of eucalyptus trees are often fatal.
8. A newborn koala is about an inch long.
9. It crawls into its mother's pouch for further development.
10. At six months the fully developed koala rides on its mother's shoulders.

☐ EXERCISE 5

1. There was not a cloud in the sky.
2. A lizard darted from cactus to cactus.
3. Locusts swarmed over the prairie like a thundercloud.

4. Louder and louder grew the sound of the insects.
5. Here and there we saw prairie flowers.
6. The wind shifted the prairie soil constantly.
7. In the distance were the mountains.
8. Rapidly the sun sank below the horizon.
9. Then the prairie suddenly became cold.
10. We were glad for the warmth of our car.

□ **EXERCISE 6**

1. The skiers wanted snowy weather.
2. At the end of the little path was a deer.
3. Juncos came to my bird feeder all winter.
4. During my vacation I made the most of every minute.
5. The wistful-looking child stood in front of the toy shop window.
6. Her house contained all kinds of laborsaving devices.
7. At that dinner I exceeded the feed limit.
8. The exhibits at the fair were entertaining.
9. There were many educational exhibits too.
10. The letter for his dad is probably still in his pocket.

□ **EXERCISE 7**

1. Stand with your weight on the balls of your feet.
2. Swimming is probably the best kind of exercise.
3. He dived off the cliff into the deep water.
4. In spite of the undertow he swam safely to shore.
5. Do 25 pushups without stopping.
6. She seems happy in her new job.
7. There was no excuse for his absence.
8. Slowly the crowds moved into the stadium.
9. It was a close game.
10. Then in the last few seconds our team made a touchdown.

□ **EXERCISE 8**

1. The Persians built the first windmill in the seventh century.
2. Today windmills meet some energy needs.
3. But windpower provides less than one percent of U.S. energy.
4. The future of windpower, however, looks bright.
5. The government supports the design and testing of large wind generators.
6. It also encourages residential windmills for individual homeowners.
7. It gives income-tax credits for such additions to property.

8. Residential windmills at $5,000 to $10,000 are hardly cheap.
9. Furthermore, they provide only part of a household's electrical needs.
10. Yet windpower has possibilities for the future.

☐ EXERCISE 9

1. During his early years Picasso burned his sketches for warmth.
2. Van Gogh often applied paint to the canvas with a pallet knife.
3. Seurat, however, used tiny daubs of pure color.
4. The picture above the fireplace is a copy of a Seurat.
5. In the National Gallery of Art in Washington, we saw the collection of French impressionist paintings.
6. Shakespeare used several spellings of his name during his lifetime.
7. The United Nations receives more brickbats than bravos.
8. Yet it remains the only real hope for peace.
9. A mature person knows the important from the unimportant.
10. The amoeba is a transparent little animal no bigger than the period at the end of this sentence.

☐ EXERCISE 10

1. Every state in the Union now has a state bird.
2. The cardinal is the most popular.
3. Seven states chose it as their state bird.
4. Those states are Kentucky, Illinois, Indiana, Ohio, North Carolina, Virginia, and West Virginia.
5. The second most popular bird is the western meadowlark.
6. It belongs to Kansas, Wyoming, Nebraska, Montana, North Dakota, and Oregon.
7. The Hawaiian nene is on the endangered species list.
8. The smallest state bird is the black-capped chickadee of Maine and Massachusetts.
9. The cactus wren was a natural choice for Arizona.
10. Perhaps the most beautiful state bird is the ring-necked pheasant of South Dakota.

SUBJECTS NOT IN PREPOSITIONAL PHRASES

A prepositional phrase is simply a preposition and the name of something or someone. We don't use many grammatical terms in this book, and the only reason we're mentioning prepositional phrases is to get them out of the way. They're a bother in analyzing sentences. For example, you might have difficulty finding the subject and verb in a long sentence like this:

> Under these circumstances one of the fellows drove to the North Woods during the first week of his vacation.

But if you cross out all the prepositional phrases like this:

> Under these circumstances one of the fellows drove to the North Woods during the first week of his vacation.

then you have only two words left—the subject and the verb. And even in short sentences like the following, you might pick the wrong word as the subject if you didn't cross out the prepositional phrases first.

> One of my friends lives in Sacramento.
> Most of the team went on the trip.

The subject is never in a prepositional phrase. Read this list several times to learn to recognize prepositional phrases.

about the desk	**in** the desk
above the desk	**inside** the desk
across the desk	**into** the desk
after vacation	**like** the desk
against the desk	**near** the desk
along the street	**of** the desk
among the desks	**off** the desk
around the desk	**on** the desk
at the desk	**outside** the desk
before the desk	**over** the desk
behind the desk	**past** the desk
below the desk	**since** vacation
beneath the desk	**through** the desk
beside the desk	**to** the desk
between the desks	**toward** the desk
beyond the desk	**under** the desk
by the desk	**until** vacation
down the street	**up** the street
during vacation	**upon** the desk
except the desk	**with** the desk
for the desk	**within** the desk
from the desk	**without** the desk

EXERCISES

Cross out the prepositional phrases. Then underline the subject once and the verb twice. Correct each group of ten sentences before going on.

□ EXERCISE 1

1. All ~~of my classes~~ are ~~in the main building~~.
2. Most ~~of my courses~~ require a lot of homework.
3. Many ~~of us~~ prefer true-false tests.
4. ~~In my economics course~~ that book is basic.
5. Much ~~of my time~~ goes ~~to my economics~~ project.
6. ~~In most classes~~ an ability ~~in writing~~ helps.
7. A third of the students really studied for the exam.
8. Most of them passed.
9. One of the students passed with honors.
10. The end of the term is always hectic.

□ EXERCISE 2

1. Many of the spectators left at the end of the first half.
2. In spite of everything we won.
3. Three of the members of the team were on probation.
4. During the game the atmosphere was tense.
5. In the last quarter we made a touchdown.
6. The result of the game was a tie between the two rival teams.
7. Most of my time after classes and on weekends goes into sports.
8. All of the club members went to the tournament.
9. Under the most trying circumstances she won the match.
10. All of the members cheered.

□ EXERCISE 3

1. Two of my friends went with me on a motor trip.
2. All of us wanted to see more of California.
3. Most of all we wanted to see Muir Woods.
4. The road to the woods is long and winding.
5. But all of us were enchanted with the cathedral-like woods.
6. The quietness of the scene among the big trees was breathtaking.
7. All of us learned a great deal that day about redwoods.
8. The next place on our list was Golden Gate Park.
9. With its aquarium, arboretum, and museums, it kept us busy for an entire day.
10. Finally the three of us had tea in the Oriental Tea Garden.

□ EXERCISE 4

1. Hibernation differs from sleep.
2. In sleep animals merely relax.
3. In hibernation, however, their life almost stops.
4. The breathing of the animals becomes very slow.
5. And the beating of their hearts becomes irregular.
6. During hibernation, a woodchuck's body is only a little warmer than the air in its burrow.
7. Some kinds of insects freeze solid.
8. Animals generally prepare for hibernation by eating large amounts of food.
9. They store the food in thick layers of fat.
10. Groundhogs, for example, become very plump before hibernation.

□ EXERCISE 5

1. The national bird of the United States is the bald eagle.
2. With its white head and white tail it is easy to identify.
3. But bald eagles are now an endangered species.
4. Cedar Glenn along the Mississippi River in Illinois is a haven for these birds.
5. After their breeding season in the northern states and Canadian provinces, they gather here for the winter.
6. For five or six months each winter they stay in this protected place.
7. An area of about 580 acres around Cedar Glenn is now an eagle sanctuary.
8. On frigid winter nights the eagles perch side-by-side on the branches of large sycamore trees.
9. More bald eagles spend the winter at Cedar Glenn than at any other place in the United States.
10. Havens like this ensure a future for our national bird.

□ EXERCISE 6

1. Along the railroad track and between the rails, California poppies grew profusely.
2. On one side of the lake a mountain rose abruptly.
3. On the other side was a huge garden with beds of exotic plants.
4. In the garden we found a small reflecting pool.
5. During that afternoon we spent much of our time beside it.
6. At the edge of the pool a sandpiper scuttled away.
7. Beyond the pool we saw two deer.
8. During our stay in the area we hiked many miles.

9. Our farthest trip was to the cliffs by the ocean.
10. Few forms of sea life survive in the pounding surf at the base of the cliffs.

☐ EXERCISE 7

1. Sugar maples are the most common hardwoods in Vermont.
2. In early spring the sap in the maples rises.
3. Throughout the countryside farmers tap the trees for sap.
4. From it they make Vermont's famous maple syrup and maple sugar.
5. One of the most striking natural phenomena is the Natural Bridge in Virginia.
6. The 90-foot stone arch spans the 215-foot gorge of Cedar Creek.
7. In southern Utah is the still larger Rainbow Bridge.
8. With a height of 309 feet and a length of 278 feet, it is the largest natural bridge in the world.
9. Of the original Seven Wonders of the World, only the Great Pyramid exists today.
10. The splendid temples at Nikko in Japan stand in a grove of giant cryptomeria trees at the top of a hill.

☐ EXERCISE 8

1. The exact composition of the core of the earth is a subject for much conjecture.
2. Hundreds of scientists speculate about it after every volcanic eruption.
3. The longest recorded flight of a banded bird during migration is 12,000 miles by an Arctic tern.
4. The redwing blackbird builds its nest on the ground among the rushes beside a stream.
5. A monument to the sea gulls stands in Temple Square in Salt Lake City.
6. Between the blocks of the pyramids, the Egyptians used no mortar.
7. The faces of gargoyles grinned down from the medieval cathedral.
8. Artists in the Dark Ages produced beautiful stained-glass windows.
9. The glass in such windows has deep, rich tones.
10. With only 6 percent of the world's population, America uses 60 percent of the world's resources.

☐ EXERCISE 9

1. One of my hobbies is the restoration of furniture.
2. In my spare time I pursue my hobby.
3. For example, a rung in one of our chairs was loose.
4. From some old wood I made a new rung.

5. After a good sanding, the rung was ready to glue in place.
6. A coat of dull varnish finished the job.
7. One of my next projects was an antique barrel-top trunk.
8. The embossed metal on the top was grimy with age.
9. With the help of an electric sander, I cleaned the metal.
10. Then a coat of dull varnish made it look old again.

□ EXERCISE 10

1. Neither of my best friends owns a car.
2. Each of them drives the family car.
3. There are advantages to such an arrangement.
4. Both of the cars are large and expensive.
5. Furthermore, someone in the family pays for the gas.
6. In her new job she found challenging problems and congenial associates.
7. Many of her associates were long-time employees.
8. Most of them helped her on occasion.
9. One of them became her closest friend.
10. In that organization there was a good feeling of cooperation.

WRITING ASSIGNMENT

As you do the writing assignments that begin on page 186, are you keeping a list of your misspelled words on the inside back cover of this book?

MORE ABOUT VERBS AND SUBJECTS

Sometimes the verb is more than one word. Here are a few of the many forms of the verb *drive*:

I drive	I will be driving	I may drive
I am driving	I will have been driving	I could drive
I have driven	I will have driven	I might drive
I have been driving	I am driven	I should drive
I drove	I was driven	I would drive
I was driving	I have been driven	I must drive
I had driven	I had been driven	I could have driven
I had been driving	I will be driven	I might have driven
I will drive	I can drive	I should have driven

Note that words like *not, ever, never, only, always, just, really, already, often* are not part of the verb even though they may be in the middle of the verb.

Keith had never driven to the cottage before.

I had always before driven to the cottage by myself.

She should just have driven around the block.

Two other forms—*driving* and *to drive*—look like verbs, but neither can ever be the verb of a sentence. No *ing* word by itself can ever be the verb of a sentence; it must have a helping verb in front of it.

Larry driving home. (not a sentence because there is no proper verb)
Larry was driving home. (a sentence)

And no verb with *to* in front of it can ever be the verb of a sentence.

To drive down the river road. (not a sentence because there is no proper verb and no subject)
I like to drive down the river road. (a sentence)

These two forms, *driving* and *to drive*, may be used as subjects, or they may have other uses in the sentence.

Driving is fun.   To drive is fun.

But neither of them can ever be the verb of a sentence.

Not only may a verb be composed of more than one word, but also there may be more than one verb in a sentence:

<u>Steve</u> <u>painted</u> the house and <u>planted</u> trees in the yard.

Also there may be more than one subject.

<u>Steve</u> and <u>Marie</u> <u>painted</u> the house and <u>planted</u> trees in the yard.

EXERCISES

Underline the subject once and the verb twice. Be sure to include all parts of the verb. Also watch for more than one subject and more than one verb. It's a good idea to cross out the prepositional phrases first.

☐ EXERCISE 1
1. There have always been periodic forest fires.
2. Before the coming of people, fires were started by lightning.
3. Conditions must be right for vegetation to burn.
4. Vegetation usually contains too much water and will not burn.
5. During dry seasons, fires start and burn easily.
6. Fire can race across a forest at express-train speed.
7. The land can change in minutes from an area of life to an area of ashes.
8. Sometimes only heavy rain will put out a fire.
9. With the coming of people, the number of forest fires has increased.
10. Constant vigilance is necessary to save our forests.

☐ EXERCISE 2
1. For years she had been collecting shells.
2. She would identify each one carefully.
3. Then she would place it in a cabinet with a neatly typed label.
4. Limpets had always been her favorites.
5. Those shells could be found only at low tide.
6. Others could be found only on the ocean floor.
7. That morning she awoke at sunrise and looked out at the lake below.
8. She went down to the shore and wandered for several miles.
9. She picked up shells and took them home to identify.
10. In the evening she and her friends went for a boat ride on the lake and later had their supper on the shore under the stars.

☐ EXERCISE 3

1. Yellow has always been the favorite color for pencils.
2. Pencils in other colors simply have not sold.
3. Over two billion pencils are sold in the United States annually.
4. An ordinary pencil can draw a line 35 miles long.
5. America could conserve huge amounts of energy by the recycling of steel cans.
6. Steel cans can be separated magnetically from waste and can be put back to work.
7. Many cities are recovering billions of steel cans in modern recovery plants.
8. The farmers had been hoping for rain for three weeks.
9. The heat had been oppressive all afternoon.
10. Then during the night a heavy rain came and flooded the area.

☐ EXERCISE 4

1. Dr. Salk discovered a vaccine for polio and freed the country from that dread disease.
2. The House and the Senate passed the bill.
3. The incumbent and his opponent engaged in a bitter campaign.
4. We visited the United Nations building and listened to a debate.
5. Lincoln has been called the best-loved American.
6. Many books have been written about Martin Luther King, Jr.
7. He rose, steadied himself, and launched into his speech.
8. A college education broadens and deepens a person's outlook.
9. Great tragedy both sobers and uplifts the human spirit.
10. Music echoed and reechoed in the narrow chamber.

☐ EXERCISE 5

1. Through the years Miriam has always been my best friend.
2. I confide in her and take her advice.
3. We have always spent much of our time in the country.
4. We walk along country roads and identify plants.
5. Today we came to an old bridge and wondered about it.
6. It didn't look strong enough for automobile traffic.
7. Farther on we saw a lake calm and bright in the sunlight.
8. Beside it a heron was teetering along on its spindly legs.
9. Then the sun sank slowly in the west and disappeared.
10. Darkness did not come, however, for several hours.

□ EXERCISE 6

1. The Library of Congress is probably the world's largest library.
2. In its holdings are included over 74 million items.
3. And over 7,000 new items are added to the collection every working day.
4. All forms of preserved thought from papyrus to microfilm are included.
5. It was established in 1800 as a reference library for Congress.
6. Today It has become a library for all Americans.
7. Libraries in all parts of the country can borrow from it.
8. Or people can go to the Library of Congress and use the materials there.
9. Besides books there are manuscripts, photographs, recordings of folklore, and reels of motion pictures.
10. It also houses the world's largest collection of maps, with 3½ million maps and atlases.

□ EXERCISE 7

1. The papers of 23 American Presidents are stored in the Library of Congress.
2. And four million pieces of music from classical to rock may be found there.
3. A collection of rare Stradivarius violins is also included in the library.
4. Two-thirds of the 18 million books are in 470 different foreign languages.
5. Perhaps the most famous book is the Gutenberg Bible.
6. The copy is one of three surviving copies in the world.
7. The vast collections are housed in a complex of buildings on Capitol Hill.
8. The main building, of course, is the ornate Library of Congress Building.
9. In that main building the sculptures, paintings, and murals were produced by 50 American artists.
10. Visitors are given free tours through the building.

□ EXERCISE 8

1. I have been reading about volcanoes.
2. The most famous volcanic explosion in history was that of Mount Vesuvius in A.D. 79.
3. It buried Pompeii and Herculaneum and killed at least 2,000 people.
4. The 1980 blast of Mount St. Helens was of about the same magnitude but was in a less populated area.
5. It was the first volcanic explosion in the continental U.S. since the eruption of Mount Lassen, 400 miles to the south, in 1914.

6. The Mount St. Helens blast blew down 150 square miles of timber and caused millions of dollars' worth of damage to crops and streams.
7. About 5,900 miles of roads were buried under ash.
8. The largest volcanic eruption in North American history occurred at remote Mount Katmai in Alaska in 1912.
9. That blast had a magnitude ten times that of Mount St. Helens but caused no fatalities.
10. Today there are 600 active volcanoes on the earth's surface.

□ **EXERCISE 9**
1. At that time of year in Alaska days were short.
2. Night came quickly in midafternoon and lasted until late morning.
3. The mountains and ice-covered cliffs appeared inaccessible.
4. After a heavy fall of snow, cars could not climb the hills.
5. Bears and deer roamed near the cabin all winter.
6. The young man opened the cabin door and looked out into the semi-darkness.
7. Only the tracks of rabbits and wolves could be seen.
8. Van Allen is known as the discoverer of the doughnut-shaped radiation belts around the earth.
9. The northern lights are perhaps caused by a leakage of radiation particles from the Van Allen belts.
10. The International Geophysical Year was planned for a time of great solar activity.

□ **EXERCISE 10**
1. Astronomers have never been able to see the stars clearly through their telescopes.
2. The atmosphere of the earth has always interfered.
3. Even the largest telescopes can't get a good view from the earth.
4. Now plans are being made for a space telescope.
5. It will orbit the earth and get a view without the interference of earth's atmosphere.
6. It will provide images ten times sharper than those of the big telescopes on the ground.
7. It will operate under radio control from earth and circle the earth once every 100 minutes at an altitude of 310 miles.
8. Galileo made the first telescope in 1609.
9. Improvements have been made on that first crude instrument ever since.
10. Now the most effective telescope yet will open whole new worlds to astronomers.

GETTING RID OF RUN-TOGETHER SENTENCES

Any group of words having a subject and verb is a clause. The clause may be independent (able to stand alone) or dependent (unable to stand alone). Every sentence you have worked with so far has been an independent clause because it has been able to stand alone. It has made a complete statement.

If two such independent clauses are written together with no punctuation, or merely a comma, they are called a run-together sentence. We noted some run-together sentences on page 50. Here are some more:

> The girls made the fire the boys cooked the steaks.
> The girls made the fire, the boys cooked the steaks.
> The book was interesting therefore I read it rapidly.
> The book was interesting, therefore I read it rapidly.

Such run-together sentences can be corrected in one of three ways:

1. Make the two independent clauses into two sentences.

> The girls made the fire. The boys cooked the steaks.
> The book was interesting. Therefore I read it rapidly.

2. Separate the two independent clauses with a semicolon. Note the connecting words (underlined) that may follow the semicolon.

> The girls made the fire; the boys cooked the steaks.
> The book was interesting; I read it rapidly.
> The book was interesting; <u>therefore</u> I read it rapidly.
> The book was interesting; <u>consequently</u> I read it rapidly.
> I worked overtime; <u>thus</u> I finished my project early.
> I was late; <u>nevertheless</u> I made the plane.
> I was too busy to go; <u>also</u> I wasn't really interested.
> I wrote a thesis statement; <u>then</u> I began my paper.

Other words that may come between independent clauses are *finally, furthermore, however, likewise, moreover, otherwise*. All of these connecting words require a semicolon in front of them when they come between independent clauses.

But be sure that such words really do come between independent clauses. Sometimes they are merely interrupters (see p. 162) and do not require a semicolon, as in the following sentences:

> I decided, therefore, to paint the kitchen.
> It took me weeks, however, to get started.

3. Connect the two independent clauses with a comma and one of the following words: <u>and, but, for, or, nor, yet, so</u>.

The book was interesting, and I read it rapidly.
The girls made the fire, but the boys cooked the steaks.
I must hurry, or I'll never finish.
I haven't seen that movie, nor do I want to.
He was not outgoing, yet I liked him.

But be sure there are two independent clauses. The first sentence below has two independent clauses. The second is merely one independent clause with two verbs and therefore needs no comma.

The girls made the fire, and the boys cooked the steaks.
The girls made the fire and cooked the steaks.

THE THREE WAYS TO PUNCTUATE INDEPENDENT CLAUSES

The girls made the fire. The boys cooked the steaks.
The girls made the fire; the boys cooked the steaks.
The girls made the fire, and the boys cooked the steaks.

Learn these three ways, and you will avoid run-together sentences.

You may wonder when to use a period and capital letter and when to use a semicolon between two independent clauses. In general, use a period and capital letter. Only if the clauses are closely related in meaning should you use a semicolon. But either way is correct. Therefore your punctuation of the sentences that follow may differ from the answers at the back of the book.

EXERCISES

In each independent clause underline the subject once and the verb twice. Be ready to tell why the sentence is punctuated as it is.

☐ EXERCISE 1

1. Pronunciations change over the years, and new words are constantly being added to the language.
2. Read with your dictionary beside you; then you can look up interesting words.
3. Note derivations, for they will help you to remember words.
4. Keeping a vocabulary list is a good idea too; then you can review your words.
5. Use the new words. It's a good way to fix them in your memory.
6. Use a new word three times, and you'll not forget it.
7. Forty million handguns circulate in this country, and two and a half million are sold annually.
8. Half of all suicides and murders are committed with handguns.
9. Many people believe in their right to own guns and resent any effort to curb that right.
10. But others complain of the hazards of gun ownership; they are working for gun control.

☐ EXERCISE 2

1. I'm writing a term paper on Arthur Erickson; he's a famous Canadian architect.
2. He has designed universities and public buildings, and at Japan's Expo '70 he won the top architectural award among entries from 78 countries.
3. He has now designed a three-block complex in downtown Vancouver. His achievement has restored vitality to the downtown area.
4. The complex consists of buildings and plazas, and it has the most extensive urban plantings of trees, shrubs, and vines of any North American city.
5. A luxurious office building for the local government and a seven-story courthouse are included in the complex.
6. The courthouse is more open and less forbidding than most courthouses, and its glass roof is one of the biggest in the world.
7. Robson Square is the greatest attraction, for it is a place for outdoor lunches, shows, and theater groups.
8. Robson Square also has an outdoor ice- or roller-skating rink as well as indoor theaters, restaurants, and an exhibition hall.
9. An energy tank for the complex is heated or cooled during cheaper off-peak hours, and the buildings are then heated or cooled from the tank.
10. I've learned a lot about Erickson, and I hope to see his work someday.

Most—but not all—of the following sentences are run-together. In each independent clause, underline the subject once and the verb twice. Then if the sentence is run-together, separate the two clauses with the correct punctuation—comma, semicolon, or period and capital letter. Remember that the semicolon and the period with a capital letter are interchangeable; thus your answer may differ from the one at the back of the book.

☐ EXERCISE 3

1. He plays on a softball team he's the captain.
2. I'm going to the park it's too nice a day to stay inside.
3. He'll have to take the bus, I can't wait any longer.
4. She's been all over the United States, and now she's going to Europe.
5. The day dawned clear, not a cloud was in the sky.
6. We gathered firewood from the nearby woods and built a fire.
7. I caught a tiny trout we had it for breakfast.
8. Then we broke camp and started home.
9. At that time my family was living near a small town in the heart of the mining country, and the hills were full of deserted mine shafts.
10. My pals and I explored them. We didn't realize the dangers.

☐ EXERCISE 4

1. I can't go to the play tonight I have too much homework.
2. I'd like to go for I've heard good reports about it.
3. Could you understand the lecture this morning I couldn't.
4. I always listen in class but I seldom take part in class discussion.
5. I've studied for that exam all day moreover I intend to study tonight.
6. My desk is untidy my mind has been on other matters.
7. Answer the phone it's probably for you.
8. I have been trying to keep within the speed limit it's difficult.
9. I stay at 55 for a while then I creep up to 70.
10. I get better mileage at 55 so I keep trying.

☐ EXERCISE 5

1. A strong wind was blowing, our boat nearly capsized.
2. The rain came down in torrents consequently we abandoned our boat and swam ashore.
3. We were grateful to get to shore we should not have ventured out in such weather.
4. We saw a cabin nearby and knocked on the door.
5. All was quiet only the wind could be heard.
6. We went inside but found no traces of recent occupants.
7. The cabin was cold, moreover there was no firewood.

8. The wind blew through the cracks and the shutters rattled.
9. Even so we were grateful for shelter and stayed there until the storm was over.
10. The next day we found our boat downstream it had been a wild adventure.

□ EXERCISE 6

1. Clement had grown up on the family farm he had played under the 100-year-old sycamore trees in the yard.
2. In his day there was no TV he had to make his own entertainment.
3. He read books then he read more books.
4. He was determined to succeed he worked far into the night on his studies.
5. Furthermore he made his own way he never had help from anyone.
6. His industriousness later paid off he was successful in his career.
7. His success was due to his hard work and also it was due to his belief in his work.
8. Now he had come back and he was looking once more at the sycamore trees.
9. The old house and the trees had shared that yard for more than a hundred years but now the trees were being cut down.
10. He would have liked to save them but they were his no longer.

□ EXERCISE 7

1. Of all the kinds of winds, tornadoes are the most violent they do millions of dollars worth of damage each year.
2. Tornadoes are made up of winds with speeds of 30 or 40 miles an hour some have speeds even higher and they cause the most deaths.
3. These winds rotate in a counterclockwise direction and look like a funnel at the bottom of a cloud.
4. Tornadoes are usually only a quarter of a mile wide and not more than 15 miles long furthermore they don't last very long.
5. Their coverage is small and their time is short yet in a few seconds they can leave a path of destruction.
6. A few safety tips are worth knowing they could save lives.
7. Stay away from windows, doors, and outside walls shield your head.
8. Go to a basement or the interior part of a first floor closets or interior halls are the best places.
9. In the outdoors go to a sturdy shelter or lie in a ditch with your hands protecting your head.
10. Spring is the tornado season but tornadoes can strike at any time.

☐ **EXERCISE 8**

1. The 856-mile border between East Germany and West Germany is a heavily fortified wire mesh fence.
2. Watchtowers can see every yard of the fence and the crossing spots are heavily guarded.
3. At places the fence goes three feet underground to prevent tunneling furthermore the top is sharpened mesh to prevent a fingerhold.
4. East Germany claims the fence is for protection against the West but many of the watchtowers don't even have a view of West Germany.
5. The fence was first fortified in 1961 to stop the flood of East Germans to the West more than 200,000 a year were leaving.
6. In the first year 5,761 people escaped across the fence but few make it today.
7. In 1979 two families made a balloon out of bedsheets and curtains and sailed across the fence at night but most are not so lucky.
8. It is safer to try to get out through a neighboring country only the desperate risk the "death strip" today.
9. Many West Germans have relatives on the other side but communication is difficult.
10. East Germany has spent an estimated $7 billion on the barrier and more is being spent.

☐ **EXERCISE 9**

1. One of the most popular museums in Washington is the National Air and Space Museum it takes in the age of the airplane from the flight of the Wright brothers to the landing on the moon 66 years later.
2. Here may be seen the Wright brothers' first plane and Lindbergh's *Spirit of St. Louis* here too is the command module for the first voyage to the moon.
3. In all there are more than 200 original air and spacecraft vehicles they are housed in a three-block-long marble building.
4. Each of the largest galleries is more than six stories high and three times larger than a basketball court.
5. Three of these galleries house historic aircraft such as the linked *Apollo-Soyuz Spacecraft* and the *Skylab Orbital Workshop* here also are historic commercial airliners.
6. The exhibits are suspended from the glass-roofed ceiling or they seem to rise from below the floor level.
7. Smaller galleries show examples of vertical flight, balloons, combat flying in World War I, air traffic control, and man-made satellites.
8. A motion picture *To Fly* is sensational it begins with a balloon ascension in 1831 and ends in a voyage to outer space.

9. In the film the viewer feels the thrill of flying upside down or of sailing along in a tiny hang glider.
10. The Air and Space Museum is part of the Smithsonian Institution it would take weeks to see all of that great institution.

Punctuate the following paragraphs so there will be no run-together sentences.

☐ EXERCISE 10

1. Last spring we were driving through Arizona and decided to see the Petrified Forest therefore we took the 27-mile drive through that strange landscape trees have turned to stone and thousands of great stone logs lie on the ground we learned a great deal about petrified wood and were glad for the experience we had seen a new part of our country the National Park Service is preserving the area for future generations.

2. The most striking feature of the oceans is their vast size the next most striking feature is the constant motion of their surfaces one cause of the motion is the wind it may make waves from an inch to over 60 feet in height another cause of waves is geologic disturbances such as earthquakes and volcanic eruptions below the surface of the oceans waves from geologic disturbances are sometimes incorrectly called tidal waves but they have no relationship to the tides.

WRITING YOUR OWN SENTENCES

On a separate sheet, or in your journal, write three sentences, each containing two independent clauses, and punctuate them correctly. Master this section before you go on. It will take care of many of your punctuation errors.

WRITING ASSIGNMENT

Continue with your writing assignments that begin on page 186. Are you listing all your misspelled words on the inside back cover?

GETTING RID OF FRAGMENTS

There are two kinds of clauses—independent, which we have just finished studying, and dependent. A dependent clause has a subject and verb just like an independent clause, but it can't stand alone because it begins with a dependent word such as

after	since	where
although	so	whereas
as	so that	wherever
as if	than	whether
because	that	which
before	though	whichever
even if	unless	while
even though	until	who
ever since	what	whom
how	whatever	whose
if	when	why
in order that	whenever	

Whenever a clause begins with one of the above dependent words (unless it is a question, which would never give you any trouble), it is dependent. If we take an independent clause such as

We finished the game.

and put one of the dependent words in front of it, it becomes dependent:

After we finished the game
Although we finished the game
As we finished the game
Before we finished the game
If we finished the game
Since we finished the game
That we finished the game
When we finished the game
While we finished the game

The clause can no longer stand alone. As you read it, you can hear that it doesn't make a complete statement. It leaves the reader expecting something more. It is a fragment and must not be punctuated as a sentence.

To correct such a fragment, simply add an independent clause:

After we finished the game, we went to the clubhouse.
While we finished the game, the others waited.
We gave up the court when we had finished the game.
We were happy that we had finished the game.

In other words **EVERY SENTENCE MUST HAVE AT LEAST ONE INDEPENDENT CLAUSE.**

Note in the examples above that when a dependent clause comes at the beginning of a sentence, it is followed by a comma. Often the comma prevents misreading, as in the following sentence:

When he entered, the room became quiet.

Without a comma after *entered,* the reader would read *When he entered the room* before realizing that that was not what the author meant. The comma makes the reading easy. Sometimes if the dependent clause is short and there is no danger of misreading, the comma is omitted, but it is easier and safer simply to follow the rule.

Note that sometimes the dependent word is the subject of the dependent clause:

I took the highway that was finished just last month.

Sometimes the dependent clause is in the middle of the independent clause:

The highway that was finished last month goes to Indianapolis.

And sometimes the dependent clause is the subject of the entire sentence:

What I was doing was not important. (Here no comma is necessary after the dependent clause because it flows right into the rest of the sentence.)

Also note that sometimes the *that* of a dependent clause is omitted:

This is the house that Jack built.
This is the house Jack built.
I thought that you were coming with me.
I thought you were coming with me.

And finally the word *that* does not always introduce a dependent clause; it may be a pronoun (That is my book) or a describing word (I like that book).

EXERCISES

Underline the subject once and the verb twice in both the independent and the dependent clauses. Then put a broken line under the dependent clause.

☐ EXERCISE 1

1. I refused to go because I had homework to do.

2. I could make good grades if I studied.

3. After I finish college, I'll get a job.

4. They were out playing Frisbee while he was studying.

5. Her essay would have been better if she had rewritten it.

6. Unless you return your library book today, you'll have to pay a fine.

7. A large vocabulary is the characteristic that most often accompanies outstanding success.

8. He was searching for the money that he had dropped in the snow.

9. Although he looked a long time, he couldn't find It.

10. Until you understand subjects and verbs, you cannot understand clauses.

Underline each dependent clause with a broken line.

☐ EXERCISE 2

1. You can't do your best when you are tired.
2. I'd have been waiting still if you hadn't called.
3. The crowd cheered when one of the Navy players came onto the field.
4. They roared with excitement as he raced down to the goal line.
5. I have always hoped that I could someday go to the Super Bowl.
6. He took his car although he really preferred his motorcycle.
7. If it's nice tomorrow, we'll hike up Old Baldy.
8. While the leaves are still on the trees, let's take some pictures.
9. I thought that you were coming with me.
10. While she is away, someone will take her place.

☐ EXERCISE 3

1. If you are too busy for a vacation, at least get some exercise.
2. Although I studied, I still found the exam difficult.
3. If you want to learn to write, you must rewrite and rewrite.
4. After I rewrite, I'm more satisfied with my papers.
5. When the sun went down, the air became cool.
6. As It became dark, we looked at the stars through our telescope.
7. Astronomers have located a quasar that may be the largest object in the universe.
8. Whereas the earth's diameter is about 8,000 miles, the diameter of the newly discovered quasar is 468,000,000 miles.
9. If you stood on the moon and looked back toward Earth, you could see with the naked eye only one man-made structure.
10. That structure is the Great Wall of China, which was built in the third century B.C.

If the clause is independent and therefore a sentence, put a period after it. If the clause is dependent and therefore a fragment, add an independent clause either before or after it to make it into a sentence. Remember that if the dependent clause comes first in the sentence, it should have a comma after it.

☐ EXERCISE 4

1. As he ran to catch the ball

2. Then he finally caught it

3. She couldn't find the necessary reference material

4. Because no one had told me about the new ruling

5. When I make up my mind to really work

6. Therefore I'm going to stay at home tonight

7. If I can just spend a couple of hours on my math

8. Moreover I should study my psychology

9. When I'm finished with both of them

10. I'll feel confident for those tests

□ **EXERCISE 5**

1. The people flocked around the injured man

2. As the ambulance came racing down the street

3. When a book is really interesting

4. Come into the office

5. As we learned more about the problem

6. Because I had so much homework for that evening

7. Unless something goes wrong

8. While everyone else was studying

9. Therefore I decided to go

10. The far-off hills are green

□ **EXERCISE 6**

1. But the news from him was always reassuring

2. When he had drunk his fill from the cool spring

3. After the sun sank behind the hills

4. The desert air became cold

5. Even though she is my best friend

6. Nevertheless she went to live on the coast

7. As he jumped into the air to catch the Frisbee

8. Then there was a sudden rumbling sound

9. Begin at the beginning

10. Since I had had nothing for lunch but an apple

WRITING YOUR OWN SENTENCES

Now that you are aware of independent and dependent clauses, you can vary the sentences you write. On a separate sheet write eight sentences, **each containing two independent clauses** connected by one of the following words. Be sure to use the correct punctuation—comma or semicolon.

consequently	and
but	or
therefore	nevertheless
however	then

Now make up eight sentences, **each containing one independent and one dependent clause,** using the following dependent words. If you put the dependent clause first, put a comma after it.

although	unless
after	until
while	because
since	if

MORE ABOUT FRAGMENTS

We have seen that a dependent clause alone is a fragment. Any group of words that does not have a subject and verb is also a fragment.

Paid no attention to his parents (no subject)

Rick thinking about all his problems (no adequate verb. Although *ing* words look like verbs, no *ing* word by itself can ever be the verb of a sentence. It must have another verb in front of it.)

Speeding along the highway (no subject and no adequate verb)

The announcement that we had expected (no verb for the independent clause)

To change these fragments into sentences, we must give each a subject and an adequate verb:

He paid no attention to his parents. (We added a subject.)

Rick was thinking about all his problems. (We put a helping verb in front of the *ing* word to make an adequate verb.)

Speeding along the highway, he had an accident. (We added an independent clause.)

The announcement that we had expected finally came. (We added a verb for the independent clause.)

Sometimes you can tack a fragment onto the independent clause before or after it; other times it is better to change some of the words and make it into a new sentence.

Are fragments ever permissible? Increasingly, fragments are being used in advertising and in other kinds of writing. In Exercise 6 you will find an advertisement that makes use of fragments effectively to give a dramatic pause between individual parts of the sentence. But such fragments are used by writers who know what they are doing. They are used intentionally, never in error. Until you are an experienced writer, stick with complete sentences. Especially in college writing, fragments should not be used.

EXERCISES

Put a period after each sentence. Make each fragment into a sentence either by adding an independent clause before or after it or by changing some words in it. Sometimes changing just one word will change a fragment into a sentence.

☐ EXERCISE 1

1. After answering the telephone and taking the message

2. Having washed my only pair of jeans, I crawled into bed

3. After falling on the ice and breaking his leg

4. The announcement that there would be no classes on Friday

5. Perspiration is often more needed than inspiration

6. Whether I should continue my education

7. My parents wanting desperately to give me more than they had

8. Not wanting to disappoint them

9. My father being a man of very decided opinions

10. Having always done his best in school

☐ EXERCISE 2

1. Having walked through the forest all day without even a break for lunch

2. Where no man had ever set foot before

3. Trying to keep the fire burning

4. Weakened by lack of food and sleep, we were glad to go home

5. Having traveled almost 200 miles

6. A boring evening in which we did nothing but watch TV

7. Not having anything to do all day but wait for the phone to ring

8. The gracious house that she had so carefully planned

9. A place where she could feel secure

10. Finishing the day by vacuuming and doing the washing

☐ **EXERCISE 3**

1. Facts that no educated person could deny

2. My hobby being one that is not expensive

3. At a time when I was too busy to be bothered

4. Although neither of us was eager to undertake the job

5. Each of us hoping the other would volunteer

6. Being a fellow who was always ready to help

7. Even though we were told that the game might be postponed

8. Since I was sure I could get there on time if I kept up my present speed

9. Keep to the right

10. The audience applauding wildly and calling for more

Get rid of the fragments in the following paragraphs. Each of these particular fragments can be tacked onto the sentence before it. Just change the punctuation and the capital letter. To change a capital letter to a small letter, simply put a diagonal line through it.

☐ **EXERCISE 4**

Individuals can help save our forests. Americans waste vast amounts of paper. Because they don't think of paper as forests. They think nothing of wasting an envelope. Because an envelope is only a tiny piece of paper. But it takes two million trees to make the yearly supply of 112 billion envelopes. Even small savings can encourage others to save. Until finally the concerted efforts of enough individuals can make a difference.

☐ **EXERCISE 5**

Future historians will probably call our age the time when humans began the exploration of space. Some historians say that space exploration marks a turning point in the history of the world. Some people criticize space exploration. Saying that the money should have been spent on the poor here on earth. Others say, however, that we wouldn't have spent the money on anything of greater human value. The annual space budget is less than one percent of federal spending. Whereas the bulk of federal spending goes to defense and to health, education, and welfare. There have been practical payoffs from space exploration. One is the transoceanic television broadcasts that can be relayed by communications satellites. Another payoff is the daily weather picture. That appears on television screens. Still another payoff is the earth-resources satellites. That circle the earth and help map remote regions, search for water and minerals, and monitor crops and timber. And the final payoff is military reconnaissance. That helps make possible arms limitation agreements among nations.

In the following advertisement, the writer has chosen to use a number of fragments. Although they are effective in the ad, they would not be acceptable in formal writing. Make all the changes necessary to turn the paragraph into acceptable college writing.

□ EXERCISE 6

When curiosity flourishes, worlds can be changed. Why? How? What if?

Young people question. Taking joy in the search for solutions. Their worlds

abound with endless possibilities. So, too, it is with scientists. Whose

laboratories are as limitless as the universe. Whose ideas shape worlds.

To interest young minds in the wonders of science, Phillips Petroleum has

made possible a film series called "The Search for Solutions." Stimulating

films aired on PBS and seen by over two million students per month. They

capture the excitement of discovery. And the discoverer. To teach. To en-

courage. But most of all, to interest. Because childlike curiosity in the right

hands can help turn darkness into light.

—Phillips 66

Review of Run-together Sentences and Fragments

SIX SENTENCES THAT SHOW HOW TO PUNCTUATE CLAUSES

I gave a party. Everybody came.   (two independent clauses)
I gave a party; everybody came.

I gave a party; moreover every- (two independent clauses con-
body came.   nected by *also, consequently,*
furthermore, however, likewise,
moreover, nevertheless, other-
wise, therefore, then, thus)

I gave a party, and everybody   (two independent clauses con-
came.   nected by *and, but, for, or, nor*
yet, so)

When I gave a party, everybody   (dependent clause at beginning
came.   of sentence)

Everybody came when I gave a   (dependent clause at end of sen-
party.   tence) The dependent words are
after, although, as, as if, because,
before, even if, even though, ever
since, how, if, in order that,
since, so, so that, than, that,
though, unless, until, what,
whatever, when, whenever,
where, whereas, wherever,
whether, which, whichever,
while, who, whom, whose, why

If you remember these six sentences and understand the rules for their punctuation, most of your punctuation problems will be taken care of. It is essential that you learn the words in the above table. If your instructor reads some of the words, be ready to tell which ones come between independent clauses and which ones introduce dependent clauses.

Make the necessary changes in these paragraphs so that there will be no run-together sentences or fragments.

1. In the 1960s Lake Erie was so polluted that experts feared there wouldn't be a single living organism in it within 20 years strict antipollution laws in the United States and Canada, however, have eliminated much of the industrial pollution also better sewage-treatment methods have reduced the flow of phosphorus into the lake now the waters are alive with fish again and the beaches are crowded with swimmers.

2. How to dispose of hazardous chemical wastes is one of the greatest environmental problems society has benefited from the chemicals that control pain and disease and those that create new industrial products but almost 35,000 chemicals used in the United States are classified as possibly hazardous to human health the Environmental Protection Agency estimates that the United States is generating more than 77 billion pounds of hazardous chemical wastes a year and that only 10 percent are being handled safely at least half of the wastes are being dumped indiscriminately, poisoning the earth and the underground water supplies toxic chemicals are adding to disease according to the Surgeon General and virtually the entire population is carrying some body burden of these chemicals.

3. The science of medicine has had a long history it began with superstitions and illness was attributed to evil spirits the ancient Egyptians were among the first to practice surgery anesthesia was, of course, unknown therefore the patient was made unconscious by a blow on the head with a mallet surgery was also practiced in early Babylonia and the Code of Hammurabi lists the penalties that an unsuccessful surgeon had to pay for example, if a patient lost an eye through poor surgery, the surgeon's eye was put out.

4. In 1598 the famous Globe Theater was built across the Thames from London Shakespeare became a shareholder and his plays were produced there the theater was octagonal and held about 1,200 people the "groundlings" stood on the floor and watched the play but the wealthier patrons sat in the two galleries those paying the highest fees could sit upon the stage the stage jutted out into the audience thus the players and the audience had a close relationship.

USING STANDARD ENGLISH VERBS

This chapter and the next are for those who need practice in using Standard English verbs. Many of us grew up speaking a dialect other than Standard English, whether it was in a farm community where people said *I ain't* and *he don't* and *they was* or in a black community where people said *I be* and *it do* and *they has*. Such dialects are colorful and powerful in their place, but in college and in the business and professional world, the use of Standard English is essential. Frequently, though, after students have learned to speak and write Standard English, they go back to their home communities and are able to slip back into their community dialects while they are there. Thus they have really become bilingual, able to use two languages—or at least two dialects.

The following tables compare four verbs in one of the community dialects with the same four verbs in Standard English. Memorize the Standard English forms of these important verbs. Most verbs have endings like the first verb *walk*. The other three verbs are irregular and are important because they are used not only as main verbs but also as helping verbs. We'll be using them as helping verbs in the next chapter.

Don't go on to the exercises until you have memorized the forms of these Standard English verbs.

REGULAR VERB: WALK

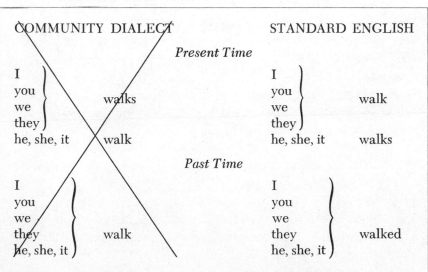

COMMUNITY DIALECT   STANDARD ENGLISH

Present Time

I, you, we, they — walks
he, she, it — walk

I, you, we, they — walk
he, she, it — walks

Past Time

I, you, we, they, he, she, it — walk

I, you, we, they, he, she, it — walked

IRREGULAR VERB: HAVE

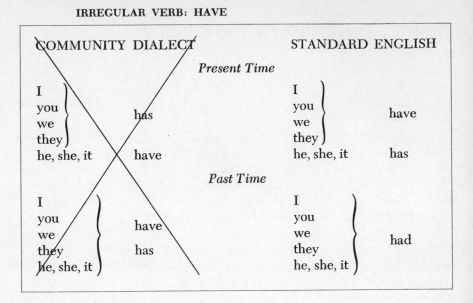

COMMUNITY DIALECT   STANDARD ENGLISH

Present Time

COMMUNITY DIALECT		STANDARD ENGLISH	
I, you, we, they	has	I, you, we, they	have
he, she, it	have	he, she, it	has

Past Time

COMMUNITY DIALECT		STANDARD ENGLISH	
I, you, we, they, he, she, it	have / has	I, you, we, they, he, she, it	had

IRREGULAR VERB: BE

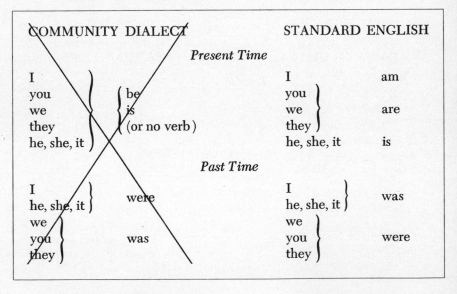

COMMUNITY DIALECT   STANDARD ENGLISH

Present Time

COMMUNITY DIALECT		STANDARD ENGLISH	
I, you, we, they, he, she, it	be / is (or no verb)	I	am
		you, we, they	are
		he, she, it	is

Past Time

COMMUNITY DIALECT		STANDARD ENGLISH	
I, he, she, it	were	I, he, she, it	was
we, you, they	was	we, you, they	were

IRREGULAR VERB: DO

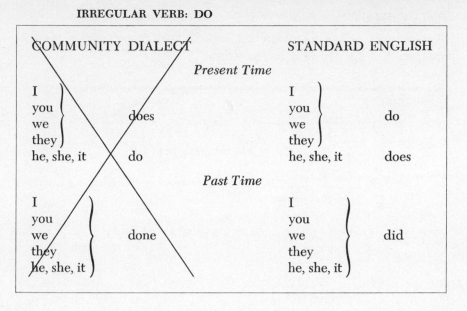

COMMUNITY DIALECT		STANDARD ENGLISH	
Present Time			
I you we they	does	I you we they	do
he, she, it	do	he, she, it	does
Past Time			
I you we they he, she, it	done	I you we they he, she, it	did

Sometimes students have difficulty with the correct endings of verbs because they do not hear the words correctly. As you listen to your instructor or to TV, note carefully the *s* sound and the *ed* sound at the end of words. Occasionally the *ed* is not clearly pronounced, as in *He asked me to go*, but most of the time you can hear it if you listen.

Try reading the following sentences aloud, making sure that you say every sound.

1. He seems to enjoy his two new friends.
2. He likes his job and hopes to stay with it.
3. It costs a quarter to go by bus, so she walks.
4. He rests for ten minutes before he starts again.
5. I was interested in his story.
6. He composed a piece for the piano.
7. She learnèd all I hoped she would.

Now read some other sentences aloud from this text, making sure that you sound all the *s*'s and *ed*'s. Listening to others and reading aloud will help you use the correct verb endings automatically.

EXERCISES

In these pairs of sentences, use the present form of the verb in the first sentence and the past form in the second.

☐ EXERCISE 1

walk   1. I often _____ in the park these days. I

_____ in the park yesterday.

be   2. I _____ happy now. I _____ not happy last week.

have   3. She _____ a moped now. She _____ a bike last year.

do   4. I _____ as I please. I _____ as I pleased last year.

need   5. He _____ help right now. He _____ help last fall.

help   6. Her tutoring _____ me now. Her tutoring

_____ me last semester.

want   7. I _____ it right now. I _____ it yesterday.

attend   8. He _____ a four-year college now. Last year

he _____ a community college.

talk   9. He _____ with her frequently now. He

_____ with her last week.

suppose   10. I _____ I'm late. They _____ that I had already gone.

☐ EXERCISE 2

be   1. I _____ tired now. I _____ tired last night too.

do   2. I always _____ my best now. I _____ my best last year too.

have   3. She _____ a scholarship now. She _____
a scholarship last year.

ask   4. I _____ for help if I need it. I _____
for help when I needed it.

enjoy   5. They _____ their garden now. They _____
their garden last summer.

finish   6. She _____ work at two now. She _____
work at four last fall.

learn   7. She _____ when she tries. She _____
a lot last year.

work   8. He _____ hard these days. He _____
hard on his last job.

listen   9. I _____ to her now. I _____ to
her then.

play   10. Now I _____ the drums. Last year I _____
the cello.

Underline the Standard English verb form. All the verbs follow the pattern
of the regular verb *walk* except the three irregular verbs *have*, *be*, and *do*.
Keep referring to the tables if you are not sure which form to use.

☐ **EXERCISE 3**
1. It (doesn't don't) matter to me what you (do does).
2. I (expect expects) to hear that she (change changed) her mind.
3. I (suggest suggests) that you (watch watches) your step.
4. It (bother bothers) me that I (miss missed) that play.
5. I (did done) what I (want wanted) to do.
6. They (was were) here a short while ago, but where (are is) they now?
7. I (did done) my best, but he (did done) still better.
8. Yesterday I (ask asked) her to a movie, but she (wasn't weren't) in
the mood.
9. You (was were) there, (wasn't weren't) you?
10. All of us (was were) there, and we all (return returned) together last
night.

□ EXERCISE 4

1. I (join joined) the college orchestra last fall and (like likes) it.
2. I (play played) the drums in high school, but I (play plays) the flute in the college orchestra.
3. The orchestra director (need needs) more players and (hope hopes) to get some.
4. It (doesn't don't) matter whether you (are be) a music major.
5. We (work works) hard at each practice and (learn learns) a lot.
6. The director (expect expects) perfection and (insist insists) on it.
7. We (practice practices) two hours and (has have) a short break in the middle.
8. Everyone (enjoy enjoys) those practices and (benefit benefits) from them.
9. We (watch watches) the director's baton and (do does) our best to follow.
10. Last night we (was were) pleased when the director (praise praised) us.

□ EXERCISE 5

1. I never (like liked) English before, but now I (work works) hard at it.
2. Last week we (learn learned) about possessives and (discuss discussed) how to form them.
3. Our instructor (explain explained) what we (did done) wrong.
4. I (do does) my best in the course and (hope hopes) to pass.
5. Last semester I (like liked) the course in psychology, but I (drop dropped) chemistry.
6. I (check checked) into the possibilities and (decide decided) not to major in math.
7. I (pick picked) this college because it (did done) well in football last fall.
8. The athletic coach (encourage encouraged) me to enroll, and I (listen listened) to his advice at that time.
9. Now when the going (be is) rough, he always (be is) there.
10. He (advise advises) me and (treat treats) me like a friend.

□ EXERCISE 6

1. I (start started) to collect stamps when I (was were) small.
2. I still (collect collects) them and (has have) quite a good collection.
3. Last year I (ask asked) all my friends to save foreign stamps, and they (was were) glad to.

4. At first I (want wanted) stamps from all countries; then I (decide decided) to specialize.
5. Now I (want wants) only stamps from the South Pacific.
6. I (dispose disposed) of my other stamps last winter and (receive received) some money for them.
7. The South Pacific stamps (is are) pretty, and I (has have) quite a few.
8. The biggest stamps (be are) from Tonga; they (measure measures) more than two inches wide.
9. The stamps (help helps) me to learn about other countries; they also (impress impresses) me with their beauty.
10. I (intend intends) to go to the South Pacific some day.

□ EXERCISE 7

1. When I (finish finished) that book yesterday, I (return returned) it to the library.
2. Then I (ask asked) for another book by the same author, but the library (had have) no other.
3. An accident (occur occurred) when I (was were) on my way home.
4. I (happen happened) to see the accident and (report reported) it to the police.
5. No one (expect expected) the police to arrive so soon, but they (appear appeared) in five minutes.
6. The driver of the truck (did done) the best he could to avoid the accident, but it (happen happened) in spite of him.
7. Three people (was were) involved, but they (wasn't weren't) hurt.
8. It (was were) lucky that it (wasn't weren't) more serious.
9. When I (arrive arrived) home later, I (rest rested) a while before dinner.
10. I always (enjoy enjoys) my dinner more if I (am be) rested.

□ EXERCISE 8

1. She (listen listened) to my advice and then (did done) what she (please pleased).
2. My sister and I (volunteer volunteered) last week to help with the Cub Scouts.
3. We (are is) eager to help, and they (need needs) us.
4. The letter (contain contained) his resignation and (list listed) his reasons for resigning.
5. I (attend attended) an assertiveness training workshop last week and (benefit benefited) from it.
6. He (help helps) his students and (listen listens) to their problems.

7. I (celebrate celebrated) my twentieth birthday last week and (enjoy enjoyed) myself.
8. He (discuss discussed) the problem and (offer offered) to help.
9. She (change changed) her plans last week and (surprise surprised) me with a visit.
10. I (plan plans) a big dinner for Sunday and (hope hopes) you can come.

□ EXERCISE 9

1. The lecture (impress impressed) me and (change changed) my thinking on the subject.
2. Cleaning the house (bore bores) me, but I (do does) it.
3. She (need needs) support, and I (intend intends) to give it to her.
4. I (ask asked) him to help me, and he (did done) what he could.
5. He (seal sealed) the letter and (drop dropped) it in the mailbox.
6. I (discover discovered) some violets this morning; they (are be) early this year.
7. Yesterday I (happen happened) to see a horned lark in a field; it (was were) the first of the season.
8. I (ask asked) for directions yesterday and (walk walked) to her house.
9. It (occur occurs) to me now that they (complain complained) before.
10. My friends (expect expects) me to call them tonight.

□ EXERCISE 10

1. It (please pleased) me that she (want wanted) to come.
2. I (order ordered) a pizza last night and (finish finished) all of it.
3. I (hand handed) my paper in when it was (finish finished).
4. She (loan loaned) me a dollar, and I (want wants) to return it now.
5. No one (complain complained) about the meal, but I (dislike disliked) it.
6. He (drop dropped) the course because he (had have) no interest in it.
7. It (occur occurs) to me that I (need needs) a haircut.
8. I (observe observed) all the traffic rules when I (start started) to drive last year.
9. He (want wants) to speak Standard English and (doesn't don't) want to give up.
10. She (hope hopes) to speak well too and (do does) her best.

WRITING YOUR OWN SENTENCES

On a separate sheet, or in your journal, write three sentences using verbs you may formerly have used incorrectly.

STANDARD ENGLISH VERBS (compound forms and irregular verbs)

In the last chapter we talked about the present and past forms of the regular verb *walk*. Other forms of the regular verb may be used with helping verbs. Here is a table showing all the forms of some regular verbs and the various helping verbs they are used with.

REGULAR VERBS

BASE FORM (Use after *can, may, shall, will, could, might, should, would, must, do, does, did.*)	PRESENT	PAST	PAST PARTICIPLE (Use after *have, has, had.* Or use after some form of *be* to describe the subject or to make a passive verb.)	*ING* FORM (Use after some form of *be.*)
ask	ask (*s*)	asked	asked	asking
dance	dance (*s*)	danced	danced	dancing
decide	decide (*s*)	decided	decided	deciding
enjoy	enjoy (*s*)	enjoyed	enjoyed	enjoying
finish	finish (*es*)	finished	finished	finishing
happen	happen (*s*)	happened	happened	happening
learn	learn (*s*)	learned	learned	learning
like	like (*s*)	liked	liked	liking
need	need (*s*)	needed	needed	needing
open	open (*s*)	opened	opened	opening
start	start (*s*)	started	started	starting
suppose	suppose (*s*)	supposed	supposed	supposing
walk	walk (*s*)	walked	walked	walking
want	want (*s*)	wanted	wanted	wanting

Sometimes a past participle is used after some form of the verb *be* (or verbs that take the place of *be* like *appear, seem, look, feel, get, act, become*) to describe the subject.

He is satisfied.
He was confused.
He has been disappointed.
He was supposed to go.
He appeared pleased. (He was pleased.)
He seems interested. (He is interested.)
He looked surprised. (He was surprised.)

He feels frightened. (He is frightened.)
He gets bored easily. (He is bored easily.)
He acts concerned. (He is concerned.)
He became disillusioned. (He was disillusioned.)

Usually these past participles are called describing words that describe the subject rather than being called part of the verb of the sentence. What you call them doesn't matter. The only important thing is to be sure you use the correct form of the past participle (*ed* for regular verbs).

Sometimes the subject of the sentence neither *does* nor *is* anything. It just stays there passive in the sentence and is acted upon.

The lesson was studied by the children.

The subject is *lesson.* It doesn't do anything. It is passive. It is acted upon by the children. Thus we say that *was studied* is a passive verb. All you really need to remember is that whenever a form of *be* is used with a past participle, you must be sure to use the correct past participle form (*ed* for regular verbs).

Note that when there are several helping verbs, it is the last one that determines which form of the main verb should be used: she could *have* finished; he should have *been* finished by now.

When do you write *finish, suppose, ask?* And when do you write *finished, supposed, asked?* Here's a rule that may help you decide.

Use *finished, supposed, asked* rather than *finish, suppose, ask*

1. when it's past time:
   She *finished* her paper yesterday.
   When I saw you, I *supposed* you had had lunch.
   He *asked* her for a date last night.
2. when some form of *be* or *have* comes before the word:
   She is *finished* with her paper now.
   I am *supposed* to give you this note.
   He has *asked* her to go with him.

IRREGULAR VERBS

All the verbs in the table on page 93 are regular. That is, they are all formed in the same way—with an *ed* ending on the past form and on the past participle. But many verbs are irregular. Their past and past participle forms change spelling instead of just adding an *ed*. Here is a table of some irregular verbs. (The present and the *ing* forms are not usually given in a list of principal parts because they are formed easily from the base form and cause no trouble.) Refer to this list when you aren't sure which verb form to use. Memorize all the forms you don't know.

BASE FORM	PAST	PAST PARTICIPLE
be	was, were	been
become	became	become
begin	began	begun
break	broke	broken
bring	brought	brought
buy	bought	bought
build	built	built
catch	caught	caught
choose	chose	chosen
come	came	come
do	did	done
drive	drove	driven
eat	ate	eaten
fall	fell	fallen
feel	felt	felt
fight	fought	fought
find	found	found
forget	forgot	forgotten
forgive	forgave	forgiven
freeze	froze	frozen
get	got	got *or* gotten
give	gave	given
go	went	gone
grow	grew	grown
have	had	had
hold	held	held
keep	kept	kept
know	knew	known
lead	led	led
leave	left	left
lose	lost	lost
make	made	made

BASE FORM	PAST	PAST PARTICIPLE
meet	met	met
pay	paid	paid
read	read	read
ride	rode	ridden
rise	rose	risen
run	ran	run
say	said	said
see	saw	seen
sell	sold	sold
sing	sang	sung
sleep	slept	slept
speak	spoke	spoken
spend	spent	spent
stand	stood	stood
take	took	taken
teach	taught	taught
tell	told	told
think	thought	thought
throw	threw	thrown
wear	wore	worn
win	won	won
write	wrote	written

EXERCISES

Write the correct form of the verb. Refer to the tables and explanations on the previous pages if you aren't sure which form to use after a certain helping verb. Do no more than ten sentences at a time before checking your answers.

□ EXERCISE 1

finish 1. I should _____ my paper today, but I may not

be _____ until tomorrow.

finish 2. I could _____ in a few hours if I worked hard.

finish 3. I have often _____ a paper rapidly, and I might

_____ this one rapidly.

finish 4. I am _____ it so that I can hand it in on Monday.

finish   5. I wish that I had _____ it earlier.

finish   6. It was _____ yesterday, but then I made some changes in it.

finish   7. Now I must _____ it all over again.

finish   8. When my paper is _____, I'll be glad.

finish   9. I _____ the things I start.

finish   10. Most students have _____ their papers by now.

☐ EXERCISE 2

be, change   1. I thought you _____ coming with me, or

have you _____ your mind?

see, ask   2. I _____ my cousin yesterday, and she

_____ about you.

break, eat   3. I have _____ my rule and have _____ dessert every day this week.

look, see   4. Yesterday I _____ at the scales and

_____ what was happening.

decide, go   5. I _____ right then that I had _____ too far.

eat, begin   6. I have not _____ dessert today, and I think

I have already _____ to lose a little.

speak, learn   7. We had _____ to our son's teacher and

had _____ that our son needs extra help.

intend, begin   8. We now _____ to help him; in fact we

_____ last night.

be, realize   9. Last night as we _____ helping him, we

_____ how much we can do.

help, be,   10. As we _____ him last night, we _____
begin

impressed with how quickly he was _____
to catch on.

☐ EXERCISE 3

see, eat   1. I _____ her in the cafeteria after I had

_____ my lunch.

need, take   2. I find that I _____ exercise, and I

_____ some every day.

jog, play   3. I now _____ every morning before break-

fast, and I _____ a little tennis each
afternoon.

be, impress   4. You _____ the best skater in the tourna-

ment yesterday; your skating has always _____
me.

speak, begin   5. Newscasters always _____ Standard

English, and I now have _____ to imitate
them.

seem, want   6. That _____ to be a good way to learn

Standard English, and I _____ to learn it
now as fast as possible.

know, become 7. I _____ that it will help me in my job; in

fact it has _____ a requirement in my
field.

imitate, use   8. I am _____ my teachers too because they

all _____ Standard English.

teach, begin   9. I must _____ my ears to hear the correct

endings of verbs, and I now am _____ to
hear them.

like   10. I _____ the feeling now of knowing two
dialects.

☐ EXERCISE 4

be, see   1. We _____ delighted when we _____
his car come in the driveway yesterday.

see, begin   2. We hadn't _____ him for a year, and we

had _____ to miss his visits.

drive, eat   3. He had _____ 500 miles that day and had

_____ very little.

ask, do   4. We _____ him to have some food immedi-

ately and _____ what we could to make him
comfortable.

eat, ask   5. He sat down then and _____ ravenously and

_____ for more.

write, ask,   6. Then he said he had _____ to us and
  receive

_____ whether we had _____
his letter.

come, begin   7. The letter hadn't _____, and we told him

we had _____ to think he had forgotten us.

see, suggest   8. We _____ that he was tired and _____ that he go to bed.

go, wash,   9. After he had _____ to his room, we
prepare
_____ the dishes and _____ for the next day.

see, be, run   10. I _____ then that we _____

low on food and _____ to the grocery for more supplies.

□ EXERCISE 5

want, give   1. Last year my parents _____ me to succeed

and _____ me lots of help.

make, do   2. This year I have _____ most of my spend-

ing money because I have _____ odd jobs.

become,   3. I have _____ more independent, and my
appreciate,
do   parents have _____ what I have _____.

watch, say   4. People are _____ more and more TV now-

adays; the pollsters _____ the average is
29 hours per week per citizen.

spend, be   5. And children are _____ more time in front

of the TV than they _____ in any other
activity except sleeping.

have, continue   6. Protests against violence on TV _____ had

little effect, and the violence _____.

make, be   7. Educational television now _____ some
good use of the medium, however, and children

_____ learning from it.

take, sing   8. He has _____ voice lessons for a year and

has _____ in several programs.

choose, learn   9. He has _____ music as his major and has

_____ a lot.

ask, do   10. He was _____ to be in an opera last year

and _____ well in it.

□EXERCISE 6

decide, see   1. Last winter I _____ to go to see the annual ice carnival at the college because I had never

_____ one before.

freeze, reach   2. I was almost _____ by the time I

_____ the rink.

be, go   3. As I watched, however, I _____ glad I

had _____.

observe, see   4. A friend of mine was competing in the figure skating,

and as I _____, I _____ that

she was good.

announce, win   5. Finally when the judges' decision was _____,

she had _____ first place.

smile, receive 6. She _____ through her tears then as she

_____ the trophy.

be, do   7. All her friends that night _____ pleased

that she had _____ so well.

be, accept 8. _____ you there when she _____
her trophy?

discuss, 9. That book that we _____ in class yester-
impress
day really _____ me.

analyze, give 10. Our instructor _____ it yesterday and
_____ some quotations from it.

□ **EXERCISE 7**

say, visit 1. Our friends from Texas had _____ that they
would _____ us when they came east.

hope, come 2. We were _____ that they would _____
last weekend.

be, drive 3. We _____ delighted, therefore, when they
_____ in Friday evening.

see, grow 4. We had not _____ them for years, and their
children had _____ tall.

take, take 5. Their son has _____ up skiing, and their
daughter is _____ ballet lessons.

be, stay 6. I _____ impressed with their good family
relationship and was pleased that they would _____
for two days.

occupy, take 7. Our time was _____ mainly with talking, but
we _____ a few excursions.

see, be 8. They had never _____ our lake and _____
eager to have a sail on it.

ask, like   9. Also we _____ them if they would _____

to see our antique museum.

be, collect   10. They _____ interested because they have

_____ antiques for years.

WRITING YOUR OWN SENTENCES
Write five sentences using some verbs you may formerly have used incorrectly.

Avoiding Dialect Expressions

Whereas verbs cause the most trouble for those who have grown up speaking a dialect other than Standard English, certain other expressions, more common in speech than in writing, should be avoided. Some (such as *he don't, you was*) are discussed elsewhere in the book. A few others are listed here.

DIALECT	STANDARD ENGLISH
anywheres, nowheres, some- wheres	anywhere, nowhere, somewhere
anyways	anyway
hisself, theirselves	himself, themselves
this here book, that there book, those there books	this book, that book, those books
he did good, she sang good	he did well, she sang well
my brother he plays ball	my brother plays ball
haven't no, haven't none, haven't never, haven't nothing, wasn't no, wasn't never (These are called double negatives.)	have no, have none, have never, have nothing, was no, was never

MAKING SUBJECTS, VERBS, AND PRONOUNS AGREE

All parts of a sentence should agree. In general if the subject is singular, the verb should be singular; if the subject is plural, the verb should be plural.

<u>Each</u> of the boys <u>has</u> his own room.

<u>Both</u> of the boys <u>have</u> their own rooms.

<u>Jennifer</u> and <u>Matthew</u> <u>have</u> a good friendship.

<u>He</u> and <u>I</u> <u>were</u> there.

There <u>were</u> two <u>places</u> at the long table.

The following words are singular and take a singular verb:

(*one* words)	(*body* words)	
one	nobody	each
anyone	anybody	either
someone	somebody	neither
everyone	everybody	

<u>One</u> of my friends <u>is</u> a freshman.

<u>Each</u> of the students <u>is</u> responsible for one report.

<u>Either</u> of the girls <u>is</u> a good choice.

The following "group" words take a singular verb if you are thinking of the group as a whole, but they take a plural verb if you are thinking of the individuals in the group:

group	band	heap
committee	flock	lot
crowd	class	audience
team	dozen	jury
family	kind	herd
number	public	

My family *is* behind me. . . . . My family *are* all scattered.
The number present *was* small. . . . A number *are* going to the rally.
A dozen *is* enough. . . . . A dozen *are* going.
A lot *was* accomplished. . . . . A lot *were* late to class.

Not only should subject and verb agree. A pronoun, too, should agree with the word it refers to. If that word is singular, the pronoun should be singular; if that word is plural, the pronoun should be plural.

Each of the boys has *his* own room.

The pronoun *his* refers to the singular subject *Each* and therefore is singular.

Both of the boys have *their* own rooms.

The pronoun *their* refers to the plural subject *Both* and therefore is plural.

If you have trouble deciding whether a verb should be singular or plural, put *he* or *they* in front of it. For example, if you are wondering whether to write *my parents insist* or *my parents insists*, try putting *he* or *they* in front of the verb.

he insists
they insist

Thus you will know that you must write *my parents insist.*

Modern usage allows some exceptions to the rules for agreement, especially in conversation. Sometimes, for example, the verb and the pronoun may agree with the *intent* of the subject rather than with its grammatical form.

Neither of *them* were in. (The intent of the sentence is to show that both were not in, and therefore a plural verb is used.)
Everybody took off *their* hats as the parade went by. (The intent of the sentence is to show that all the people took off their hats, and therefore a plural pronoun is used.)

Today many people write *he or she* and *him or her* in an attempt to avoid sex bias, but such writing can be awkward and wordy. To avoid such wordiness, the pronouns *they, them,* and *their* are frequently used, particularly in conversation.

> If *anyone* wants a ride, *they* can go in my car (less awkward than the grammatically correct *he or she* can go in my car).
>
> If *anybody* calls, tell *them* I've left (less awkward than the grammatically correct tell *him or her* I've left).
>
> *Somebody* has left *their* textbook here (less awkward than the grammatically correct *his or her* textbook).

A better way to avoid the awkward *he or she* and *him or her* is to make the words plural. Instead of writing, "Each of the students was in his or her place," write, "All of the students were in their places," thus avoiding sex bias and still having a grammatically correct sentence.

Although the above nonstandard forms are acceptable in conversation, they are not acceptable in formal writing. For all your college writing, therefore, stick with the strict grammatical rules.

Here are some subject-verb pairs you can *always* be sure of. No exceptions!

you were	(*never* you was)
we were	(*never* we was)
they were	(*never* they was)
he doesn't	(*never* he don't)
she doesn't	(*never* she don't)
it doesn't	(*never* it don't)

EXERCISES

Cross out the prepositional phrases so you can find the subject. Underline the subject with a single line. Then underline the correct verb with a double line. In some sentences you will also need to underline the correct pronoun. Use the correct grammatical form even though an alternate form may be acceptable in conversation. Check your answers ten at a time.

☐ EXERCISE 1

1. Everybody in our family (are is) planning a trip this summer.
2. Each of us (are is) going to a different part of the country.
3. One of my brothers (are is) going fishing in the Far North.
4. My other brother (doesn't don't) know yet where he'll go.
5. Each of them (are is) taking (his their) own motorcycle.
6. My sister and I (was were) planning to go to Wyoming.
7. But my sister decided she (doesn't don't) want to go.
8. No one in our family (has have) ever been to California.
9. So my sister and one of her friends (think thinks) they'll go there.
10. My parents (intend intends) to drive to Pennsylvania.

☐ EXERCISE 2

1. Each member of the family (are is) sure to have a good experience.
2. One of my friends (has have) just come back from Jersey City.
3. Nobody in our family (has have) been in the New York area.
4. Each of us (hope hopes) someday to go there.
5. Everybody in our family (like likes) to travel.
6. It has been two years since we (was were) at my grandfather's farm.
7. Both of my cousins (live lives) near his farm.
8. They (was were) expecting us to visit them last summer.
9. I thought you (was were) going to Pittsfield this weekend.
10. (Doesn't Don't) your father live there anymore?

☐ EXERCISE 3

1. Each of these rules (are is) important.
2. And doing the exercises (help helps) me remember the rule.
3. Some of the rules (are is) harder than others.
4. Each of the rules (has have) been a challenge to me.
5. A few of them (was were) familiar, but most of them (was were) new.
6. Every one of the rules (depend depends) on the previous rule.
7. It (doesn't don't) do any good to learn one isolated rule.
8. All of them (work works) together.
9. For example, the punctuation of sentences (require requires) a knowledge of subjects and verbs.
10. Each of the rules (are is) going to be of value in my writing.

☐ EXERCISE 4

1. Each of my sisters (has have) (her their) own apartment.
2. Both of them (like likes) independence.
3. One of them (live lives) in the center of the city.
4. She (doesn't don't) like to have far to walk to work.
5. The other one of my sisters (has have) her apartment in the suburbs.
6. Each of them (has have) (her their) own car.
7. It (doesn't don't) take either of them long to drive to our house.
8. Both of them (was were) over here last night.
9. Two of their friends (was were) with them.
10. All of them (spend spends) an evening with us now and then.

☐ EXERCISE 5

1. A number of women (are is) going to the conference.
2. Each of the women (has have) to make (her their) own reservation.
3. A few of them (has have) made (her their) reservations already.
4. It (doesn't don't) matter when they are made.
5. The conference planners (expect expects) a good attendance.
6. Some of the women (hope hopes) to go by car, but most of them (intend intends) to go by plane.
7. My friend and I (enjoy enjoys) going to the country to ski.
8. We (spend spends) quite a bit of time that way.
9. Some of our friends usually (go goes) with us too.
10. Each of us (take takes) ski equipment and food for the weekend.

☐ EXERCISE 6

1. All of the buildings on our campus (are is) modern Gothic.
2. Each one (exhibit exhibits) a slightly different style of architecture.
3. Each of the buildings (was were) built to conform to the master plan.
4. Every one of the buildings (are is) fireproof.
5. Most of the students (come comes) to the free movie each week.
6. All of them (like likes) a break from studying.
7. You (was were) there too, (wasn't weren't) you?
8. There (was were) 50 people in line, and we (was were) at the end.
9. Both of us (was were) successful in getting in though.
10. Each of us (feel feels) it was a worthwhile movie.

☐ EXERCISE 7

1. All of the children (watch watches) the magician eagerly.
2. Some of those tricks (are is) easy.

3. A box of oranges (was were) sent to our house by mistake.
4. There (was were) packages from all of her friends.
5. One of her friends (are is) here for the weekend.
6. He plans to stay until Sunday night, (doesn't, don't) he?
7. There (was were) 20 people at her house for dinner.
8. One of my friends (expect expects) to be here tomorrow.
9. You (was were) on my mind all day yesterday.
10. One of us (are is) making a mistake.

☐ EXERCISE 8

1. Each of the stamps (was were) distinctive in (its their) own way.
2. Everyone in the chorus (enjoy enjoys) the practices.
3. He (doesn't don't) ask for any help.
4. Most of the magazine stories (contain contains) some humor.
5. There (remain remains) a number of insoluble problems.
6. (Wasn't Weren't) you surprised at her answer?
7. It (doesn't don't) matter whether you go or not.
8. Everybody on the committee (are is) in favor of the proposal.
9. (Doesn't Don't) she like her new position?
10. There (has have) been many reasons for my inability to concentrate.

☐ EXERCISE 9

1. Each of the boys (are is) working on (his their) own project.
2. All of the boys (are is) going to finish (his their) work by Christmas.
3. Most of the boys (intend intends) to give their projects as gifts.
4. Each of the lessons (present presents) a different problem.
5. There never (are is) enough books to go around.
6. (Doesn't Don't) she go to college now?
7. Marv and Sam (plan plans) to work at the polling booth.
8. Sam (doesn't don't) know much about the candidates.
9. A number of the delegates (are is) voting against the incumbent.
10. It (doesn't don't) matter to me who wins.

☐ EXERCISE 10

1. My parents (insist insists) on an attractive garden.
2. That house (fulfill fulfills) my mother's dreams because the yard (contain contains) many trees.
3. I never knew you (was were) from Pearl City.
4. Each of the boys (has have) (his their) own style of swimming.
5. I'm sure she (doesn't don't) believe all those compliments.

6. There (are is) three apples in the dish on the table.
7. Ice skating takes strong muscles, (doesn't don't) it?
8. Each of us (have has) been at fault.
9. All of us (sleep sleeps) late on Saturday mornings.
10. We slept late this morning because we (was were) up late last night.

WRITING YOUR OWN SENTENCES
On a separate sheet, or in your journal, write three sentences with correct agreement that you may formerly have had trouble with.

WRITING ASSIGNMENT
As you do the writing assignments that begin on page 186, are you keeping a list of your misspelled words on the inside back cover of this book?

CHOOSING THE RIGHT PRONOUN

Of the many kinds of pronouns, the following cause the most difficulty:

SUBJECT GROUP	NONSUBJECT GROUP
I	me
he	him
she	her
we	us
they	them

A pronoun in the Subject Group may be used in two ways:

1. as the subject of a verb:

   He is my brother. (*He* is the subject of the verb *is.*)
   We girls gave a party. (*We* is the subject of the verb *gave.*)
   He is taller than *I.* (The sentence is not written out in full. It means "He is taller than I am." *I* is the subject of the verb *am.* Whenever you see *than* in a sentence, ask yourself whether a verb has been left off. Add the verb, and then you will be able to figure out the correct pronoun.)

2. as a word that means the same as the subject:

   That boy in the blue jeans is *he.* (*He* is a word that means the same as the subject *boy.* Therefore the pronoun from the Subject Group is used.)
   It was *she* all right. (*She* means the same as the subject *It.* Therefore the pronoun from the Subject Group is used.)

   Modern usage allows some exceptions to this rule however. *It is me* and *it is us* (instead of the grammatically correct *It is I* and *it is we*) are now established usage; and *it is him, it is her,* and *it is them* are widely used, particularly in informal speech.

Pronouns in the Nonsubject Group are used for all other purposes. The following pronouns are not subjects, nor are they words that mean the same as subjects. Therefore they come from the Nonsubject Group.

He came with Lynn and *me.*

A good way to tell which pronoun to use is to leave out the extra name: *He came with me.* You would never say *He came with I.*

> We saw Lynn and *him* last night. (We saw *him* last night.)
> He gave *us* boys a pony. (He gave *us* a pony.)
> The firm gave my wife and *me* a trip to the Virgin Islands. (They gave *me* a trip to the Virgin Islands.)

EXERCISES

Underline the correct pronoun. Remember the trick of leaving out the extra word in order to decide which pronoun to use. Also if you find *than* in a sentence, remember that the sentence may not be written out in full.

□ EXERCISE 1

1. It cost Dave and (I me) a dollar apiece to make that long-distance call.
2. He asked for a ride home with my sister and (I me).
3. My cousin is smarter than (I me), but she doesn't work as hard.
4. Consequently I usually get better grades than (her she).
5. No one could be better prepared for the exam than (he him).
6. I gave all the tickets to (she her) and her sister to sell.
7. They sent a telegram to (she her) and her father.
8. They asked whether (she her) and her father would come to the wedding.
9. I hope that my boyfriend and (I me) will be invited.
10. I hope they will invite my boyfriend and (I me).

□ EXERCISE 2

1. I don't think there's much in common between (he him) and his father.
2. Dad gave my brother and (I me) a motorcycle for Christmas.
3. My aunt asked my girlfriend and (I me) to visit her.
4. My aunt asked whether my girlfriend and (I me) would like to go to the carnival.
5. The noise was blamed on my roommate and (I me).
6. Actually he was more to blame than (I me).
7. Some of (we us) freshmen are always being blamed for something.
8. Most of the lecture seemed to be directed at (we us) freshmen.
9. This is strictly between you and (I me).
10. (Me and my sister, My sister and I) share an apartment.

☐ EXERCISE 3

1. The director asked (we us) girls to help serve.
2. (We Us) girls did most of the decorating.
3. The program was left up to (we us) girls too.
4. It was a close game of chess between my friend and (I me).
5. Did you watch (he him) and Karla dancing last night?
6. No one could be more of a clown than (he him).
7. There's difficulty between (he him) and his parents.
8. While we were traveling in Nevada, time went fast for Lou and (I me).
9. (Lou and I, Me and Lou) were gone three weeks.
10. It was one of the best trips Lou and (I me) ever took.

☐ EXERCISE 4

1. (He and I, Him and me) went skiing last weekend.
2. It was the first ski trip (he and I, him and me) had taken.
3. Several others joined (we us) two.
4. I wonder why (he him) and his brother don't play football.
5. You should have heard the conversation between Noel and (I me).
6. Mom asked Dad and (I me) what we intended to do about the dented fender.
7. No one could decide that problem except Dad and (I me).
8. Dad and (I me) sat down to talk it over.
9. My dad and (I me) now have an agreement between us.
10. We may disagree, but there are never hard feelings between (we us) two.

☐ EXERCISE 5

1. The bus rolled away leaving Don and (I me) standing there.
2. They left it up to Joan and (I me) to plan the refreshments.
3. Between you and (I me), I think we have the best coach in the state.
4. The coach has left it to Robert and (I me) to arrange the rides.
5. I am older than (them they).
6. The president of the firm invited my wife and (I me) to a reception.
7. (Me and my wife) (My wife and I) will enjoy going.
8. (David and I) (Me and David) have always been the best of friends.
9. Don't you think you should leave that for Fran and (I me) to decide?
10. Don't you think that Fran and (I me) should decide that?

WRITING YOUR OWN SENTENCES

On a separate sheet, or in your journal, write three sentences using pronouns you may formerly have used incorrectly.

MAKING THE PRONOUN REFER TO THE RIGHT WORD

When you write a sentence, *you* know what it means, but your reader may not. What does this sentence mean?

Joe told his father he would have to take the car to the garage.

Who would have to take the car? We don't know whether the pronoun *he* refers to Joe or to his father. The sentence might mean

Joe said that his father would have to take the car to the garage.
or
Joe told his father that he was planning to take the car to the garage.

A simpler way to get rid of such a faulty reference is to use a direct quotation:

Joe said to his father, "I will have to take the car to the garage."

Here is another sentence with a faulty reference:

I have always been interested in nursing and finally have decided to become one.

Decided to become a nursing? There is no word for *one* to refer to. We need to write

I have always been interested in nursing and finally have decided to become a nurse.

Another kind of faulty reference is a *which* clause that refers to an entire idea:

No one could tell him where the bike had been left which made him angry.

Was he angry because no one could tell him or because the bike had not been left in its proper place? The sentence should read

It made him angry that the bike had not been left in its place.
or
It made him angry that no one could tell him where the bike had been left.

EXERCISES

Most of the following sentences are not clear because we don't know what word the pronoun refers to. Revise such sentences, making the meaning clear. Remember that using a direct quotation is often the easiest way to clarify what a pronoun refers to. Since there are more ways than one to rewrite each sentence, yours may be as good as the one on the answer sheet. Just ask yourself whether the meaning is clear.

☐ EXERCISE 1

1. I put the omelet on the table, took off my apron, and began to eat it.

2. They offered me a job which pleased me.

3. I've been trying to decide what trip to take which isn't easy.

4. She told her sister that her room was a mess.

5. I have a pair of glasses, but my eyes are so good that I don't use them except for reading.

6. The president told the dean he had been too lenient.

7. When I praised the child's finger painting, it was pleased.

8. I thought he would phone, and I waited all evening for it to ring.

9. The teachers established a play center where they can spend their leisure.

10. Ray told the professor that his watch was wrong.

☐ EXERCISE 2

1. When I picked up the dog's dish, it began to bark.

2. I have always been interested in coaching football ever since I was in high school, and now I have decided to become one.

3. I decided not to get a summer job which annoyed my family.

4. She asked her sister why she wasn't invited to the party.

5. Jay's father let him take his new tennis racket to school.

6. I have always liked French Provincial furniture and have finally decided to buy one.

7. She told her instructor she didn't understand what she was saying.

8. She likes to swim; in fact she spends most of her summer doing it.

9. She is good in her studies although not very good in sports. This is why she was chosen student body president.

10. When the boss talked with Ed, he was really despondent.

☐EXERCISE 3

1. His motorcycle swerved into the side of a house, but it wasn't damaged.

2. As I approached the baby's playpen, it began to cry.

3. As soon as the fender was repaired, I drove it home.

4. I stopped at the old Wiley Schoolhouse, which has been designated a state historical site.

5. The instructor told him his typewriter needed a new ribbon.

6. He told his father he ought to wash the car.

7. I walked into the room, climbed on the ladder, and began to paint it.

8. I'm taking lessons in golf, which is my favorite sport.

9. She told her mother she needed to be positive before making such a big decision.

10. We couldn't find a single bottle and blamed Rudy for drinking all of them.

☐ **EXERCISE 4**

1. Andy told his brother that his car had a flat tire.

2. It would be cold in New England at this time of year which I don't like.

3. He asked the mechanic why he was having trouble.

4. When her sister came in at 4 a.m., she was crying.

5. As I tried to attach the dog's leash, it jumped away.

6. Yesterday I turned in a paper that came back with an *A* grade.

7. The cars whizzed past, but they didn't even look my way.

8. As soon as I approached the robin's nest, it flew away.

9. I've decided to save all my money for a trip which won't be easy.

10. She told her daughter that she had missed her appointment.

☐ **EXERCISE 5**

1. He told his dad he needed a new suit.

2. We couldn't find the cake plate and realized the children must have eaten it.

3. She served me a pizza, which was cold.

4. When I moved the child's tricycle, it screamed.

5. I have adjusted the steering wheel, and you can take it home.

6. After I had read the story of Lindbergh's life, I decided that is what I want to be.

7. He asked the man to come back when he had time to talk.

8. When Jerome talked to his father, he was very angry.

9. Ben told his father he ought to get a refund for the faulty tire.

10. When I opened the door of the kennel, it ran away.

GETTING RID OF MISPLACED OR DANGLING MODIFIERS

A modifier gives information about some word in a sentence, and it should be as close to that word as possible. In the following sentence the modifier is too far away from the word it modifies to make sense:

Leaping across the road we saw two deer.

Was it *we* who were leaping across the road? That is what the sentence says because the modifier *Leaping across the road* is next to *we*. Of course it should be next to *deer*.

We saw two deer leaping across the road.

The next example has no word at all for the modifier to modify:

At the age of six my family moved to North Dakota.

Obviously the family was not six when it moved. The modifier *At the age of six* is dangling there with no word to attach itself to, no word for it to modify. We must change the sentence so there will be such a word:

At the age of six I moved to North Dakota with my family.

Now the modifier *At the age of six* has a proper word—I—for it to modify. Or we could get rid of the dangling modifier by turning it into a dependent clause:

When I was six, my family moved to North Dakota.

Here the clause has its own subject—I—and there is no chance of misunderstanding the sentence. Here is another dangling modifier:

After running six blocks, the bus pulled away as I reached it.

Had the bus run six blocks? Who had? You can change the sentence one of two ways. Either insert *I* to make clear who did the running:

After running six blocks, I saw the bus pull away as I reached it.

Or turn the dangling modifier into a dependent clause:

After I had run six blocks, the bus pulled away as I reached it.

Either way of getting rid of the dangling modifier makes the sentence clear.

EXERCISES

Most—but not all—of these sentences contain misplaced or dangling modifiers. Some you may correct simply by shifting the modifier so it will be next to the word it modifies. Others you'll need to rewrite. Since there is more than one way to correct each sentence, your way may be as good as the one at the back of the book.

☐ EXERCISE 1

1. You will enjoy looking at the pictures that you took years later.

2. Sound asleep on the front porch I came across my grandfather.

3. Crawling across the dusty road I saw a furry little caterpillar.

4. Taking her in his arms the moon hid behind a cloud.

5. While talking on the phone the cake burned.

6. By concentrating Intently, I at last understood the meaning of the paragraph.

7. Lincoln Park is the most interesting park in the city that I have seen.

8. She was engaged to a man with a Cougar named Smith.

9. At the age of fourteen my sister was born.

10. We gave all the food to the dog that we didn't want.

☐ EXERCISE 2

1. After cleaning my room, my dog wanted to go for a walk.

2. A son was born to Mr. and Mrs. N. L. Larson weighing eight pounds.

3. Being a bore, I don't enjoy his company.

4. Except when pickled, I don't care for cucumbers.

5. Screaming and kicking, I tried to quiet the child.

6. I bought a car from a used-car dealer with a leaky radiator.

7. Leaning against the barn, I saw the broken ladder.

8. After watching TV all evening, the dirty dishes were still on the table.

9. At the age of six my grandfather paid us a visit.

10. Slamming the door he marched out of the house.

☐ EXERCISE 3

1. Badly in need of a bath, I brought the dog into the laundry room.

2. Quietly munching hay, I watched the horses in the pasture.

3. Having been born and raised in the country, the old cookstove naturally appeals to me.

4. Excited and eager to go, the bus was in front of the building waiting for us.

5. The house is surrounded by a grove of catalpa trees where I was born.

6. Crying pitifully, I stopped and talked to the child.

7. Unwrapping gift after gift, the puppy had a great time playing with all the tissue paper.

8. I decided to give the clothes to a charity that I had no use for.

9. Although almost eight years old, he refused to turn his car in on a newer model.

10. She put the sandwiches back in the bag that she had not eaten.

☐ EXERCISE 4

1. At the age of ten my father became manager of his company.

2. Falling from the top of the Empire State Building we could see little white pieces of paper.

3. While on a two-week vacation, the office had to take care of itself.

4. I saw that the murderer had been captured in the evening paper.

5. After playing Frisbee all evening, my English paper did not get finished.

6. Consulting the Lost and Found section of the paper, the dog was soon safe at home again.

7. The youngster went careening down the driveway just as we arrived on a scooter.

8. After eating lunch hurriedly, the two taxis then started for Yosemite.

9. Moving slowly down the street, we saw the parade.

10. Looking at the dress closely, I saw that the material was coarse.

☐ EXERCISE 5

1. While tobogganing down the hill, a huge bear came into view.

2. The class made me aware of little speech habits I have while speaking with my friends which I got rid of very soon.

3. I watched a monkey running up a coconut tree.

4. The monkey watched us peeling a banana in the cage.

5. While hiking up the mountain, we saw three porcupines.

6. Dressed in a long blue evening gown, he thought she had never looked prettier.

7. Being a small town, one doesn't have to worry about crime.

8. Darting here and there through the bushes, we watched the first spring warblers.

9. Because of going to too many parties, my term paper was late.

10. We are having a series of lectures on religions of the world which will end May 30.

USING PARALLEL CONSTRUCTION

Your writing will be clearer if you use parallel construction. That is, when you make any kind of list, put the items in similar form. If you write

I enjoy *swimming, skiing,* and *to hunt.*

the sentence lacks parallel construction. The items don't all have the same form. But if you write

I enjoy *swimming, skiing,* and *hunting.*

then the items are parallel. They all have the same form. They are all *ing* words. Or you could write

I like *to swim, to ski,* and *to hunt.*

Again the sentence uses parallel construction because the items all have the same form. They all use *to* and a verb. Here are some more examples. Note how much easier it is to read the column with parallel construction.

LACKING PARALLEL CONSTRUCTION	HAVING PARALLEL CONSTRUCTION
He expected a woman *to have* a good job, *to be* beautiful, and *who would pamper* his every whim.	He expected a woman *to have* a good job, *to be* beautiful, and *to pamper* his every whim. (All three items start with *to* and a verb.)
His experience made him *sullen, bitter,* and a *cynic.*	His experience made him *sullen, bitter,* and *cynical.* (All three are words describing him.)
She asked me *whether I could take shorthand* and *my experience.*	She asked me *whether I could take shorthand* and *what experience I had had.* (Both items are dependent clauses.)
By hard work and *because I invested my savings* in the company, I won a promotion.	*By hard work* and *by investing my savings* in the company, I won a promotion. (Both items are prepositional phrases.)
She wanted a house with *seven rooms, a two-car garage,* and *it should be in a good location.*	She wanted a house with *seven rooms, a two-car garage,* and *a good location.* (All three are words that can be read smoothly after the preposition *with.*)

Here are examples of thesis statements (see pp. 190–192 for an explanation of thesis statements), which of course should always use parallel construction. Note how each item in the last column can be read smoothly after the main statement. Those in the first column cannot.

My summer job at a resort was worthwhile because it gave me
1. money for college.
2. I hadn't had a full-time job before.
3. had time for recreation.

My summer job at a resort was worthwhile because it gave me
1. *money* for college.
2. *experience* in a full-time job.
3. *time* for recreation.

College students should not live at home because
1. they need to be independent.
2. friendships in a dorm.
3. waste time commuting.

College students should not live at home because
1. they need to be independent.
2. they'll make more friends in a dorm.
3. they won't waste time commuting.

Using parallel construction will make your writing more effective. Note the effective parallelism in these well-known quotations:

We cannot dedicate, we cannot consecrate, we cannot hallow this ground.
—Abraham Lincoln

Ask not what your country can do for you; ask what you can do for your country.
—John F. Kennedy

With this faith we will be able to work together, to pray together, to struggle together, to go to jail together, to stand up for freedom together, knowing that we will be free one day.
—Martin Luther King, Jr.

EXERCISES

Most—but not all—of these sentences lack parallel construction. Make whatever changes are necessary.

☐ EXERCISE 1

1. I like staying up late at night and to sleep late in the morning.

2. She taught her preschool son by reading to him, by teaching him songs, by giving him constructive toys, and she took him on neighborhood excursions.

3. Each student was given a choice of writing a term paper, taking a written exam, or an oral report could be given.

4. She wants a house near the city and having modern conveniences.

5. I had read the textbook, read the reference books, written the term paper, and I had studied for the exam.

6. After we had eaten our supper, we put water on the fire, washed the dishes, and we packed the car for an early morning start.

7. Among the advantages of my new job are the short hours, the boss is pleasant, and the good salary.

8. I enjoy hiking, mountain climbing, and love camping out.

9. I have learned to adapt myself to new environments and how to get along with other people.

10. My small brother likes candy, popcorn, and chewing bubble gum.

☐ EXERCISE 2

1. She liked to play solos and performing before an audience.

2. He arrived in the ancient city of Damascus, threaded his way through the narrow streets, and was taking pictures of the children.

3. The cat was meowing pitifully and scratched at the screen door.

4. He will learn to work with other people and the value of cooperation.

5. At the auction she bought a victrola, two old chairs, and she also bought an old popcorn popper.

6. If you want to create a beautiful room, it is more essential to have a knowledge of decorating than having a great deal of money.

7. The speaker was interesting, inspiring, and entertained the audience too.

8. I'm learning to read more rapidly, to improve my vocabulary, and I'm also reading better books.

9. He spoke with authority, illustrated his talk with personal incidents, and then he concluded with a poem.

10. The weather was cold, damp, and often raining.

☐ EXERCISE 3

1. With tact, kindness, and having understanding, one can usually help a disturbed child.

2. They chose a house in the country because they wanted to grow their own vegetables, to give their children a country environment, and to enjoy the quiet of rural life.

3. A coaching career offered him a good salary, enjoyable work, and he would have security.

4. Her garden included evergreens, deciduous trees, bushes, and there were all kinds of flowers.

5. She weeded them, pruned them, watered them, and sometimes she even sat and enjoyed them.

6. We tried to teach our puppy to sit up, to beg, and come when called.

7. I finished studying, had a snack, and then I went to bed.

8. The box is six inches long and five inches in width.

9. My father worked, saved, and finally made his way through college.

10. Radiation is something you can't see, can't feel, and you can't even smell it.

☐ EXERCISE 4

1. She took her children to art classes, skating classes, and to judo lessons.

2. The preschool gave Justin experience in working with his hands, in developing rhythm, and in getting along with others.

3. When Justin started kindergarten, however, he was shy, frightened, and he was unhappy.

4. A concerned teacher and children who were friendly soon changed his attitude.

5. He lost his shyness and his being afraid.

6. He became outgoing, happy, and he was interested in all that was going on.

7. His father bought him a paint set, wrapped it in fancy paper, and then he placed it at Justin's place at the table.

8. Justin's father was even-tempered, kind, and thought of others before himself.

9. He showed Justin how to root a plant, how to plant it, and finally the way fertilizer should be added.

10. That we give our children too many material things, that we don't develop values, and that we don't help them become creative were his main beliefs.

☐ EXERCISE 5

1. Michelle has wanted a new job for a long time, has been offered several, and finally has accepted one in a dress shop.

2. She has previously worked as a secretary, a bookkeeper, and she has worked as a bank teller too.

3. Now she is responsible for checking the new shipments, pricing the clothes, and then she has to make the window displays.

4. The rest of the clerks merely have to keep the racks in order, the display counters should be kept neat, and of course wait on customers.

5. Her job is demanding, but she feels satisfied with what she is accomplishing; it's really challenging.

6. She likes a job where she meets people, where she can help people, and have some job security.

7. Her supervisor reports that she knows the stock well, is pleasant with customers, and that she gets along well with the other employees.

8. Last winter she went to Phoenix to attend a convention and for a vacation.

9. She brought back from Arizona turquoise beads, some Indian baskets, and she also brought back an Indian blanket.

10. She traveled by car, by bus, and train.

☐ EXERCISE 6

1. When our family went on a camping trip, we had rain, sleet, and it was cold the first day.

2. After we had set up camp, we cooked our supper, walked down to the beach, and watched the children playing in the water.

3. Then we went to a lecture that taught us the names of flowers and trees, the songs of birds, and to recognize the sounds of insects.

4. The lecture was informative and good entertainment.

5. The next morning on our walk through the woods, we saw the buds on the maple trees opening, the tightly rolled leaves of the May apples showing their heads above ground, and the anemone blossoms were waving in the wind.

6. We watched the waxwings eating berries, the starlings pecking in the grass, and a redheaded woodpecker was tapping away on a tree trunk.

7. Walking along the stream, looking for wild flowers, and to watch for birds fascinated me.

8. I enjoy living on a beach because I can sunbathe, sail, or I can go in swimming without driving miles to a resort.

9. I waxed my car, vacuumed the interior, and polished the chrome.

10. We found the summer camp challenging, enjoyable, and it taught us some things as well.

□ EXERCISE 7

1. Her study contained an old rolltop desk, a typing table, and in one corner was her bulging file cabinet.

2. He washed the dishes, tidied the house, and was waiting for Sue to return.

3. His talk was about law enforcement, gun control laws, and that crime is increasing.

4. He had traveled by land, by sea, and air.

5. He wrote his paper, had a friend read it, rewrote it, read it aloud, and rewrote it once more.

6. By careful planning, by smart shopping, and cooking economy meals, she stayed within their budget.

7. He suggested doing all the exercises and that we rewrite all our papers.

8. She is a woman with infinite charm and who always says the tactful thing.

9. By then I had learned how to change the oil, how to check the battery, and the way to change a tire.

10. "Go back to Mississippi, go back to Alabama, go back to South Carolina, go back to Georgia, go back to Louisiana, go back to the slums and ghettos of our northern cities, knowing that somehow this situation can and will be changed." —Martin Luther King, Jr.

Make the supporting points of these thesis statements parallel.

☐ **EXERCISE 8**

1. Every college student should know how to type because
   1. some instructors require typed papers

   2. saves time

   3. get higher grades

2. Going home every weekend is unwise because
   1. I spend too much time on the bus

   2. I get behind in my college work

   3. expensive

   4. miss out on weekend activities at college

3. Commercial billboards along highways should be prohibited because
   1. they often cause accidents

   2. mar scenery

4. Learning to sew is valuable because
   1. sewing your own clothes saves money

   2. creative

5. My chief objectives in this course are
   1. to learn to spell

   2. to learn to write well-constructed sentences

   3. being able to write a clear composition

WRITING YOUR OWN SENTENCES

On a separate sheet, or in your journal, write two sentences using parallel construction, one telling the fields you might consider going into and one telling the kind of house you'd like to have.

AVOIDING SHIFT IN TIME

If you begin writing a paper in past time, don't shift now and then to the present; and if you begin in the present, don't shift to the past. In the following paragraph the writer starts in the present and then shifts to the past.

> In *The Old Man and the Sea* there are various conflicts. The Old Man has to fight not only the marlin and the sharks; he has to fight the doubts in his own mind. He wasn't sure that he still had the strength to subdue the giant marlin.

It should be all in the present:

> In *The Old Man and the Sea* there are various conflicts. The Old Man has to fight not only the marlin and the sharks; he has to fight the doubts in his own mind. He isn't sure that he still has the strength to subdue the giant marlin.

Or it could be all in the past:

> In *The Old Man and the Sea* there were various conflicts. The Old Man had to fight not only the marlin and the sharks; he had to fight the doubts in his own mind. He wasn't sure that he still had the strength to subdue the giant marlin.

EXERCISES

These sentences have shifts in time, either from past to present or from present to past. Change the verbs in each sentence to agree with the first verb used. Cross out the incorrect verb and write the correct one above it.

☐ EXERCISE 1

1. In my excitement I stumbled over rocks and dirt and then finally I see what looks like a path.

2. We hiked to the end of the trail, and then we come back.

3. We rented a boat, went out on the lake, and watched the sunset before we come in for supper on the beach.

4. In the short story "The Secret Life of Walter Mitty," Mr. Mitty is first driving his car, but then in his mind the car became an airplane.

5. When Mr. Mitty's wife asks him why he isn't wearing his gloves, he suddenly thought of surgeon's gloves and became a doctor performing an operation on a millionaire banker.

6. I heard a knock, and then in comes my old high school friend.

7. I went to my room to dress but suddenly remember that my clothes were all in the washer.

8. The heroine was rescued after the speedboat turns over.

9. He tells us he'll write, but he never wrote.

10. Berne's book lists the games people play and told why they play them.

☐EXERCISE 2

1. The candidate gave his speech, answered questions, and then came down from the stage and goes around shaking hands with everyone.

2. We worked the entire summer at the camp, and then at the end the director surprises us with an extra week's pay.

3. The bad guy shoots at the good guy, but of course the good guy escaped.

4. The heroine gives up her right to the fortune, but she got it finally anyway.

5. I wanted to do my best in that course; I give it all I have.

6. I finished the dishes, set the table for morning, and crawl into bed.

7. Friends are important to me, especially because I had no close relatives.

8. She loved that little house and goes back to see it again and again.

9. I took one look at the clock and run for the bus.

10. The book gave an account of Freud's work, but it doesn't tell much about his life.

The following paragraphs shift back and forth between past time and present. Change the verbs in each paragraph to agree with the first verb used.

☐ EXERCISE 3

As I traveled down the highway, I signal to turn left. I start the turn, and all of a sudden I heard a braking noise that could be heard for miles. A man had tried to pass me and had not seen my signal, probably because of the glaring sunlight. The man stopped finally. Really not knowing what I was doing, I pull off the road. Then it hit me, a sick feeling that reached all parts of my body. I stop the truck and get out, stunned but relieved.

☐ EXERCISE 4

That summer I decided to buy a radio receiver with the money I had earned mowing lawns. I set it up in my bedroom, and then I spent an afternoon putting an antenna on the roof. My mother stands down there on the lawn hollering advice at me because she's afraid I'm going to fall off the roof. In spite of her I finally get it up, and then I went inside and connected the antenna to the receiver. Presto! I am listening to radios all over the world. Eventually I decide I want a ham radio operator's license too so I could transmit back to some of the stations I was hearing. I got the license all right, but being young and shy, I never did much talking. Mostly I just listen and work on my equipment. After a few months I tired of my new toy and never did any more with it. The challenge of striving for the set was more fun than actually having it.

□ EXERCISE 5

The astronomer Carl Sagan says that life elsewhere in the cosmos is probable. He said there are many places where life could develop. In the Milky Way, for example, there are 400 billion suns, and most may have planetary systems. Sagan says that the building blocks of life form readily and that there are billions of years of time for evolution. He said it's likely that life has emerged in a large number of places and that intelligence has emerged in a smaller number of places.

□ EXERCISE 6

Early people had to find shelter in nature. In warm climates trees provide shelter, but in cold climates caves were the best protection. The people built a fire at the mouth of the cave to keep fierce animals away, and they live near the fire rather than in the damp, chill interior of the cave. Several families live together in a cave and hunted together. This was the beginning of group living.

□ EXERCISE 7

Even though Robert Frost eventually became the most beloved of New England poets, his early career was not promising. After a few months in college, he decides that the routine of study is too much for him, and he became a bobbin boy in a mill. Later he married and once more tried college at Harvard but gave up after two years. Then followed a period in which he tramps, teaches school, makes shoes, and edits a weekly paper. Finally his grandfather took pity on him and bought him a farm. For eleven years he tried with scant success to wrest a living from the stony hills. During all this time he is writing poetry, but no magazine wanted it. Not until he sold his farm and went to England, where his first book of poems was published, did he become known. When he returned to America three years later, he finds himself famous.

□ **EXERCISE 8**

In Eudora Welty's short story "A Worn Path," old Phoenix Jackson encounters all sorts of hazards as she takes the long walk through the woods and fields on her way to Natchez to get some medicine for her grandson. The thorny bush caught her dress; the barbed wire fence was difficult to get through; the scarecrow frightened her; and a passing dog made her tumble into a ditch like a little puff of milkweed. But she lightheartedly overcomes all the obstacles and eventually gets to the doctor's office, where she was given the soothing medicine as well as a nickel, which she planned to spend on a paper windmill for her grandson. The author seems to be saying that it is possible for a person to be so full of love, so in tune with nature and man, so free of fear, that she was able to overcome obstacles that for anyone else would be insurmountable.

WRITING YOUR OWN PARAGRAPHS

1. Write a brief paragraph in past tense describing an accident you once had.
2. Now describe the same accident as if it is happening at this moment.

AVOIDING SHIFT IN PERSON

You may write a paper in

First person—*I, we*
Second person—*you*
Third person—*he, she, one, anyone, a person, they*

but do not shift from one group to another.

Wrong: In making experiments in chemistry *one* should read the directions carefully. Otherwise *you* may have an explosion.

Right: In making experiments in chemistry *one* should read the directions carefully. Otherwise *one* (or *he* or *she*) may have an explosion.

Right: In making experiments in chemistry *you* should read the directions carefully. Otherwise *you* may have an explosion.

Wrong: Few *people* get as much enjoyment out of music as *they* could. *One* need not be an accomplished musician to get some fun out of playing an instrument. Nor do *you* need to be very far advanced before joining an amateur group of players.

Right: Few *people* get as much enjoyment out of music as *they* could. *One* need not be an accomplished musician to get some fun out of playing an instrument. Nor is it necessary to be very far advanced before joining an amateur group of players.

Too many *one's* in a paper make it sound stilted and formal. Often a sentence can be revised (as in the last sentence of the last example) to avoid using either *one* or *you*.

Sometimes an inexperienced writer uses *you* when the meaning is not *you, the reader*.

You could tell that no one had been there in weeks.

Such a sentence is almost always improved by getting rid of the *you*.

Obviously no one had been there in weeks.

EXERCISES

Revise these sentences and paragraphs from student papers so there will be no shift in person. You may simply cross out some words and write your corrections above, or you may wish to rewrite an entire sentence.

□ EXERCISE 1

1. If you do all these exercises, one should be able to get an *A*.

2. I like the feeling that comes when you have reviewed thoroughly and feel ready for any exam.

3. If you don't get enough sleep at night, one won't be able to concentrate during the day.

4. I'm learning to spell, but I find you really have to work at it.

5. One's grades are usually in proportion to the time you spend studying.

6. I studied until midnight; after that your brain just doesn't function well.

7. I discovered when I got to college that you can't take it easy the way you did in high school.

8. One should get some exercise every day if you want to stay healthy.

9. Anyone who wants to lose weight has to cut out sugar, and you have to stick to some rigid diet.

10. When we went into the woods, you could see deer tracks in the snow.

□ EXERCISE 2

1. After we got our seat belts fastened, the plane took off, and you could see the little farms like a checkerboard below.

2. Then as we looked down, you couldn't see anything but clouds.

3. I work harder when I know an instructor really wants to help you.

4. If you want to improve your reading ability, one should read a great deal.

5. If parents expect their children to be unselfish, you have to set the example.

6. I always enjoy myself more if no one says when you have to be in.

7. If you want to prevent air pollution, one's car should have a tune-up twice a year.

8. We used to fight a lot when we were kids, but as you grow up you become more friendly.

9. Those who want to go on the field trip should get your equipment now.

10. You shouldn't strive to possess things, for eventually they'll possess you.

□ EXERCISE 3

1. In high school I took a course called General Woods in which you made a piece of furniture. You did this on your own with a little help from the teacher. I made a coffee table, which my teacher encouraged me later to enter in a state content.

2. Mr. Martin was one of the best teachers I ever had. He would give you two work sheets every day, and if you didn't do them, he would keep after you until you did. And he was the kind of teacher you could tell your problems to. I'll never forget the talks I had with him.

3. The part of the accounting course I liked best was the practice sets. We did four sets during the semester. Doing them made you feel you were getting the experience of working for a company because we wrote checks, filed papers, and wrote in journals and ledgers. The practice sets prepared you for the business world.

Revise these student papers so there will be no shift in person.

□ EXERCISE 4

FREEDOM COSTS FREEDOM

I had worked all summer to save money for my first car. For months I'd kept at my job every day and saved every penny I earned. I'd never buy donuts at coffee break or dessert at lunch because every dollar saved brought me closer to the car I wanted so much. Finally for a few hundred dollars I bought a car that was just right for me.

A car is more than just a means of getting around. It's a status symbol. It's your sign of independence. It's your ticket to freedom. You don't have to ask to borrow the family car, and you don't have to explain where you are going or when you'll be back. Now I could drive where I wanted when I wanted.

The one thing I hadn't counted on, though, was how much it cost to keep a car running. With insurance, gas, and repairs, I found myself working just to support my car. My paychecks went for new wheel rims, car stereo components, and every accessory you could think of. I worked extra evenings to buy plush seatcovers and overtime on weekends to buy new tires.

Funny how it costs so much of your freedom to support your freedom.

□ EXERCISE 5

FLOATING ON A CLOUD

Ever since I'd seen pictures of hot air balloons, I knew I'd have to try one. They looked so beautiful and peaceful as they floated along. Finally I made arrangements for a flight, and today was the day.

Driving to a field outside the city, I joined the pilot and some friends. Together we unloaded the balloon from a trailer, spread it on the grass, and inflated it. It was amazing to watch a bundle of fabric expand to such an enormous size, its bright yellow and red colors lit up by the morning sun.

When a balloon is inflated with hot air, it really wants to fly, so I hopped in the basket with the pilot, and he turned up the gas burner until the others outside couldn't hold us down. As we rose silently and slowly into the morning sky, you could see the people below getting smaller and smaller. The serenity was marred only by the noise from the burner that the pilot turned on periodically to keep the air in the balloon hot.

Flying in a balloon is about as close to floating on a cloud as you can get. You can't feel the wind, of course, because you are drifting with it, but you can see the ground moving along beneath you. We rose higher by running the burner and then drifted lower as the air cooled off. When we went low, a dog in a yard barked wildly at us; when we went high, you could see for miles. Then sometimes we just hung there quietly in the sky.

After a couple of hours the pilot carefully let the balloon cool off, and we descended gently into a field. The landing was so soft it almost seemed as if we were still in the air. Our friends drove up, and as we deflated the balloon and loaded it back on the trailer, they congratulated us on a beautiful flight.

Few experiences you could have could compare with floating on a cloud.

WRITING YOUR OWN PARAGRAPHS

1. Write a brief paragraph telling someone how to develop good study habits. It will, of course, be a "you should" paragraph.
2. Then write the same paragraph to yourself—an "I should" paragraph.
3. Finally write the same paragraph using "students should" and using the pronoun *they*.

GETTING RID OF WORDINESS

Good writing is concise writing. Don't say something in ten words if you can say it as well, or better, in five. "In this day and age" is not as effective as simply "today." "At the present time" should be "at present" or "now."

Another kind of wordiness comes from saying something twice. There is no need to say "in the month of July" or "7 a.m. in the morning" or "my personal opinion." July *is* a month, 7 a.m. *is* the morning, and my opinion obviously *is* personal. All you need to say is "in July," "7 a.m.," and "my opinion."

Still another kind of wordiness comes from using expressions that add nothing to the meaning of the sentence. "The fact of the matter is that I'm tired" says no more than "I'm tired."

Below are more examples of wordiness.

WORDY WRITING	CONCISE WRITING
at that point in time	then
there is no doubt but that	no doubt
he is a person who	he
a person who is honest	an honest person
there are many boys who	many boys
he was there in person	he was there
personally I think	I think
my father he	my father
surrounded on all sides	surrounded
during the winter months	during the winter
brown in color	brown
refer back	refer
repeat again	repeat
two different kinds	two kinds
free complimentary copy	complimentary copy
free gift	gift
very unique	unique
past history	history
end result	result
and etc.	etc.
usual custom	custom

EXERCISES

Cross out words or rewrite parts of each sentence to get rid of the wordiness. Doing these exercises can almost turn into a game to see how few words you can use without changing the meaning of the sentence.

☐ EXERCISE 1

1. I woke up at 4 a.m. this morning.

2. We were considering the question as to whether we should charge admission.

3. There are many people who never read a book from one end of the year to the other.

4. After our lengthy hike that lasted over eight hours, we were hungry for food.

5. He had tried several different sports. These sports included football, basketball, and hockey.

6. He is a man who can be depended upon to do what he says he will do.

7. I had an unexpected surprise yesterday when the guy who had roomed with me in college stopped in to see me.

8. I think if I am not mistaken, that she is really planning to go.

9. I found that I had no money at all by the end of the year.

10. All of the three different kinds of stones we found were very unique.

☐ EXERCISE 2

1. There is no doubt but that our team will win.

2. They carried him to his place of residence in an intoxicated condition.

3. At this point in time there is a lot more permissiveness than there used to be in years gone by.

4. In my personal opinion there is no doubt but that justice is too slow in this country of ours.

5. What I am trying to say is that in my opinion justice should be swift and sure.

6. He is a man who has worked hard all his life.

7. It is his height that makes him such a good basketball player.

8. The melons were large in size and sweet in taste.

9. The great percentage of students do not leave the campus on weekends.

10. The last point that I will try to make in this paper is the idea that one should learn more at college than just what is learned from one's courses.

□ **EXERCISE 3**

1. There were a lot of people there.

2. At the present time thousands of acres of land are under water along the river.

3. Personally I think something should be done to prevent all this flooding.

4. It is my opinion that no one seems to be working on the problem.

5. Finally the doctor arrived on the scene, but absolutely nothing could be done for her.

6. The plane circled around the airport for half an hour and then disappeared from view.

7. I was unaware of the fact that she had arrived.

8. The reason he left college was that he wanted some experience in the world of business.

9. In this modern day and age, it is important for the wealthier countries to help the developing countries all over the world by giving them aid.

10. In the year of 1981 my brother accepted a new job with the Bell and Howell Company, which is located in the city of Chicago.

☐ EXERCISE 4

1. It is my personal opinion that most people these days are spending entirely too much of their leisure time watching programs presented on TV.

2. The fact of the matter is that I completely forgot about the meeting that was scheduled for last night.

3. Most writers use too many words, repeating themselves and saying things over and over again.

4. When driving a new car for the first time, one must take care not to drive too fast for the first 500 miles.

5. With reference to your letter, I may say that I really appreciate your kind invitation and am happy that I am able to accept.

6. What I intend to do is to finish my year here and then look for a job that will bring in some money.

7. Most people, you will find, want a business form that is clear, concise, and easy to understand.

8. It seems to me that the president should take it upon herself to see that the motion comes to a vote of the members of the organization.

9. I couldn't help but think that she was just pretending to be ill.

10. I am making an effort to try to get rid of wordiness in my papers.

On a separate sheet rewrite this paragraph from a university publication, cutting its 117 words to about 47 and see how much more effective it will be.

□ EXERCISE 5

One of the main problems of a student entering university is how to find his way around the twelve floors of the Library and how to use the materials. The students are confronted by rows of books, journals, complicated indexes, abstracts and ponderous reference works, and need help in finding the information they seek amid the mass of material. The Library staff recognizes its responsibility to help them utilize all this material. Orientation programs are given to all new students. Many faculty members bring their classes to a particular subject area or to the Government Publications for an orientation. Short printed handouts are available, such as special subject bibliographies, how to use periodical indexes or psychological abstracts.

Review of Sentence Structure

One sentence in each pair is correct; the other is incorrect. Read both sentences carefully before you decide. Then write the letter of the *correct* sentence in the blank. You may find any one of these errors:

run-together sentence
fragment
wrong verb form
lack of agreement between subject and verb and pronoun
wrong pronoun
faulty reference of pronoun
dangling modifier
lack of parallel construction
shift in time or person

_____ 1. A. You're right this can't go on.
              B. My sister and I planned the program.

_____ 2. A. The tutor helped both Renée and me.
              B. It don't matter if you're a little late.

_____ 3. A. One of my friends is getting a job for the summer.
              B. I intended to study, but I watch a TV program instead.

_____ 4. A. I held her books she ran back to the house.
              B. She had lost her camera but hoped she would find it.

_____ 5. A. If one wants a thrill, you should try water-skiing.
              B. Our team won the first game but lost in the finals.

_____ 6. A. We was planning a get-together after the game.
              B. I worked for hours but didn't get my paper finished.

_____ 7. A. Each of my sisters has her own car now.
              B. Getting that *A* pleases me and gave me new confidence.

_____ 8. A. He had worked as a farmhand, chauffeur, and in a mine.
              B. That sports car belongs to my fiancé and me.

_____ 9. A. Hoping for years that I could go to college and then finally making it.
              B. I liked his good humor, his easygoing way, and his generosity.

_____ 10. A. He was surprise to hear from her.
               B. They invited my boyfriend and me to their cottage.

_____ 11. A. The professor told my friend and I that we had passed.
               B. One of us is making a mistake.

_____ 12. A. Each of the candidates is well qualified for the job.
               B. Working for five hours last night, my term paper was finished.

_____ 13. A. The group leader asked my wife and me to canvass our block.
               B. Because he wanted people he could depend on.

_____ 14. A. You was certainly the best runner we had.

B. We freshmen were entertained by the upperclassmen.

_____ 15. A. They invited Nan and me to dinner.

B. An invitation which of course pleased us.

_____ 16. A. She ask me to help her with the refreshments.

B. Drive carefully.

_____ 17. A. When I entered the cottage, you could see that someone had been there.

B. I've finished mowing the lawn and now am going to rest.

_____ 18. A. The president asked Vic and me to be on the nominating committee.

B. I can't decide whether to become a teacher, a secretary, or go into social work.

_____ 19. A. Having finished all my homework, I went to bed.

B. He told his dad that his car needed a tune-up.

_____ 20. A. Every one of my plants are withering.

B. They expected us students to keep our rooms tidy.

_____ 21. A. One of my cousins is getting married in the spring.

B. Which is what we had been expecting her to do.

_____ 22. A. Running to catch the bus, she slipped and fell.

B. I hope to have my paper finish by classtime on Friday.

_____ 23. A. Because most of us intend to get jobs during vacation.

B. Having finished play practice, they went out for some food.

_____ 24. A. A list of readings was posted in the library.

B. He always comes late therefore he often misses the assignment.

_____ 25. A. You can improve your vocabulary it just takes determination.

B. Winning that trophy was the best thing that ever happened to him.

Punctuation
and
Capital Letters

3 Punctuation and Capital Letters

PERIOD, QUESTION MARK, EXCLAMATION MARK, SEMICOLON, COLON, DASH

Every mark of punctuation should help your reader. Just like Stop and Go signals at an intersection, marks of punctuation will keep the reader, like the traffic, from getting snarled up.

Here are the rules for six marks of punctuation. The first three you have known for a long time and have no trouble with. The one about semicolons you learned when you studied independent clauses (p. 66). The one about the colon will be less familiar.

Use a period at the end of a sentence and after an abbreviation.

Mr.	Ms.	Dr.	Wed.	sq. ft.
Mrs.	etc.	Jan.	p.m.	lbs.

Use a question mark after a direct question (but not after an indirect one).

Shall we go?
He asked whether we should go.

Use an exclamation mark after an expression that shows strong emotion.

Great! You're just in time!

Use a semicolon between two closely related independent clauses unless they are joined by one of the connecting words *and, but, for, or, nor, yet, so.* (Refer to pp. 66–72 for more practice in the use of the semicolon.)

The rain came down in torrents; we ran for shelter.
I have work to do; therefore I must leave.

Use a colon after a complete statement when a list or long quotation follows.

We took the following items: hot dogs, fruit, and coffee. (*We took the following items* is a complete statement. You can hear your voice fall at the end of it. Therefore a colon is used before the list.)

150

We took hot dogs, fruit, and coffee. (Here *We took* is not a complete statement; it needs the list to make it complete. Therefore since we don't want to separate the list from the first part of the sentence, no colon is used.)

Use a dash when there is an abrupt change of thought.

The little old lady sat in front of her spinning wheel—in Las Vegas. And the dash—well, don't use it too often.

EXERCISES

Add the necessary punctuation to these sentences (period, question mark, exclamation mark, semicolon, colon). Not all sentences require additional punctuation. Also your answer may not always agree with the one at the back of the book because clauses can be separated either with a semi-colon or with a period and capital letter. In general, use a period and capital letter. Only when the clauses are closely related in meaning should a semicolon be used.

□ EXERCISE 1

1. Hurry We've only two minutes until takeoff.
2. He asked whether we had seen his wife.
3. She was late however she still made the plane.
4. It was an hour's flight to Toronto we'd never been there before.
5. The snow was deep and crusty it was a perfect day for skiing.
6. That was the beginning of a good week I'll never forget it.
7. I couldn't decide what I liked best the skiing, the scenery, or the food.
8. That was only the first of our trips it made us want more.
9. We visited the following national parks Yellowstone, Glacier, and Yosemite.
10. We visited Yellowstone, Glacier, and Yosemite.

□ EXERCISE 2

1. Laughter is an indication of mental health some people never laugh.
2. I had to do three things that morning mail a package, pay the light bill, and get the concert tickets.
3. I stood in line for an hour to get the concert tickets then when I got to the window, they were sold out.
4. People usually minimize their own mistakes they magnify those of others.
5. Her hobby was decorating eggs she had learned the art from her Ukrainian mother.
6. Did you know I'm taking karate lessons.

7. First the horse trotted then it broke into a gallop.
8. That was the first time I had ever galloped I almost fell off.
9. Help I've lost Archie.
10. And what about Tommy Where's he.

□ EXERCISE 3

1. Ervin has been collecting fossils for years he now has a large collection.
2. He finds the fossils in various places creek beds, gulleys, ravines.
3. He has found most of them in the surrounding countryside a few he has bought.
4. His practiced eye can always spot a likely rock he's always on the lookout for them.
5. Fossils are the hardened remains or traces of prehistoric plants or animals they were embedded in the earth's crust in past geological ages.
6. Some fossils are on the surface of rocks others appear only when the rock is broken open.
7. One fossil may show the fronds of a fern another may show the skeleton of a small fish.
8. Still another may be the imprint of a leaf another may reveal the outline of a worm.
9. Fossils reveal much about the age of the earth, about prehistoric plants and animals, and about the evolution of the species.
10. Ervin is now giving his collection to a state park it will be an exhibit worth seeing.

□ EXERCISE 4

1. Our friends have moved they live on the north side of town now.
2. We'd like a house and garden just like theirs it's our ideal.
3. Last week a flock of Bohemian waxwings descended on their garden all the pyracantha berries were gone in an hour.
4. A scrub jay has become tame it will hop on their patio table and accept bits of food.
5. On my trip to Georgia my car broke down all my money went for repairs.
6. I had to buy a fan belt, a fuel pump, and a gas filter.
7. Finally my car was ready I started once more on my trip.
8. All that was left in my lunch bag was a sandwich, an apple, and a few cookies.
9. I stopped at a drive-in and sat there trying to decide what to order chicken, hamburger, or fish.
10. Finally I made my decision the waiter seemed relieved.

□ EXERCISE 5

1. Lincoln at six-feet-four was our tallest president Taft at 332 pounds was our heaviest.
2. Nine presidents never attended college three had been college or university presidents.
3. Among those who never went to college were the following Washington, Lincoln, and Truman.
4. The three who had been college or university presidents were Garfield, Wilson, and Eisenhower.
5. Ronald Reagan at 69 became the oldest elected president John Fitzgerald Kennedy at 43 was the youngest elected president.
6. Theodore Roosevelt became president at 42 he was not, however, elected president but merely moved up from the vice-presidency at the death of William McKinley.
7. The Panama Canal was opened in 1914 it was a great boon to navigation.
8. The most unusual buildings in town are the old courthouse, the one-room schoolhouse, and the Thatcher residence.
9. The cast includes the following students Craig, Stanley, Rita, and Kevin.
10. The cast includes Craig, Stanley, Rita, and Kevin.

□ EXERCISE 6

1. Did you know that horses are making a comeback on farms.
2. For years horses were considered an outmoded source of energy now they are the latest thing.
3. On many farms giant draft horses are being used for the following jobs planting, plowing, mowing, and hay-loading.
4. Horses don't compact the soil thus they are better in that way than tractors.
5. They have no trouble starting on a cold morning tractors sometimes do.
6. They will work for 15 or 20 years the average life of a tractor is about half that.
7. Horses are a source of power that reproduces itself other kinds of power deplete the source.
8. But of course the main advantage of horses is that they are fueled by homegrown food furthermore they add fertilizer to the soil.
9. It is true that a tractor can move more than three times as many logs in a day as horses can however the horses don't tear up tree roots or skim away the bark of other trees.
10. Horses will never take the place of tractors on huge farms they are useful, however, as an alternate energy source for smaller jobs.

☐ **EXERCISE 7**

1. Have you ever been to Greenfield Village in Dearborn, Michigan.
2. It's not only a reconstructed historical village it's almost an autobiography of Henry Ford.
3. In his early years Ford wasn't interested in the past then in 1919 he began to reconstruct the old Ford family farm.
4. Later he moved the buildings to Dearborn then he began to add other buildings.
5. He reconstructed the shop where he had built his first horseless carriage next he added the first factory of the Ford Motor Company.
6. No expense was too great he spent half a million, for example, to restore an old country inn.
7. The 107 houses and shops in the village span 300 years of American history and include a toy store, drugstore, barbershop, baker's shop, milliner's shop, and locksmith's shop.
8. Ford scoured the country to find furniture and china to refurnish the buildings he wanted an example of every article that had been used in America from the days of the first settlers to his own day.
9. Nothing was too small or insignificant for his museum one collection, for example, shows the evolution of the clothespin.
10. His Model T Ford had just about abolished the old way of life Ford tried, however, to reconstruct that way of life in Greenfield Village.

☐ **EXERCISE 8**

1. Ancient civilizations had no clocks they had, however, simple devices to measure time.
2. The early timekeepers were sundials, notched candles, and hourglasses.
3. No one knows the date of the first hourglass it was probably about 2,000 years ago.
4. A huge mechanical clock was installed in the Cathedral of Strasbourg in France in 1354 it was far from accurate however.
5. In 1656 a Dutch scientist invented the pendulum his invention revolutionized timekeeping.
6. By 1800 pocket watches became popular not until 1914, however, were wristwatches accurate enough to compete with pocket watches.
7. The early Egyptians divided their nights into 12 parts each part represented the rising of a certain star.
8. They divided their days into 12 parts too the length of the hours varied, however, according to the season.
9. In winter the hours were short in summer they were long.
10. Today we still follow the Egyptian custom of dividing our days into 24 parts the parts, though, have now become of equal length.

☐ EXERCISE 9

1. Our candidate will be at the party therefore I want to go.
2. The candidate's strong points are the following sincerity, adaptability, and dependability.
3. Their petition asked for three things shorter hours, double pay for overtime, and two-week summer vacations.
4. We worked at party headquarters all morning then we canvassed all afternoon.
5. I'm taking English, American history, political science, and French.
6. I'm taking the following subjects English, American history, political science, and French.
7. I worked a year after finishing high school therefore I won't graduate from college when my friends do.
8. I never used to worry about miles per gallons now I do.
9. I used to jump in my car for every small errand now I usually walk.
10. It's making a difference I now fill my gas tank less often.

☐ EXERCISE 10

1. Terry Fox was an outstanding Canadian soccer and basketball player then he lost his right leg to cancer.
2. But he refused to give up he decided to run a "marathon of hope" across Canada to aid cancer research.
3. He started in Newfoundland in April 1980 his goal was to finish in Vancouver.
4. Terry ran with a kind of hop and a skip on his artificial leg some days he ran as much as 30 miles.
5. He endured all kinds of weather rain, snow, hailstones, and blistering heat.
6. Everyone admired his plunk and perseverance they came out to see him and give him money or pledges.
7. In Toronto 10,000 people greeted him he had become a national hero.
8. Then in September, halfway across Canada, he had to give up the disease had spread to his lungs.
9. In 4½ months he had run 3,317 miles furthermore he had collected over $20 million for the Canadian Cancer Society.
10. And he had made his point "I wanted to show people," he said, "that just because they're disabled, it's not the end."

WRITING YOUR OWN SENTENCES

On a separate sheet, or in your journal, write two sentences with lists, one requiring a colon and the other not requiring one.

COMMAS

Students often sprinkle commas through their papers as if they were shaking pepper out of a pepper shaker. Saying "I thought there should be one" or "There seemed to be a pause" is not a good reason for using a comma. Never use a comma unless you know a rule for it. But commas are important. They help the reader. Without them, a reader would often have to go back and reread a sentence to find out exactly what the writer meant.

Actually you need only six comma rules. MASTER THESE SIX RULES, and your writing will be easier to read. The first rule you have already learned (p. 66).

1. **Put a comma before <u>and, but, for, or, nor, yet, so</u> when they connect two independent clauses.**

   We lost our oars, and that was the end of our boating.
   We may leave Friday, or we may wait until Monday.
   I wanted to go but could not get my car started.

The last example does not have two independent clauses (it has two verbs but just one subject); therefore no comma is needed.

2. **Put a comma between items in a series.**

   Hurrah for the red, white, and blue.
   She put down the phone, picked up her purse, and left.

Some words "go together" and don't need a comma between them even though they do make up a series.

   The dear little old lady
   The eager little boy
   The dilapidated old building

The way to tell whether a comma is needed between two words in a series is to see whether *and* could be used naturally between them. It would sound all right to say *red and white and blue*; therefore commas are used. But it would not sound right to say *dear and little and old lady* or *eager and little boy*; therefore no commas are used. Simply use a comma where an *and* could be used. (It is permissible to omit the comma before the *and* connecting the last two members of a series, but more often it is used.)

If an address or date is used in a sentence, treat it as a series, putting a comma after every item, including the last.

> He was born on May 17, 1959, in Beverly, Massachusetts, and grew
>   up there.
> She lived in Las Cruces, New Mexico, for two years.

When only the month and year are used in a date, the commas may be omitted.

> In May 1980 he moved to Kentucky.

3. Put a comma after an introductory expression that does not flow smoothly into the sentence. It may be a word, a group of words, or a dependent clause.

> Yes, I'll go.
> Well, that was the end of that.
> Moreover, the umpire agreed with me.
> Running down the hill, she slipped and fell.
> When everyone had left, the auditorium was locked for the night.

When you studied dependent clauses, you learned that a dependent clause at the beginning of a sentence usually needs a comma after it. In the last example you can see that a comma is necessary. Otherwise the reader would read *When everyone had left the auditorium* . . . before realizing that that was not what the writer meant. A comma prevents misreading.

EXERCISES

Punctuate these sentences according to the first three comma rules. Correct your answers ten at a time.

☐ **EXERCISE 1**
1. When I am going on a trip, I plan long in advance.
2. I read travel brochures, and I make lists of what I want to see.
3. If I have time, I consult books in the library.
4. I also look at newspapers, encyclopedias, and travel magazines.
5. Yes, planning is half the fun of travel.
6. Even if I'm not going far away, the planning is enjoyable.
7. When I've done a lot of planning, the entire trip goes more smoothly.
8. After I finish college, I intend to take a really long trip.
9. I might go to Hawaii, Tahiti, or Australia.
10. Even if I don't go that far, it's fun to think about it.

□ EXERCISE 2

1. I've been having trouble concentrating lately and I have to do something about it.
2. Since I've been out of school for several years it's difficult to get back in the swing.
3. Although my professors aren't dull my mind still wanders.
4. I'll be listening to an interesting lecture and then suddenly my mind is miles away.
5. Just a word can ensnare me and I'm off.
6. Since I've got to quit this daydreaming I'm trying a new plan.
7. Whenever my mind drifts off I put down a mark on a sheet of paper.
8. Then I yank my mind back and concentrate for a while.
9. At the end of every period I have a lot of marks but each day they become fewer.
10. One of these days I'll have no marks at all and then I'll have arrived.

□ EXERCISE 3

1. I write all my papers and do all my exercises without fail.
2. After I've finished ten sentences I check my answers.
3. If I miss an answer I go back and reread the rules.
4. When I've done all the exercises I start my paper.
5. As soon as I have a good thesis statement I begin to write.
6. I often work on my paper all evening and finish about midnight.
7. When I finish my paper is usually three or four pages long.
8. After I've finished I have a sense of accomplishment.
9. I've learned something about writing and I'm proud of the result.
10. Even though I don't always like writing I enjoy having written.

□ EXERCISE 4

1. If fish in rivers die during the winter it is not necessarily because they freeze to death.
2. When the snow covers the ice the water plants can't achieve photosynthesis.
3. Lack of photosynthesis lowers the oxygen content of the water and the fish may suffocate.
4. In Jamaica there are no snakes and bats are the only native mammals.
5. With the help of radar naturalists can follow the flight of birds through fog.
6. We stayed at a camp near Conway South Carolina for a week.
7. Then we spent another week at Turkey Run State Park in Indiana.
8. For scenic beauty in nature trails that's the place to go.

9. Big billowy white clouds rolled over the area.
10. The greatest loss of life in the history of the world occurred in the earthquake in Shensi Province China on January 23 1556 when an estimated 830,000 people were killed.

□ EXERCISE 5

1. He had always been an eager conscientious student.
2. His studies had included the English American and French Revolutions.
3. Although known as the chief interpreter of New England Robert Frost was born in San Francisco California March 26 1875.
4. The child was surprised hurt and resentful.
5. She wore a light blue cotton dress.
6. Fireworks were common in Europe in the 14th century but no one knows who invented them.
7. From September 2 to September 6 1665 the Great Fire swept through London.
8. When I entered the door was wide open.
9. The exhibit included water colors oils and etchings.
10. When a dependent clause comes first in a sentence put a comma after it.

□ EXERCISE 6

1. More than any other animal the buffalo is a symbol of the West.
2. Nearly wiped out in the 1800s the buffalo are now making a comeback.
3. When Lewis and Clark explored the West there were about 60 million buffalo.
4. But in the 1800s they were slaughtered by the settlers by sportsmen and by hide and meat hunters.
5. Hoping to subdue the Indians by cutting off their food supply the U.S. Army also slaughtered the buffalo.
6. By 1889 only 551 buffalo were alive in the United States and of those a herd of 20 was almost wiped out by poachers.
7. Under careful management the buffalo have now made a comeback and there are at present about 25,000 in the United States and Canada.
8. They are kept in preserves such as Yellowstone National Park National Bison Range in Montana and Theodore Roosevelt National Park in North Dakota.
9. While they are not completely free they are given adequate space to roam.
10. These shaggy beasts are part of our national heritage and they must be helped to survive.

☐ EXERCISE 7

1. Of the 39 national parks in the United States only five are in the East.
2. They are Acadia in Maine Shenandoah in Virginia Mammoth Cave in Kentucky Everglades in Florida and Great Smoky Mountains in Tennessee and North Carolina.
3. Perhaps the best known is Mammoth Cave in Kentucky.
4. When I was in the South last summer I decided to visit Mammoth Cave.
5. I had read about stalactites and stalagmites but I was not prepared for their amazing variety.
6. A stalactite projects downward from the ceiling of the cave and a stalagmite projects upward from the floor.
7. Both are formed by the dripping of mineral-rich water and both have taken many years to form.
8. Some are tinted with manganese or iron oxide and have a purple brown or reddish tint.
9. While I was in the cave I also saw gypsum and crystal formations in the shapes of flowers.
10. There are 150 miles of passages on five levels and I walked along a few of the passages.

☐ EXERCISE 8

1. Some of the most striking formations in Mammoth Cave are Crystal River Frozen Niagara and Cathedral Domes.
2. Before I left I took a boatride on the underground Echo River.
3. Now I want to see more national parks for they include the most striking natural scenery of our country.
4. Our national parks cover some 16 million acres and they have about 275 million visitors a year.
5. Yellowstone was the first national park to be created and no other park the same size has as many natural wonders.
6. In Yellowstone are geysers hot springs lakes rivers and cataracts.
7. Of the 200 active geysers in Yellowstone Old Faithful is the most famous.
8. Ever since it was discovered in 1870 it has been spouting on an average of every 65 minutes.
9. Since the intent of national parks is to preserve the balance of nature animal and plant life are disturbed as little as possible.
10. Hunting and lumbering are prohibited but fishing is allowed.

□EXERCISE 9

1. With a galloping speed of up to 35 miles an hour the giraffe is one of the swiftest animals.
2. The Arabs called it *zarafa* or "swift creature" and thus it got its name.
3. Few animals are so delicate yet giraffes have survived for 25 million years.
4. Of the 400,000 giraffes that exist today most are in East Africa.
5. Of those that have been measured the tallest was 19 feet and 3 inches.
6. Since a giraffe's eyes are set in sockets bulging from its head it has almost 360-degree vision.
7. Giraffes feed high in the trees and each giraffe may eat 100 pounds of leaves twigs and branches in a day.
8. The giraffe curls its 1½ foot tongue around a branch draws it between its thick lips and skims off a mouthful of twigs.
9. Its favorite tree is the acacia and some acacia seeds won't take root unless they've been through a giraffe's digestive system.
10. The female giraffe gives birth while standing and drops her calf five or six feet to the grass.

□EXERCISE 10

1. Since giraffes do little harm they are likely to survive.
2. They seldom molest anyone and they don't kill people as lions do.
3. They won't bend down for the grass that sheep and cattle eat and they don't trample crops as elephants do.
4. Among the most graceful of animals the giraffe adds to the interest of the African countryside.
5. In national parks throughout the world the feeding of wild animals is forbidden.
6. But the law is often ignored and people feed wild animals potato chips bread cheese anything.
7. Even though signs warn that such food is not good for animals the public cannot resist giving handouts.
8. The animals are thus lured to the highways and may be struck by trucks or cars.
9. Since there are never enough wardens to enforce the antifeeding laws hundreds of animals are killed in this way each year.
10. Through thoughtlessness the public is depleting the number of animals in national parks.

WRITING YOUR OWN SENTENCES

On a separate sheet write the first three comma rules with a sentence to illustrate each.

COMMAS (continued)

4. Put commas around the name of a person spoken to.

I think, Sylvia, that you are absolutely right.
Kim, how about a game of tennis?
I've finished washing the car, Phil.

5. Put commas around an expression that interrupts the flow of the sentence (such as *however, moreover, finally, therefore, of course, by the way, on the other hand, I am sure, I think*).

I hope, of course, that they'll come.
We took our plates, therefore, and got in line.
It should, I think, take only an hour.

Read the above sentences aloud, and you will hear how those expressions interrupt the flow of the sentence. Sometimes, however, such expressions flow smoothly into the sentence and don't need commas around them. Whether a word is an interrupter or not often depends on where it is in the sentence. If it is in the middle of a sentence, it is more likely to be an interrupter than if it is at the beginning or the end. The expressions that were interrupters in the above sentences are not interrupters in the following sentences and, of course, don't require commas.

Of course I hope they'll come.
Therefore we took our plates and got in line.
I think it should take only an hour.

Remember also that the above expressions (*however*, etc.) often come between two independent clauses and then require a semicolon in front of them.

He was busy; however he took time to help.
It's an important meeting; therefore I'm going.

Thus words like *however* are used in three ways:

1. as an interrupter (commas around it)
2. as a word that flows into the sentence (no commas)
3. as a connective between two independent clauses (semicolon in front of it)

6. Put commas around nonessential material.

The material may be interesting, but the main idea of the sentence would be clear without it. In the following sentence

Dorothea Land, who is running for mayor, will speak tonight.

the clause *who is running for mayor* is not essential to the main idea of the sentence. Without it we still know exactly who the sentence is about and what she is going to do: Dorothea Land will speak tonight. Therefore the nonessential material is set off from the rest of the sentence by commas to show that it could be left out. But in the following sentence

The woman who is running for mayor will speak tonight.

the clause *who is running for mayor* is essential to the main idea of the sentence. Without it the sentence would read: The woman will speak tonight. We would have no idea which woman. The clause *who is running for mayor* is essential because it tells us which woman. It could not be left out of the sentence. Therefore commas are not used around it. In this sentence

The Grapes of Wrath, a novel by John Steinbeck, was a best seller.

the words *a novel by John Steinbeck* could be left out, and we would still know the main meaning of the sentence: *The Grapes of Wrath* was a best seller. Therefore the nonessential material is set off by commas to show that it could be left out. But in this sentence

John Steinbeck's novel *The Grapes of Wrath* was a best seller.

the title of the novel is essential. Without it the sentence would read: John Steinbeck's novel was a best seller. We would have no idea which of John Steinbeck's novels was a best seller. Therefore the title could not be left out, and commas are not used around it.

EXERCISES
Punctuate these sentences according to Comma Rules 4, 5, and 6.

□EXERCISE 1
1. Bill who had almost fallen asleep jumped when the professor called on him.
2. She repainted the old chair that had once belonged to her grandmother.
3. The little cabin overlooking the river is over a hundred years old.
4. I'm hoping Marge that you'll come with us.
5. The car it seems was parked on the wrong side of the street.
6. We have of course given no thought to that question.
7. Of course we'll come.
8. My wife who teaches kindergarten doesn't get home until four.
9. Isn't it odd Ellen that he never even called?
10. We tried nevertheless to persuade him to go with us.

☐ EXERCISE 2

1. Yes, Warren, there's a lot to be done.
2. It should not be, imagined, moreover that the job is an easy one.
3. Commas should not be used around expressions that are essential to the meaning of the sentence.
4. This is the house that my grandfather built.
5. Of course I was glad to see her.
6. She was beyond a doubt, the most unselfish person I had ever known.
7. She should, I think, be going to see you shortly.
8. The house was filled with people, who had come for the wedding.
9. We always take our vacation in Minnesota, the land of a thousand lakes.
10. Kilauea, which was active when we were in Hawaii, is one of the world's largest volcanoes.

☐ EXERCISE 3

1. The boy carrying the flag led the parade.
2. The two longest rivers in the world are the Amazon flowing into the South Atlantic and the Nile flowing into the Mediterranean.
3. The book that I told you about is now on the best-seller list.
4. Some of the adventures that he had last summer were breathtaking.
5. The entire country of course is concerned about the increase in crime.
6. What we need many think is stricter law enforcement.
7. Swifter and surer punishment they say is the solution.
8. The senator who spoke to our group last night is sure he has the solution.
9. The town where my parents were born is a special place to me.
10. Atchison where my parents were born is a special place to me.

☐ EXERCISE 4

1. The antique picture frame that she had found in the basement now hung in her living room as a showpiece.
2. The company hired an engineer who had more experience than I.
3. Of course I was happy to have them stay with me.
4. Mel could we finish that painting now?
5. I was positive however that I had locked the door before I left.
6. I have done all the exercises that I was supposed to do.
7. The zest for gardening it seems got a boost from climbing food prices.
8. He went to his favorite fishing spot which is in Wisconsin.
9. The Amos Place thirty acres of virgin timber is a favorite nesting place for birds.
10. On the bed was a quilt that had been in the family for generations.

☐ **EXERCISE 5**

1. My paper was on the whole greatly improved by my revision.
2. It's much better I think than my previous draft.
3. Focused free writing I find helps me write more easily.
4. The position that you told me about has been filled.
5. This is the suit that I bought before Easter.
6. This suit which I bought before Easter is really too small for me.
7. More than a hundred years ago Hanson Gregory captain of a schooner and dabbler in the culinary art is said to have first put the hole in the doughnut.
8. My dad who has never cared for football really enjoyed that game.
9. The man who had been assigned to the job didn't report for work.
10. That novel by Charles Dickens a 19th-century author has been made into a movie.

☐ **EXERCISE 6**

1. The motion that we adjourn was greeted with applause.
2. Greenland the largest island in the world is partly buried under an ice cap.
3. There's more room in this car Scott.
4. Come here Debra and help me hold this ladder.
5. The people who are in charge of the project seem to be making progress.
6. He had in spite of his inexperience won the confidence of his peers.
7. And we said furthermore that we would stand back of him in anything he chose to do.
8. I am sure the man who lost his wallet will soon come back for it.
9. Those who want their term papers returned should sign this list.
10. The examination which should not worry anyone will be given on Tuesday.

☐ **EXERCISE 7**

1. The photography contest which is open to all students will be judged by a three-member panel.
2. Do you think Michael that you'll enter any photographs?
3. Conductor will you stop at the next corner?
4. The city of Nassau is located on the island of New Providence which is 21 miles long.
5. The place where Cabot landed is marked by a bronze plaque.
6. Williamsburg which was at one time the capital of Virginia has been restored to its original 18th-century appearance.
7. The area which covers 170 acres contains over 500 colonial buildings.

8. It's a place certainly that's well worth visiting.
9. The book that was at the top of the best-seller list last week is in the library now.
10. I've decided however that I don't have time to read it.

□ EXERCISE 8

1. A man's character and his garden it has been said both reflect the amount of weeding done during the growing season.
2. I tell you Jon you are making a mistake.
3. All those who had worked in the political campaign felt rewarded by the outcome of the election.
4. Getting everyone to vote we have found is a difficult job.
5. The dinner gong that she had brought from Egypt hung in the dining room.
6. The coldest permanently inhabited place in the world is a small town in Siberia where the temperature reached −96° F. in 1964.
7. My stamp collection which I've been working on for almost ten years is now quite valuable.
8. The largest and heaviest animal in the world and probably the biggest creature that has ever existed is the blue whale.
9. Hippocrates who is known as the father of medicine set forth the Hippocratic oath which is still respected by modern doctors.
10. George Bernard Shaw who became one of England's most famous writers made only thirty dollars during his first nine years of writing.

WRITING YOUR OWN SENTENCES

On a separate sheet write six sentences using the six comma rules given in the following box.

Review of the Comma

Add the necessary commas to these sentences.

1. Many Americans do not know about Highway I which is an Overseas Highway.
2. It is 109 miles long and with its 42 bridges links the string of Keys or islands that run from Miami to Key West.
3. The Keys which go southwestward from the mainland of Florida form a dividing line between the Gulf of Mexico and the Atlantic Ocean.
4. The Keys are great places for shell collecting bird watching and fishing.
5. Shell collectors who say the Keys beaches are the best places in the United States for shells have the best luck just after high tide.
6. Bird watchers are interested in the herons pelicans and egrets that stop in the Keys on their migratory routes.
7. Various kinds of coral abound but their sharp edges must be handled with gloves.
8. Many Spanish galleons were shipwrecked on these razor-sharp reefs and sank with their treasures.
9. On Grassy Key is the Flipper Sea School which trains dolphins for show business or for experiments.
10. On some of the smaller Keys are found Key deer which weigh less than 100 pounds.
11. Almost extinct 20 years ago they are now however making a comeback.
12. Key West which is the end of the Overseas Highway is nearer to Havana Cuba than it is to Miami.
13. With its freewheeling life-style and its marvelous weather it has become a popular vacation spot.
14. Walking is a good way to see Key West but bicycling is even better.
15. Among the famous artists and writers who have found inspiration at Key West over the years are James Audubon Hart Crane and Ernest Hemingway.

QUOTATION MARKS

Put quotation marks around the exact words of a speaker (but not around an indirect quotation).

> He said, "I will go." (his exact words)
> He said, "Man is mortal." (his exact words)
> He said that he would go. (not his exact words)
> He said that man is mortal. (not his exact words)

Whenever *that* precedes the words of a speaker (as in the last two examples), it indicates that the words are not a direct quotation and should not have quotation marks around them.

If the speaker says more than one sentence, quotation marks are used only before and after the entire speech.

> He said, "I will go. It's no trouble. I'll be there at six."

The words telling who is speaking are set off with a comma, unless, of course, a question mark or exclamation mark is needed.

> "I will go," he said.
> "Do you want me to go?" he asked.
> "Come here!" he shouted.

Every quotation begins with a capital letter. But when a quotation is broken, the second part does not begin with a capital letter unless it is a new sentence.

> "Genius," said Carlyle, "is the art of taking infinite pains."
> "Don't be afraid to take a big step if one is indicated," said David Lloyd
> George. "You can't cross a chasm in two small jumps."

Begin a new paragraph with each change of speaker.

> "May I have the car?" I asked.
> "What for?" Dad said.
> "To go see Kathy," I replied.

Put quotation marks around the name of a story, poem, essay, or other short work. For longer works such as books, newspapers, plays, or movies, use underlining, which means they would be italicized in print.

> I like Robert Frost's short poem "Fire and Ice."
> Have you seen the movie *Ordinary People*?
> Rachel Carson's essay "And No Birds Sing" is found in her book
> *Silent Spring*.
> We went to see the play *Twelve Angry Men*.

EXERCISES

Punctuate the quotations, and add any other necessary punctuation marks. Underline or put quotation marks around each title. Correct each group of ten sentences before continuing.

☐ EXERCISE 1

1. Let's get something to eat she said.
2. Do you want to go now or after the movie he asked.
3. Why not both times she said.
4. Snow and adolescence are the only problems that disappear if you ignore them long enough said the lecturer.
5. Some people stay longer in an hour than others can in a week said William Dean Howells.
6. After her weekend visitors left, she remarked that guests always bring pleasure—if not in the coming, then in the going.
7. Doing work I like is more important to me than making a lot of money my sister said.
8. With all its sham, drudgery, and broken dreams said Adlai Stevenson it is still a beautiful world.
9. We went to see The Wild Duck, a play by Henrik Ibsen.
10. Our future as a nation is going to depend not so much on what happens in outer space as on what happens in inner space—the space between our ears said the lecturer.

☐ EXERCISE 2

1. The actions of some children said Will Rogers suggest that their parents embarked on the sea of matrimony without a paddle.
2. The best time to tackle a small problem said my father is before he grows up.
3. When Mom goes shopping says Kip she leaves no store unturned.
4. I agree with the Spanish proverb how beautiful it is to do nothing and then rest afterward.
5. He found her munching chocolates and reading a book entitled Eat, Drink, and Be Buried.
6. Mark Twain said when I was a boy of 14, my father was so ignorant I could hardly stand to have the old man around. But when I got to be 21, I was astonished at how much the old man had learned in seven years.
7. Mark Twain said the parts of the Bible which give me the most trouble are those I understand the best.
8. Work consists of whatever a body is obliged to do, and play consists of whatever a body is not obliged to do said Mark Twain.

9. On observing the great number of civic statues, Cato, the Roman, remarked I would rather people would ask why there is not a statue of Cato than why there is.
10. One does not complain about water because it is wet said Abraham Maslow nor about rocks because they are hard.

□ EXERCISE 3

1. I've just read Barn Burning, a short story by William Faulkner.
2. The construction of an airplane wrote Charles Lindbergh is simple compared to the evolutionary achievement of a bird.
3. If I had the choice Lindbergh continued I would rather have birds than airplanes.
4. Of war, George Bernard Shaw said that the men should all shoot their officers and go home.
5. An art critic once said that there are three kinds of people in the world: those who can't stand Picasso, those who can't stand Raphael, and those who've never heard of either of them.
6. Pablo Casals, the great cellist, spent hours on a single phrase. He said people say I play as easily as a bird sings. If they only knew how much effort their bird has put into his song.
7. As it is the mark of great minds to say many things in a few words wrote La Rochefoucauld so it is the mark of little minds to use many words to say nothing.
8. William James said that the essence of genius is to know what to overlook.
9. Whatever you have you must either use or lose said Henry Ford.
10. A span of time either leaves you better off or worse off wrote John Gardner there is no neutral time.

□ EXERCISE 4

1. Finish every day and be done with it said Ralph Waldo Emerson tomorrow is a new day.
2. Life can only be understood backward said Kierkegaard but it must be lived forward.
3. A friend is a person with whom I may be sincere. Before him I may think aloud wrote Ralph Waldo Emerson.
4. The only conquests which are permanent and leave no regrets Napoleon said are our conquests over ourselves.
5. Nearly all men can stand adversity, but if you want to test a man's character, give him power said Lincoln.
6. Freud said that to have mental health a person has to be able to love and to work.

7. In the novel Fathers and Sons by Turgenev the main character says that the chief thing is to be able to devote yourself.
8. Nobody can carry three watermelons under one arm says a Spanish proverb.
9. The taller the bamboo grows the lower it bends says a Japanese proverb.
10. The man who does not do more work than he's paid for said Abraham Lincoln isn't worth what he gets.

□ EXERCISE 5
1. The cost of a thing is the amount of what I call life which is required to be exchanged for it, immediately or in the long run said Henry David Thoreau.
2. A man is rich said Thoreau in proportion to the number of things he can afford to let alone.
3. Viewing the multitude of articles exposed for sale in the marketplace, Socrates remarked how many things there are that I do not want.
4. I have been reading Comfortable Words, a book about word origins by Bergan Evans.
5. Perhaps the most valuable result of all education said Thomas Huxley is the ability to make yourself do the thing you have to do, when it ought to be done, whether you like it or not.
6. James B. Conant, former president of Harvard, said that a liberal education is what remains after all you have learned has been forgotten.
7. Education does not mean teaching people to know what they do not know said John Ruskin it means teaching them to behave as they do not behave.
8. Sometimes when fate kicks us and we finally land and look around, we find we have been kicked upstairs said Carl Sandburg.
9. At the end said Richard E. Byrd only two things really matter to a man, regardless of who he is; and they are the affection and understanding of his family.
10. There are at least as many stars wrote Sir James Jeans as there are grains of sand upon all the seashores of the earth.

WRITING YOUR OWN SENTENCES
Write a conversation that might be heard at your breakfast table any morning. Start a new paragraph with each change of speaker.

CAPITAL LETTERS

Capitalize

1. The first word of every sentence.

2. The first word of every direct quotation.

He said, "You've won."
"I've done my best," he said, "and I can do no more." (The *and* is not
capitalized because it does not begin a new sentence.)
"Why do you worry?" she said. "You've done well." (*You* is capitalized
because it begins a new sentence.)

3. The first, last, and every important word in a title. Don't capitalize short prepositions, short connecting words, or *a, an, the*.

What a Property Owner Needs to Know
The Day the Saucers Flew By

4. Names of people, places, languages, races, and nationalities.

Grandfather Smith	England	Chicano
Uganda	English	Indian

5. Names of months, days of the week, and special days, but not the seasons.

February	Fourth of July	spring
Wednesday	Thanksgiving	summer

6. A title of relationship if it takes the place of the person's name, but not otherwise. If *my* is used before the word, a capital is not used.

Do you mind, Mother?	*but*	My mother doesn't mind.
I think Mother will come.	*but*	I think my mother will come.
I'm sorry, Grandfather.	*but*	My grandfather is seventy.
Come on, Sis.	*but*	My sister is coming.
I visited Aunt Margaret.	*but*	I visited my aunt.

7. Names of particular people or things, but not general ones.

Call Dr. Simmons.	*but*	Call the doctor.
I spoke to Professor Olson.	*but*	I spoke to the professor.
We sailed on the Hudson River.	*but*	We sailed on the river.
I walked down Third Street.	*but*	I walked down the street.
Are you from the Midwest?	*but*	We turned west.
Her accent shows she's from the South.	*but*	She lives in the south part of town.

I take History 301 and *but* I take history and French.
   French 10.
I went to Mercy High School. *but* I was in high school last year.
He goes to Massachusetts Bay *but* He is going to college now.
   Community College.

EXERCISES

Add the necessary capital letters.

☐ EXERCISE 1

1. I discussed the matter with my professor.
2. We were studying Robert Frost's poem "The Death of the Hired Man."
3. All freshmen take history and english.
4. Usually college classes begin the day after labor day.
5. You know, dad, I haven't had the car all week.
6. The detour took us south, then west, then north.
7. The doctor sent her to the hospital last Wednesday.
8. After graduating from high school, he went to Mesa community college.
9. My aunt is president of her club this fall.
10. There will be a hockey game at the Ft. Collins rink tonight.

☐ EXERCISE 2

1. My father wants me to go to a state university, but I want to go to Ohio institute of technology.
2. She spent the summer with her aunt in the east.
3. In high school I seldom studied, but college has changed that.
4. The headline read, "Tougher meat laws needed in ontario."
5. I hope to go to the west coast this summer and then on to the yukon.
6. We visited yosemite national park and a lot of other state parks.
7. Last spring she entered the university of southwestern Louisiana.
8. My uncle came to our house on summer evenings and told us stories.
9. Usually aunt Angela came with him.
10. My aunt and my uncle had no children of their own.

☐ EXERCISE 3

1. The fastest growing region in the world today is latin america.
2. Including mexico and central and south america, that area has grown from 86 million people in 1925 to an estimated 319 million in 1974.
3. Next year I plan to take french, history, english, and physics.
4. I have professor Olson for french.
5. After high school my dad went to community college of Philadelphia.
6. The entertainer had played before kings and presidents.

7. The John G. Shedd aquarium in grant park in Chicago is the largest aquarium in the world.
8. Have you read Eudora Welty's short story "A worn path"?
9. He shouted, "what's happening?"
10. "Nothing's happening," she called back, "except that I've fallen off the ladder and broken my back."

☐ EXERCISE 4

1. My brother and I went to Monsignor Hackett high school, but now we are both going to different colleges in Florida.
2. He is going to Gulf Coast community college, and I'm going to Miami-Dade community college.
3. May I have the car, dad, or is mother going to use it?
4. My mother usually wants the car on thursday afternoons when she goes to the Baltimore women's club.
5. We traveled east to Boston, where the pronunciation of certain words left no doubt that we were in the east.
6. We went swimming in the river every sunday when I was a boy.
7. Everyone would congregate in front of the stores on main street on saturday nights.
8. My grandmother grew up in the south, but grandfather was born in the east.
9. An Erie canal has no way of knowing how many ways a Mississippi river has of going wrong.
10. "The tragedy of life," Thomas Carlyle said, "is not so much what men suffer but rather what they miss."

☐ EXERCISE 5

1. The sugar maple and the hemlock are both native to canada.
2. She graduated from southern vocational college and now is attending the university of Alabama at Huntsville.
3. My mother likes plane travel, but dad would always rather drive.
4. Last spring we took a trip through the black hills of South Dakota.
5. Then we drove south into Nebraska and Kansas and west to Estes park in Colorado.
6. We're studying about world war II in history now.
7. I've always liked literature and have decided to make it my major.
8. Next semester I'm going to take psychology 101, history 210, and English 300; then the following semester I'll take math and physics.
9. The band from Coppin state college was on our campus last weekend.
10. "I'd rather be a big duck in a little pond," she said, "than a little duck in a big pond."

☐EXERCISE 6

1. My granddad used to take us boating on the river on weekends.
2. The Missouri river has some exceptionally swift currents.
3. But granddad was always able to maneuver the boat safely.
4. When I went away to college, I of course had no time for boating.
5. At the Missouri institute of technology, I really worked.
6. But then in the summer I got a job as a counselor at a camp at lake Bemidji, and again I had time for boating.
7. I'll always be grateful for the training granddad gave me.
8. In college my professors demand good english on all written work.
9. One who is especially insistent is professor Morris.
10. "Learn to write," he says, "or drop out."

☐EXERCISE 7

1. Sixty years ago the United Kingdom ruled over one-fourth of the human race.
2. The colonial empires of britain and france are gone.
3. We read Poe's short story "The fall of the house of Usher."
4. Are you going to take spanish or psychology as an elective?
5. A noted african explorer will speak at the high school assembly.
6. He enjoyed the fourth of July but paid up for it on the fifth.
7. Do you think everyone should go to college?
8. You have no idea, dad, what college is like today.
9. "Nothing matters now," she said, "except that you are here."
10. The university with the largest enrollment in the world is the university of Calcutta in India.

Review of Punctuation and Capital Letters

Punctuate these sentences. They include all the rules for punctuation and capitalization you have learned. Correct your answers carefully by those at the back of the book. Most sentences have several errors.

☐ **EXERCISE 1**

1. The Taj Mahal, which is in Agra, is often called the most beautiful building in the world.
2. Do you read Time or Newsweek?
3. I'm glad it's snowing, now we can go skiing tomorrow.
4. Skiing, skating, and tobogganing were their chief winter sports.
5. Figure skating, which I'm just learning, takes hours of practice.
6. His knapsack contained the following items: food matches and a water bottle.
7. As we put the horses in their stalls, we could hear Dad calling us.
8. There is much inferior paint on the market, but most consumer dissatisfaction arises from bad application.
9. A little old lady from Boston refused to travel saying, "Why should I travel I'm already here."
10. The doctor at the clinic said, however, that he didn't believe the report.

☐ **EXERCISE 2**

1. No he didn't come we'll miss him.
2. You'll find them where you left them son.
3. The boy fought bit kicked and screamed but his mother remained calm.
4. When I was in high school I memorized Robert Frost's poem the road not taken.
5. An arabian proverb says I had no shoes and complained until I met a man who had no feet.
6. You can get the document by writing to the Superintendent of Documents Government Printing Office Washington DC.
7. My mother who is not a writer herself is still a good critic of my writing.
8. The bus driver had been late in starting moreover he was now hitting all the signals wrong.
9. The gutters were full of water it was difficult to cross the street.
10. Have you read Alvin Toffler's book The Third Wave.

☐ EXERCISE 3

1. I've been reading about insects which are the most numerous of land animals.
2. Adult insects have six legs and the majority also have wings.
3. Although they are often destructive they can also be beneficial.
4. Some destroy crops but others kill more harmful insects.
5. We followed the trail into the clearing then we turned south.
6. In 1973 humans made their deepest penetration into the earth—11,391 feet—in Transvaal South Africa.
7. Although I've not read Ghosts I've read other plays by Ibsen.
8. We wanted to see that movie but couldn't get tickets.
9. The trouble with the average family said Bill Vaughan is it has too much month left at the end of the money.
10. Coming out of the capitol the senator said you save a billion here and a billion there and it soon mounts up.

☐ EXERCISE 4

1. I've been trying to teach my small son to ride a bike but it's difficult.
2. He rides a few feet then he falls off.
3. He's just not coordinated however I don't want him to get discouraged.
4. He keeps trying and I keep encouraging.
5. It's harder on me than on him but I must keep helping him.
6. Since I have learned to write a thesis statement with supporting reasons I now find writing much easier.
7. I still need to do the following things improve my spelling get rid of wordiness and use more specific details.
8. Can the story be true then that we read in the paper.
9. The Christian Science Monitor and the Wall Street Journal are excellent papers.
10. Life said Samuel Butler is like playing a violin solo in public and learning the instrument as one goes on.

☐ EXERCISE 5

1. Water is the only absolutely essential substance for all life some organisms can live without oxygen but none can live without water.
2. I finished high school two years ago and am now attending Passaic county community college.
3. Some people are affected by gloomy weather it has no effect on me.

4. The highest speed ever achieved on land is 631 mph at Bonneville Salt Flats Utah on October 23 1970.
5. The sign in the dentist's office read support your dentist eat candy.
6. Who are you going with will there be room in the car for me.
7. Have you seen the play The Glass Menagerie by Tennessee Williams.
8. He tried to improve his vocabulary by looking up new words by keeping word lists and by using the words in his conversation.
9. A girl whom I met in the east last summer is coming to visit me.
10. Reading improves your understanding of human nature writing improves your understanding of yourself.

Proofreading Exercise 1

Proofread this student paper. You will find only a few errors—eight in fact—but correcting them will improve the paper. Try to find all eight before you check with the corrections at the back of the book. This is the kind of careful proofreading you should do before you call your own papers finished.

THOSE FAULTY PARTS

I was only ten years old, but I had all the confidence of a great scientist. I had already built a little electric motor and fixed the electric parts in all the toys anyone would bring me. And now I had a magazine article that told how to build a simple battery-powered radio. The directions looked straight-forward all I needed was the parts.

My world extended only as far as my bicycle could take me, so the only place I knew of that sold radio parts was the TV repair shop five blocks away. I don't know what the men there first thought of a ten-year-old kid trying to build a radio but I persisted until one of them gathered up the parts and sold them to me. It cost a few weeks' allowance money, but I knew it was going to be worth it.

Well, after a few days of work, I had it finished. Admittedly my wiring didn't look as neat as that in the picture. As a matter of fact, those people had used a few more wires than I had, but I didn't feel that all of them were really necessary.

But my radio didn't work! And my ten-year-old mind concluded that it must be that the TV repair shop had sold me faulty parts. I bicycled back with my new radio under my arm and demanded an explanation. I was upset.

After a long discussion, one of the men finally took my radio and started working on it. I think he was afraid I might cry or something.

In about half an hour, and after many changes, he got it working.

"No charge kid," he said.

"Thank you," I said in my most polite voice, thrilled at the sound of music coming from my radio.

What a feeling of accomplishment! It was as if Id invented something great. I guess the TV repairman must have had a bit of feeling of accomplishment too as a beaming ten-year-old rode away with a little radio that worked under his arm.

Proofreading Exercise 2

This student paper is marred by one fragment and three run-together sentences. Make the necessary corrections.

I DON'T WANT TO

I must have tried to give up smoking a dozen times. Sometimes I'd last a month. And sometimes only a day or two. Always I'd start again. Then it hit me. The trouble was I didn't really want to stop I was one of those who say they want to stop but really don't. If people truly wanted to stop, I reasoned, they would. What I really needed, then, was simply to not want to smoke.

One day I added up all the negative aspects of smoking—the cost, the yellow stains on my fingers, the nervousness, the bad breath, the rotten taste in my mouth every morning, the smoker's cough, the danger to my health. Then, too, I told myself that smoking was a sign of weakness. I was unable to control myself I was caught in a habit that big tobacco companies were continuously promoting. That bothered me. I was, against my will, doing exactly what some big companies wanted me to do it was then I decided that I really didn't want to smoke.

The day I decided I didn't want to smoke, I simply stopped. Oh, it took a couple of weeks of effort to break the habit, but it's been three years now, and I haven't had another cigarette. All it took was just not to want to.

Proofreading Exercise 3

Here is another student paper to proofread. This one has seven errors. Try to find all of them before checking the answers.

CURB THAT ENTHUSIASM

There we were, the two of us, in an eight-foot rubber raft, approaching Three Forks Rapids. Neither of us had ever tried river rafting before and it was scary. We had our life jackets strapped on tight and were bracing ourselves for what might come.

As we were swept along in the incredibly swift current, I held the two oars and tried to direct the raft. Nick, in the front, was suppose to watch for rocks and yell out which direction to head but already the thunder of the water hurtling through the rapids had drowned out his voice. Anyway I was really rowing as hard as I could just to keep the raft pointing downstream, let alone directing it more specifically.

Then came the first big drop! Its an amazing feeling riding over a sudden four-foot drop in a river. But somehow we stayed upright and landed below in the white foaming water. We cheered and congratulated each other for a moment but then braced ourselves for the next big drop coming right up.

Amazingly we did it. We managed to keep the raft afloat again with both of us still in it.

"Great!" I yelled. "We made 'em both."

"We're good!" Nick shouted.

Laughing and yelling, he turned around but then as we yelled and laughed, we both happen to lean the same way, and sure enough, after running the rapids unscathed, we now found the raft tiping sideways, and over we went into the calm water . . . .

The *next* time, we told each other as we righted the raft and climbed back on board, we're going to curb our enthusiasm.

Comprehensive Test on Entire Text

In these sentences you will find all the errors that have been discussed in the entire text. Correct them by adding apostrophes, punctuation, and capital letters, and by crossing out incorrect expressions and writing the corrections above. Most sentences have several errors. A perfect—or almost perfect—score will mean you have mastered the text.

1. Its useless to wait hes probably not coming.

2. If one wants a larger vocabulary you should study word roots.

3. Spending entirely too much time on that one coarse last semester.

4. Dad ask my sister and me to water the lawn we was glad to do it.

5. While they were waiting for there daughter, they're motor stalled.

6. I cant decide whether to finish my math, study my history, or whether

    I should take it easy for a change.

7. If you're going to be hear Alice you can answer the phone for me.

8. Your going with me, aren't you.

9. We freshmen helped a upperclass student with registration he really

    appreciated it.

10. I was quiet sure that Rons car was in the driveway.

11. When we were on our trip we visited some cities in the south.

12. Which had many beautiful old homes and lovely gardens.

13. Its Mr. Petersons car but hes not driving it.

14. Each of the students are planning a individual report.

15. Looking under the car, the missing baseball was found.

16. Marks grades are always higher than Dougs.

17. Ill be ready in a minute Jeanne said.

18. This semester I'm taking french, history, and english.

19. The Doll's House which I read last year is a play by Ibsen.

20. She told her sister she needed a new purse.

21. They didnt think however that they would have time to come back.

22. She was suppose to read the short story The Elephant's Child from Rudyard Kipling's book Just So Stories.

23. Whether you agree with me or whether you follow your own ideas.

24. We waited as long as we could than we went on without her.

25. Whats done to children, they will do to society wrote Karl Menninger.

4

Writing

4   Writing

FREE WRITING

"Writing is good for us," said Oliver Wendell Holmes, "because it brings our thoughts out into the open, as a boy turns his pockets inside out to see what is in them." Try "turning your pockets inside out" by writing as fast as you can for five minutes. Write anything that comes into your mind—no one is going to read what you write. Put your thoughts down as fast as they come. If you can't think of anything to write, just write words. Write anything, but keep writing for five minutes without stopping. Look at your watch and begin.

This free writing should limber up your mind and your pen. Try it at home. Besides helping you write more freely, it will help you sort out your ideas. Sometimes after you've discussed a problem on paper, it suddenly becomes less of a problem.

Now try another kind of free writing—focused free writing. Write for ten minutes as fast as you can and say anything that pops into your head, but this time stick to one subject—travel. Look at your watch and begin.

Did you focus on travel that long? Did you think of family trips, of backpacking, of the most beautiful place you've ever seen, of trips to your grandmother's when you were small, of places you'd like to see?

You didn't have time to include all those things of course. Once more write for ten minutes and add more to your discussion of travel. Begin.

Focused free writing is a good way to begin writing a paper. When you are assigned a paper, write for ten minutes putting down all your thoughts on the subject. It will let you see what material you have and will help you figure out what aspect of the subject to write about.

GETTING RID OF CLICHÉS

A cliché is an expression that has been used so often it has lost its originality and effectiveness. Whoever first said "light as a feather" had thought of an original way to express lightness, but today that expression is outworn and boring. Most of us use an occasional cliché in speaking, but clichés have no place in writing. The good writer thinks up fresh new ways to express ideas.

Here are a few clichés. Add some more to the list.

all work and no play
apple of his eye
as luck would have it
as white as snow
better late than never
blue in the face
bright and early
by leaps and bounds
by the skin of our teeth
center of attention
cool as a cucumber
die laughing
easier said than done
few and far between
heavy as lead
last but not least

quick as a flash
sadder but wiser
short but sweet
slowly but surely
too funny for words
work like a dog

Assignment 1   My First Morning on Campus

One way to become aware of clichés so you won't use them in your writing is to see how many you can purposely put into a paragraph. Write a paragraph describing your first morning on campus, using all the clichés possible while still keeping your account smooth and clear. You might start something like this: "I was up at the crack of dawn, fresh as a daisy, and raring to go . . . ." What title will you give your paper? Why a cliché of course! Writing such a paragraph should make you so aware of clichés that they'll never creep into your writing again.

USING SPECIFIC DETAILS

Using specific details will make your writing more interesting. If you're telling about the time you received a prize, you need to do more than tell your reader it was a great moment. If you tell what you saw, what you heard, how you felt, then the reader will be able to enjoy the experience with you. In the next two assignments you will have an opportunity to use specific details.

Assignment 2   A Significant Incident

What incident in your life had a profound effect upon you? Perhaps it occurred in early childhood, in school, out of school. Write an account of the incident giving specific details so your reader will relive it with you and feel its importance.

Here are two student papers on this assignment. Both students were having difficulties with spelling and sentence structure. At first their papers were so full of errors that they were almost impossible to read, but after a number of rewritings, they are now clear and understandable. These students had something interesting to say, and it was worth their while to get rid of errors in mechanics so that their writing can be read easily.

JASON

Two years ago at the District wrestling tournament, where I was wrestling with the team, halfway through the meet I noticed an apparently retarded boy talking to and annoying everyone. Some of the crowd moved to other seats. Everybody was watching and laughing, including the guys on the bench where my team was seated. I leaned over to the guy next to me, whom I've known for several years, and I said, "Ron, look at that weirdo up there." Ron then replied proudly, "He's my older brother Jason. He's a mongoloid." I felt like a real jackass!

Later when there was a break in the tournament, Ron's brother came down on the mat and attempted to wrestle like Ron does. Of course everyone was watching Jason in hysterical laughter. Ron then lovingly and proudly walked onto the mat, embraced Jason, and they walked off together. The whole gymnasium hushed, and a tear came into my eye.

THE DAY I STOOD AND BECAME A MAN

I reached the door of my home, sweating not from exhaustion but from fear. I opened the door. A calm feeling came over me as I sat down. One more day I had escaped. But no more would I run or hide. I would stand and be a man and fight. The next day as I walked to school, out from behind a tree the bully came. We stood toe to toe and eye to eye. Fear ran through my body. Then he swung and I swung. As blood ran from his nose, my fear turned to courage. But then something happened. The fight stopped. We stood toe to toe for a minute. No words were said, and then he smiled and I smiled.

If possible write your paper several days before it is due. Let it cool for a day. When you reread it, you will see ways to improve it. Put it away for another day, and again try to improve it. Then copy it to hand in.

Now you are ready for proofreading. **Read your paper aloud.** If you read silently, you are sure to miss some errors. Read aloud slowly, pronouncing each word distinctly so you'll catch omitted words, misspelled words, faulty punctuation, and so on. Make it a rule to read each of your papers *aloud* before handing it in.

When your paper is returned, correct all the errors, and put any misspelled words on your list on the inside back cover of this book. Rewrite your paper completely if your instructor has given you suggestions for revising it. Rewriting is perhaps the best way to learn to write.

LIMITING THE SUBJECT

Finding the right subject is sometimes the hardest part of writing. For one thing, you need to limit your subject so that you can handle it in a 300- to 500-word paper. The subject *travel*, which you used for free writing, was obviously too big. You could limit it by saying

A Canoe Trip
Our Best Family Vacation
Backpacking

but even those topics are too big. Keep making your topic smaller

Backpacking in the Mountains

and smaller

Backpacking in Jasper National Park

and smaller

One Day of Backpacking in Jasper National Park

Now you have a topic that is limited enough to write about in a short paper.

Which of the following topics are small enough to handle in a short paper?

Water Pollution   Pollution of Crooked Creek
My Hometown   Our Drugstore Hangout
My Childhood   A Moment That Changed My Life

One-room Schoolhouses   The One-room School in Macomb
Pole Vaulting   Winning My Final Pole Vault
Dramatics in My High School   My Role in the Senior Play

Obviously the topics in the first column are too big; those in the second column would be more manageable. Usually the more you limit your topic, the better your paper will be, for then you will have room for plenty of specific details.

WRITING A THESIS STATEMENT

Even after you have limited your subject, you are still not ready to write. You now have to decide what point you want to get across to your reader. The topic "One Day of Backpacking in Jasper National Park" doesn't say anything. It doesn't make any point. What about that day? What did it do to you? What point about that day would you like to make? You might write

One day of backpacking in Jasper National Park taught me the importance of getting in shape before such a trip.

or

One day of backpacking in Jasper National Park taught me that I have more resourcefulness than I was aware of.

or

One day of backpacking in Jasper National Park made me a confirmed backpacker.

Now you have said something. *When you write in one sentence the point you are going to try to get across to your reader*, you have written a thesis statement.

What was the thesis statement for the paper you wrote about a significant incident? If your paper was effective, you had a thesis statement in mind even if you were not aware of it. It would have been like one of these:

An experience at a wrestling match taught me not to laugh at the handicapped.
The day I fought a bully I gained new confidence in myself.

Write the thesis statement that you had in mind (or should have had in mind) when you wrote about your significant incident.

SUPPORTING THE THESIS WITH REASONS OR POINTS

Now you are ready to support your thesis statement with reasons or supporting points. That is, you will think of ways to convince your reader that your thesis statement is true. How could you convince your reader that one day of backpacking in Jasper National Park made you a confirmed backpacker? You might write

One day of backpacking in Jasper Park National Park made me a confirmed backpacker because
1. I found that it's an inexpensive way to travel.
2. I learned a lot about nature.
3. I met interesting people.

Notice that each of the reasons can be read smoothly after the *because* of the thesis statement.

Think of some problem you are trying to solve. Are you wondering what major to choose, whether to drop out of college for a time, whether to give up smoking, whether to break up with your girlfriend or boyfriend? . . . When you have decided on your problem, write a thesis statement for *each side*. For example, if you are wondering whether to look for a part-time job, you might write

I'm going to look for a part-time job.
I'm not going to look for a part-time job.

These thesis statements now must be supported with reasons. Put a *because* at the end of each thesis statement and list your reasons underneath. You might write

I'm going to look for a part-time job because
1. I want to be partially self-supporting.
2. I'd like to get some job experience.
3. I may as well work as waste my leisure time.

I'm not going to look for a part-time job because
1. I need to spend all my energies on my studies.
2. The amount I'd earn wouldn't be great.
3. I need to spend more time with my family.

Three reasons usually work well, but you could have two or four. Be sure that your reasons are all in the same form. All of the above reasons can be read smoothly after the *because* of the thesis statement.

because   I want to be . . . .
because   I'd like to get . . . .
because   I may as well . . . .

A thesis statement does not have to end with *because*. All that is necessary is to make sure all the reasons are in the same form. You might write

I've decided to look for a part-time job.
1. I want to be partially self-supporting.
2. I'd like to get some job experience.
3. I may as well work as waste my leisure time.

When the reasons are in the same form, we say they are parallel. Be sure
the supporting reasons you write for any thesis statement are in parallel
form. For a fuller explanation of parallel form, see page 122.

Perhaps the most important thing you can learn in this course is to write
a good thesis statement. Most writing problems are not really writing
problems but thinking problems. Whether you are writing a term paper
or merely the answer to a test question, working out a thesis statement is
always the best way to organize your thoughts. If you take enough time
to think, you will be able to write a clear thesis statement, and if you have
a clear thesis statement, writing your paper won't be difficult.

WRITING A PAPER FROM A THESIS STATEMENT

Once you have a good thesis statement worked out, organizing your paper
will be easy.

First you will need an introductory paragraph. It should catch your
reader's interest and suggest in some way your thesis statement. It will
not include the supporting points because it is more effective to let them
unfold paragraph by paragraph rather than to give them all away in your
introduction. (Your instructor may ask you to write your complete thesis
statement with supporting points at the top of your paper above the title
so that it may be referred to easily.) Even though your complete thesis
statement will not appear in your paper, your reader will be perfectly
aware of it if your paper is properly constructed.

Your second paragraph will present your first supporting point—everything about it and nothing more. And be sure to use specific examples
to prove your point.

Your next paragraph will be about your second supporting point—all
about it and nothing more.

Your next paragraph will be about your third supporting point. Thus
each of your points will have its own paragraph. Keep everything about
one point in its own paragraph, and don't let anything else creep in.

Finally you will need a brief concluding paragraph. In a short paper it isn't necessary to restate all your points. Even a single clincher sentence to round out the paper is sufficient.

Here are the introductory and concluding paragraphs from a student paper. Note that the introductory paragraph arouses the reader's interest and suggests the thesis statement. And the concluding paragraph simply wraps the paper up in one good sentence.

Introductory paragraph	My superman doesn't soar through the sky or leap tall buildings in a single bound. My superman is my dad. I think my dad is super because he shows that he cares with the little things he does.
	(The paper tells in three paragraphs the kinds of little things the father does.)
Concluding paragraph	My dad may not change clothes in a telephone booth or rescue the earth from alien attack, but he's still superman to me.

Thus your paper will have five paragraphs. (If you have two or four supporting points rather than three, that of course will change the number of your paragraphs.)

---

1. Introduction arousing your reader's interest
2. Your first supporting point
3. Your second supporting point
4. Your third supporting point
5. Conclusion

Next you'll have to think of a title. Just as you are more likely to read a magazine article with a catchy title, so your reader will be more eager to read your paper if you give it a good title. (And remember that every important word in a title is capitalized.) Which of these titles from student papers would make you want to read further?

An Interesting Experience
Knees Shaking
Toss It Away
Inchworms Get There
A Place I'll Never Forget
Say Cheese

Assignment 3   A Problem I'm Trying to Solve

Now return to the two thesis statements you wrote (p. 191) about a problem you are trying to solve, and choose one to write about. Even if your mind is not completely made up, take a stand on one side. You may mention in your introduction that there are arguments on the other side, but you must take a stand on one side if your paper is to be effective.

As you write, imagine you are talking to your reader. Then when you have finished writing, read your paper *aloud* slowly word by word to catch omitted words, errors in spelling or punctuation, run-together sentences, fragments, wordiness. Finally, read it *aloud* once more at normal speed to see whether it reads smoothly.

Assignment 4   Children and My Hometown

Do you consider your hometown or your neighborhood a good place to bring up children? If so, why? If not, why not? Spend plenty of time working out a good thesis statement with two or three supporting reasons, and remember that specific details are essential to make a paper effective.

Assignment 5   A Letter to a Parent

Most of us think our parents failed in some way, large or small, in bringing us up. First do some free writing. Then work out a good thesis statement telling what you think your parents (or one parent) did wrong. Then write another thesis statement telling what you think one or both of them did right. Choose one of these thesis statements and write a paper in the form of a letter to one or both of your parents.

Even though you are writing a letter, it will still be in the form of an essay—introduction, a paragraph for each supporting reason, and a conclusion. Your introduction might well be a brief statement of the other side of the question. That is, if you are writing about the things your parents did wrong, you might in your first paragraph mention that you know they did good things too and give a brief list. But the bulk of your paper must be on one side or the other. And remember . . . specific details make any paper come alive.

Assignment 6   Getting Along with Someone

Write down the name of someone you have trouble getting along with. You may make up a name, but have a real person in mind. Write a thesis statement listing ways in which you wish that person would change so that the two of you could get along better.

As we all know, however, it's difficult to get someone else to change. Therefore now write a thesis statement listing ways in which *you* could change to make the relationship better. Perhaps you are saying, "Impossible." Think. There are always ways. Think until you have a realistic, possible thesis statement for your paper. Remember that learning to write is learning to think.

Assignment 7   How to Do Something

Nothing will get rid of the clutter in your writing like writing a "how to" paper. Every sentence will have to be clear and to the point.

Write a short paper telling someone how to do something—how to paint a table, how to choose a stereo, how to put a three-year-old to bed, how to make a piece of costume jewelry, how to change the oil in one's car . . . .

First you'll need an introductory paragraph—a sentence will do—to interest your reader, then a step-by-step explanation, and finally a concluding paragraph, which again may be just one sentence. You may want to add some humor to your introduction or conclusion to make your paper more interesting.

WRITING A SUMMARY

A good way to learn to write concisely is to write 100-word summaries. Writing 100 words sounds easy, but actually it isn't. Writing 200- or 300- or 500-word summaries isn't too difficult, but condensing all the main ideas of an essay or article into 100 words is a time-consuming task—not to be undertaken the last hour before class. If you work at writing summaries conscientiously, you will improve your reading by learning to spot main ideas, and your writing by learning to construct a concise, clear, smooth paragraph. Furthermore, your skill will carry over into your reading and writing for other courses.

Assignment 8   A 100-Word Summary

Your aim in writing your summary should be to give someone who has not read the article a clear idea of it. First read the article, and then follow the instructions given after it.

Can It!

"Put Litter in Its Place—CAN IT!" is one of the slogans of an anti-litter campaign, the CLEAN COMMUNITY SYSTEM, that is now spreading across the country and reducing litter levels sharply. Sponsored by Keep America Beautiful, Inc., a national, nonprofit, public service organization, it's not merely a cleanup campaign but rather a community action plan to change people's attitudes. And it's working.

Since its introduction in 1976, the plan has helped reduce the litter level in Chattanooga, Tennessee, 57%; in Kansas City, Missouri, 58%; in Grand Prairie, Texas, 72%; in Portsmouth, Virginia, 74%; in Farmington, New Mexico, 78%; in Riverside, California, 80%; and in Sioux Falls, South Dakota, 84%. It is proving successful in cities as large as Houston (population 1.7 million) and as small as Holly Ridge, North Carolina (population 415).

An objective litter-measuring technique developed by the American Public Works Association enables a community, with the aid of a camera and a yardstick, to keep an accurate record of its progress in getting rid of loose trash in streets and lots, and as the residents see the litter level decreasing, they want to become involved in the program. "People begin to believe they can make a difference when they learn that they *have* made a difference," says Roger Powers, President of Keep America Beautiful.

Why do people litter? A research project found that the three most common reasons given by individuals were "Everybody else does it," "It's not my problem," and "There's nothing I can do to change things." Of prime importance, therefore, is the sound program of community education, which starts in kindergarten with the "Waste in Place" program and continues throughout the schools and in public forums. An example of the effectiveness of the education program is the Earth Group in a Plainfield, New Jersey, high school that is assisting the city by identifying trash-filled alleyways and vacant lots, locating the owners, and, if necessary, helping with the cleanup. Elsewhere community education has resulted in youngsters and adults joining in the planting of trees and shrubs in empty lots to make small parks or playgrounds.

In Georgia, which had the first statewide program, 30 local communities have undertaken extensive public education programs and have made substantial reductions in the amount of loose trash along streets and in other public areas. In Atlanta, schoolchildren collect discarded aluminum cans for recycling, and the Rapid Transit Authority has installed closed-circuit TV at each new subway station. Anyone who drops a gum or candy wrapper is apt to hear a voice from a loudspeaker saying, "Pick it up, please."

Sources: Pam Proctor "How to Squash Litterbugs," *Parade*, March 30, 1980; Roger W. Powers, "Litterbugs—Beware!" *New Jersey Municipalities*, March 1980; "A Clean Sweep," *Time*, May 19, 1980.

Another aid to the program is the strict enforcement of new antilitter laws. For example, in Indianapolis the first environmental court has been established, and Judge David Jester hears cases involving litter, roaming animals, weeds, noise, zoning, and air pollution. He hands down sentences like the one he gave to a respected citizen who would not clean up his 25 rental properties—three days in jail and a fine of $25 a day until his houses were in compliance with the law. The judge's aim is not so much to punish these litterers as to change their attitudes.

The program even makes financial sense. In Cincinnati, for example, sanitation crews used to spend half a day cleaning up after outdoor events. Now a few CLEAN COMMUNITY SYSTEM workers with trash bags mingle with the crowds and encourage them to "think tidy," with the result that the cleanup time of the sanitation crews the next day is cut in half.

The CLEAN COMMUNITY SYSTEM, which depends more on popular support than on money, is succeeding in 181 cities across the land.

A good way to begin a summary is to figure out the author's thesis statement, the major idea the author wants to get across to the reader. Write that idea down BEFORE READING FURTHER.

You probably wrote something like this: *An antilitter campaign is spreading across the country and reducing litter levels as much as 70 or 80 percent in many cities.* Using your thesis statement as your first sentence, summarize the article by choosing the most important points. Since examples are not necessary in a summary, you will not need to mention specific cities. Your first draft may be 150 words or more. Now cut it down by including only essential points and by getting rid of wordiness. Keep within the 100-word limit. You may have a few words less but not one word more. By forcing yourself to keep within the 100 words, you will get to the kernel of the author's thought and understand the article better.

When you have written the best summary you can, then, *and only then,* compare it with the summary on page 283. If you look at the model sooner, you will cheat yourself of the opportunity to learn to write summaries because once you read the model, it will be almost impossible not to make yours similar. So do your own thinking and writing, and *then* compare.

Even though your summary is different from the model, it may be just as good. If you are not sure how yours compares, ask yourself these questions:

Did I include as many important ideas?
Did I omit all unnecessary words?
Does my summary read smoothly?
Would someone who had not read the article get a clear idea of it from my summary?

Assignment 9   A Summary

Summary writing is excellent practice not only for the beginning writer but also for the experienced writer because it teaches conciseness. Since it isn't necessary to include examples, your summary of the following article will require fewer than 100 words.

Digging for Roots

Why is a hippopotamus called a hippopotamus? How did daisies get their name? Why is an open-air fire called a bonfire? And how did that little dog running down the street come to be called a terrier? Where did names come from anyway?

Most names didn't just happen. They grew from roots. And when you uncover their roots, you'll often find interesting stories.

It was no accident that a hippopotamus was named a **hippopotamus.** The early Greeks thought the big animal they saw in rivers looked a bit like a fat horse, so they called it a hippopotamus or river horse (HIPP *horse*, POTAMOS *river*). In early England people called that little flower with the white petals and a large yellow disk in the center a DAY'S EYE or **daisy.** In the Middle Ages in Europe, during times of war or plague, piles of corpses were burned together in a BONE FIRE. Eventually any open-air fire came to be called a bonefire or **bonfire.** And finally, that active little **terrier** got its name from the Latin root TERR (*earth*) because it was originally a hunting dog that dug in the earth trying to get small animals out of their burrows.

Many word stories can be found in your dictionary in square brackets either just before or just after the definition. For example, such words as **gymnasium, salary, companion,** and **curfew** have histories worth looking up.

Adapted from *The Least You Should Know About Vocabulary Building,* by Teresa Ferster Glazier. Holt, Rinehart and Winston, 1981.

But digging for word roots can do more than unearth entertaining stories. It's the quickest way to improve your vocabulary.

First, looking up the roots of a word will help you remember its meaning. For example, you might find it difficult to remember a big word like **antediluvian** if you merely looked up its meaning. But if you look up its roots, you won't easily forget it. It is made up of ANTE (*before*) and DILUVIUM (*flood*) and means "before the Flood" described in the Bible. In other words, it means "very old" or "primitive." Whenever you want to exaggerate the age of something, you can call it antediluvian. A farmer without a tractor or an office without a photocopier might be said to be using antediluvian methods. And if you are trying to convince someone—or yourself—that your car is old enough to be turned in on a new model, you might refer to it as antediluvian.

Second, learning the roots of a word will help you learn other words containing the same root. For example, if you learn that **philanthropist** is made up of PHIL (*to love*) and ANTHROP (*human being*), then you've learned not only that a philanthropist is a lover or benefactor of humanity, but you have a clue to some 70 other words beginning with PHIL and to more than 60 others beginning with ANTHROP. *Webster's Third New International Dictionary* lists that many words beginning with those two roots.

Since you now know that PHIL means *to love*, you'll readily see that **philharmonic** means "love of harmony"—an appropriate name for a symphony orchestra. **Philadelphia** (ADELPH brother) is the city of "brotherly love," and a **bibliophile** (BIBL *book*) is a "lover (or collector) of books." If you're a gardener, you'll understand why the **philodendron** (DENDR *tree*) was given its name; it "loves (the shade of) trees." Even the proper name **Philip** comes from PHIL (*to love*) and HIPP (*horse*) and means "a lover of horses."

Likewise, knowing that ANTHROP means *human being* will help you understand what the ancients meant by an **anthropocentric** universe. Obviously it was a universe with "human beings at the center." After you look up **anthropoid** and find that OID means *resembling*, you'll immediately know that anthropoid apes—such as gorillas and chimpanzees—are apes that "resemble human beings." When you look up **misanthrope** and find that MIS means *to hate*, then you'll know that a misanthrope is someone who "hates people." Thus learning the meaning of ANTHROP has helped with the understanding of four words, and you'll encounter more ANTHROP words in your reading.

SYM (SYL) is another root that can unlock the meaning of many words. In fact some 450 words beginning with that root are listed in Webster's dictionary. Once you know that SYM (SYL) means *together*, you need to pay attention only to the second root of a word to discover its meaning. A **symphony** (PHON *sound*) is literally "sounds together." A **synagogue** (AGOG *to lead*) is a place where people are "led together" for worship. A **syndrome** (DROM *to run*) is a group of symptoms "running together" and indicating a specific disease or condition. **Symbiosis** (BIO life) means "living together" often for mutual benefit, as the symbiosis of ants and aphids, with the ants protecting the defenseless aphids and then "milking" them for their honeydew.

Finally, learning word roots will give more meaning to words you already know. **Escape,** for example, comes from EX (*out*) and CAP (*cape*) and originally meant to get "out of one's cape." Perhaps while a jailer was holding a prisoner by his cape, the prisoner got "out of his cape" and got free. He had escaped. **Panic** (PAN *a Greek god*) originally referred to the frantic efforts of the Greek nymphs to flee when the mischievous god Pan suddenly appeared among them. **Trivia** (TRI three, VIA *way*) refers to the meeting of "three ways" or roads in Roman times. Women on their way to market would stop at the *trivia* or "three ways" to talk about unimportant matters. Eventually that kind of talk came to be called "three ways" talk, or trivia. **Precocious** (PRE *before*, COCT *to cook*) originally meant "cooked before time." Therefore if you have a precocious child, the child has been "cooked before time" or has matured earlier than most children.

When you dig for roots, you're sure to unearth some surprising stories.

Assignment 10   A 100-Word Summary

The author of this article has been a feature writer, drama critic, film critic, editorial writer, and university professor. Here he presents some of his ideas about writing. Keep within the 100-word limit and summarize his essay. Difficult words are defined in the margin.

Simplicity
William Zinsser

Clutter is the disease of American writing. We are a society strangling in unnecessary words, circular constructions, pompous frills and meaningless jargon.

Who can understand the viscous language of everyday American commerce and enterprise: the business letter, the interoffice memo, the corporation

pompous—self-important
jargon—obscure language
viscous—not flowing readily

report, the notice from the bank explaining its latest "simplified" statement? What member of an insurance or medical plan can decipher the brochure that tells him what his costs and benefits are? What father or mother can put together a child's toy—on Christmas Eve or any other eve—from the instructions on the box? Our national tendency is to inflate and thereby sound important. The airline pilot who wakes us to announce that he is presently anticipating experiencing considerable weather wouldn't dream of saying that there's a storm ahead and it may get bumpy. The sentence is too simple—there must be something wrong with it.

But the secret of good writing is to strip every sentence to its cleanest components. Every word that serves no function, every long word that could be a short word, every adverb which carries the same meaning that is already in the verb, every passive construction that leaves the reader unsure of who is doing what—these are the thousand and one adulterants that weaken the strength of a sentence. And they usually occur, ironically, in proportion to education and rank.

components—parts

adulterants—
substances causing
impurity
ironically—contrary
to what might be
expected
mollify—calm

During the late 1960s the president of a major university wrote a letter to mollify the alumni after a spell of campus unrest. "You are probably aware," he began, "that we have been experiencing very considerable potentially explosive expressions of dissatisfaction on issues only partially related." He meant that the students had been hassling them about different things. I was far more upset by the president's English than by the students' potentially explosive expressions of dissatisfaction. I would have preferred the presidential approach taken by Franklin D. Roosevelt when he tried to convert into English his own government's memos, such as this blackout order of 1942:

potentially—possibly

> Such preparations shall be made as will completely obscure all Federal buildings and non-Federal buildings occupied by the Federal government during an air raid for any period of time from visibility by reason of internal or external illumination.

"Tell them," Roosevelt said, "that in buildings where they have to keep the work going to put something across the windows."

Simplify, simplify. Thoreau said it, as we are so often reminded, and no American writer more consistently practiced what he preached. Open *Walden* to any page and you will find a man saying in a plain and orderly way what is on his mind:

I love to be alone. I never found the companion that was so companionable as solitude. We are for the most part more lonely when we go abroad among men than when we stay in our chambers. A man thinking or working is always alone, let him be where he will. Solitude is not measured by the miles of space that intervene between a man and his fellows. The really diligent student in one of the crowded hives of Cambridge College is as solitary as a dervish in the desert.

diligent—industrious
dervish—a member of a Muslim religious order dedicated to a life of poverty and chastity and known for devotional exercises of dancing and whirling

How can the rest of us achieve such enviable freedom from clutter? The answer is to clear our heads of clutter. Clear thinking becomes clear writing: one can't exist without the other. It is impossible for a muddy thinker to write good English. He may get away with it for a paragraph or two, but soon the reader will be lost, and there is no sin so grave, for he will not easily be lured back.

Who is this elusive creature the reader? He is a person with an attention span of about twenty seconds. He is assailed on every side by forces competing for his time: by newspapers and magazines, by television and radio and stereo, by his wife and children and pets, by his house and his yard and all the gadgets that he has bought to keep them spruce, and by that most potent of competitors, sleep. The man snoozing in his chair with an unfinished magazine open on his lap is a man who was being given too much unnecessary trouble by the writer.

assail—attack

potent—powerful

It won't do to say that the snoozing reader is too dumb or too lazy to keep pace with the train of thought. My sympathies are with him. If the reader is lost, it is generally because the writer has not been careful enough to keep him on the path.

This carelessness can take any number of forms. Perhaps a sentence is so excessively cluttered that the reader, hacking his way through the verbiage, simply doesn't know what it means. Perhaps a sentence has been so shoddily constructed that the reader could read it in any of several ways. Perhaps the writer has switched pronouns in mid-

verbiage—wordiness

shoddily—poorly

sentence, or has switched tenses, so the reader loses track of who is talking or when the action took place. Perhaps Sentence B is not a logical sequel to Sentence A—the writer, in whose head the connection is clear, has not bothered to provide the missing link. Perhaps the writer has used an important word incorrectly by not taking the trouble to look it up. He may think that "sanguine" and "sanguinary" mean the same thing, but the difference is a bloody big one. The reader can only infer (speaking of big differences) what the writer is trying to imply.

sequel—continuation

sanguine—optimistic, cheerful
sanguinary—bloodthirsty
infer—guess

Faced with these obstacles, the reader is at first a remarkably tenacious bird. He blames himself—he obviously missed something, and he goes back over the mystifying sentence, or over the whole paragraph, piecing it out like an ancient rune, making guesses and moving on. But he won't do this for long. The writer is making him work too hard, and the reader will look for one who is better at his craft.

tenacious—persistent

rune—riddle

The writer must therefore constantly ask himself: What am I trying to say? Surprisingly often, he doesn't know. Then he must look at what he has written and ask: Have I said it? Is it clear to someone encountering the subject for the first time? If it's not, it is because some fuzz has worked its way into the machinery. The clear writer is a person clear-headed enough to see this stuff for what it is: fuzz.

I don't mean that some people are born clear-headed and are therefore natural writers, whereas others are naturally fuzzy and will never write well. Thinking clearly is a conscious act that the writer must force upon himself, just as if he were embarking on any other project that requires logic: adding up a laundry list or doing an algebra problem. Good writing doesn't come naturally, though most people obviously think it does. The professional writer is forever being bearded by strangers who say that they'd like to "try a little writing sometime" when they retire from their real profession. Good writing takes self-discipline and, very often, self-knowledge.

bearded—confronted

Many writers, for instance, can't stand to throw anything away. Their sentences are littered with words that mean essentially the same thing and with phrases which make a point that is implicit in what they have already said. When students give me these littered sentences I beg them to select from the surfeit of words the few that most precisely fit what they want to say. Choose one, I plead, from among the three almost identical adjectives. Get rid of the unnecessary adverbs. Eliminate "in a funny sort of way" and other such qualifiers—they do no useful work.

implicit—suggested though not directly expressed

surfeit—excess

The students look stricken—I am taking all their wonderful words away. I am only taking their superfluous words away, leaving what is organic and strong.

"But," one of my worst offenders confessed, "I never can get rid of anything—you should see my room." (I didn't take him up on the offer.) "I have two lamps where I only need one, but I can't decide which one I like better, so I keep them both." He went on to enumerate his duplicated or unnecessary objects, and over the weeks ahead I went on throwing away his duplicated and unnecessary words. By the end of the term—a term that he found acutely painful—his sentences were clean.

enumerate—list

"I've had to change my whole approach to writing," he told me. "Now I have to *think* before I start every sentence and I have to *think* about every word." The very idea amazed him. Whether his room also looked better I never found out.

Writing is hard work. A clear sentence is no accident. Very few sentences come out right the first time, or the third. Keep thinking and rewriting until you say what you want to say.

[Here are two pages of the final manuscript of the previous essay, show-ing how the author corrected them. By reading these pages and noting the author's changes, you will discover ways to improve your own writing.]

Although [these pages] look like a first draft, they have already been rewritten and retyped—like almost every other page—four or five times. With each rewrite I try to make what I have written tighter, stronger and more precise, eliminating every element that is not doing useful work, until at last I have a clean copy for the printer. Then I go over it once more, reading it aloud, and am always amazed at how much clutter can still be profitably cut.

5 —)

is too dumb or too lazy to keep pace with the ~~writer's~~ train

of thought. My sympathies are ~~entirely~~ with him.) ~~He's not~~

~~so dumb.~~ If the reader is lost, it is generally because the

writer ~~of the article~~ has not been careful enough to keep

him on the proper path.

This carelessness can take any number of ~~different~~ forms.

Perhaps a sentence is so excessively ~~long and~~ cluttered that

the reader, hacking his way through ~~all~~ the verbiage, simply

doesn't know what *it* ~~the writer~~ means. Perhaps a sentence has

been so shoddily constructed that the reader could read it in

several

any of ~~two or three different~~ ways. ~~He thinks he knows what~~

~~the writer is trying to say, but he's not sure.~~ Perhaps the

writer has switched pronouns in mid-sentence, or ~~perhaps he~~

has switched tenses, so the reader loses track of who is

talking ~~to whom~~ or ~~exactly~~ when the action took place. Per-

haps Sentence B is not a logical sequel to Sentence A — the

writer, in whose head the connection is ~~perfectly~~ clear, has

bothered to provide

not ~~given enough thought to providing~~ the missing link. Per-

haps the writer has used an important word incorrectly by not

taking the trouble to look it up. He may think
that "sanguine" and "sanguinary" mean the same thing, but
the difference is a bloody big one. The reader
can only infer (speaking of big differences) what the writer is trying to imply.

Faced with these obstacles, the reader
is at first a remarkably tenacious bird. He blames
himself. He obviously missed something, and he goes
back over the mystifying sentence, or over the whole paragraph,

6 —)

piecing it out like an ancient rune, making guesses and moving
on. But he won't do this for long. The writer is making him work too hard, and the reader will look for
one who is better at his craft.

The writer must therefore constantly ask himself: What am
I trying to say? Surprisingly often, he
doesn't know. Then he must look at what he has
written and ask: Have I said it? Is it clear to someone
encountering the subject for the first time? If it's
not, it is because some fuzz has worked its way into the
machinery. The clear writer is a person clear-headed
enough to see this stuff for what it is: fuzz.

I don't mean that some people are born
clear-headed and are therefore natural writers, whereas
others are naturally fuzzy and will never write
well. Thinking clearly is a conscious act that the
writer must force upon himself, just as if he were
embarking on any other project that requires logic:
adding up a laundry list or doing an algebra problem. Good writing doesn't come naturally, though most
people obviously think it does. The professional

Assignment 11   A 100-Word Summary

Now that you have had some practice in writing summaries, make use of your skill in reading your textbooks. When you finish reading a chapter, summarize it immediately, and you will not only understand it better but will remember it longer and have the summary ready for review.

Here is part of a chapter from an astronomy textbook. Because it contains so much important information, you will have to choose for your 100-word summary only the most striking facts, ones that you will want to remember.

The Nature of the Universe
Thomas L. Swihart

The Universe is the sum of all things that can be scientifically measured, at least in principle, so it is not possible to make a complete list of its contents. It is possible to describe a few of the major ingredients, however, and the background this gives will help to show how the details to be studied later fit into the whole.

GALAXIES

Matter is not spread evenly throughout the Universe, but is concentrated into large bunches called *galaxies*. A galaxy is an extremely large collection of stars that is held together by the force of gravity. A galaxy may contain tens or hundreds of billions of stars, each star being about as large and bright and hot as the Sun. Billions of galaxies are known to exist. There may also be large amounts of matter in space between the galaxies, although the evidence to date indicates that this isn't the case.

The size of galaxies and the distances between them are so large as to be almost beyond comprehension. Distances in astronomy tend to be so big that the speed of light is often used to measure them. Light travels at a speed of about 186,000 miles or 300,000 kilometers each second— that's nearly *eight* times around the Earth in 1 second. At this speed, light reaches us from the Moon in a little more than 1 second, while it takes 8 minutes to arrive here from the Sun. According to scientific ideas held today, it is not possible to move faster than light: It is the ultimate in speed. Yet some galaxies are so big that it takes 100,000 years or more for light just to cross from one side to the other.

In one year light can travel a distance of about 6 trillion miles. (A trillion is written 1,000,000,000,000.) This distance is called a *light year* (not a length of time), and it is convenient to measure large distances

Thomas L. Swihart, *Journey Through the Universe.* Copyright © 1978 Houghton Mifflin Company. Reprinted by permission.

in light years. We live in a large galaxy called the *Milky Way*, and it has a diameter of about 100,000 light years. The Milky Way is one of the larger galaxies, although it is by no means the largest.

A certain area of the sky is known as the constellation of Andromeda (an-DROM-e-da). On a very dark, clear night a person with good eyes might barely be able to see a faint hazy spot in Andromeda, although it is easily seen with binoculars. The object is called the *Andromeda galaxy*, and it is over 2 million light years away. This means that when you look at the Andromeda galaxy, you are seeing it as it appeared over 2 million years ago; what you are seeing is the light that was emitted by the stars in that galaxy before modern man appeared on the Earth. Thus looking out at great distances is also looking back at times far in the past. In spite of its great distance, the Andromeda galaxy is one of the closest ones to us.

. . . .

Is there a limit to how many galaxies exist and how far away they extend? Is there a limit to how far into the past they have existed and how long they will last? Or does the Universe have an infinite size and age? So far, astronomers have been able to give only very incomplete answers to these intriguing questions, and I do not believe that we will ever be able to answer them with much confidence. Past experience also reveals that when answers are found to "ultimate" questions, other ultimate questions, unimaginable earlier, arise to take their place. This continuous search for answers does give astronomers a very exciting profession.

WRITING AN APPLICATION
Assignment 12   A Letter of Application

You may not need to do much writing in the career you have chosen, but almost certainly you will at some time need to write a letter of application. Write a letter of application now, either for a job this coming summer or for a job you might want to apply for after you finish college. Then write a separate personal data sheet. Follow the forms given here.

```
                              500 West Adams Street
                              Macomb, Illinois 61455
                              February 2, 1982


Mr. John Blank, Director
Chicago Park District
425 East McFetridge Drive
Chicago, Illinois 60605

Dear Mr. Blank:

I have seen your ad in the Chicago Tribune for
helpers in the Park District Recreation Department
for the coming summer. I would like to be considered
for a position.

I am a freshman at Western Illinois University and am
majoring in Special Education. Therefore I would be
particularly pleased if I could work with mentally or
physically handicapped children.

I have listed my training and experience on the
enclosed personal data sheet, and I shall be glad to
come for an interview at your convenience.

                              Sincerely,

                              Jane Doe
                              Jane Doe
```

                         Jane Doe
                         500 West Adams
                         Macomb, Illinois 61455
                         Telephone: 000-000-0000

PERSONAL
      Age 18
      Height 5 feet, 5 inches
      Weight 135 pounds
      Unmarried

EDUCATION
      1981-1982   Freshman at Western Illinois Univer-
                  sity. Majoring in Special Education.
      1977-1981   Student at McKenzie High School,
                  Chicago.

ACTIVITIES
      Bowling
      Swimming   Won second place in a swimming meet
                 at Western in 1981.

WORK EXPERIENCE
      1981 summer   Helper in County of St. Louis
                    Department of Parks and Recreation.
                    Worked with mentally handicapped
                    children.
      1980 summer   Worked at a private camp near
                    Fond du Lac, Wisconsin, coaching
                    swimming.
      1979 summer   Took a tour with a group from my
                    high school to Washington, D.C.,
                    and then helped at the South
                    Chicago YMCA pool, working with
                    physically handicapped children.

REFERENCES
      Mr. John Jones, Director
      County of St. Louis
      Department of Parks and Recreation
      7900 Forsyth Boulevard
      St. Louis, Missouri 63105

      Mrs. Mary Johnson, Director
      Fond du Lac Camp for Girls
      Fond du Lac, Wisconsin 54935

WRITING AN EVALUATION

Assignment 13   An Evaluation of My Performance in This Course

Do five minutes of free writing on your performance in this course. Don't evaluate the course—it may have been bad or good—but simply evaluate how you performed. Although you may need to mention some weakness or strength of the course, the emphasis must be on how you reacted to that weakness or strength.

Don't be afraid to be honest. This isn't an occasion for apple-polishing. If you've gained little, you'll write a better paper by saying so than by trying to concoct phony gains. Someone who has gained little may write a better paper than someone who has gained much. How well the paper is organized and whether there are plenty of specific examples will determine the effectiveness of the paper.

After you have written your thesis statement, list your supporting points. If you have made gains, list the kinds—gains in study habits, gains in writing skills, gains in confidence . . . . Or, if you have gained little, list the reasons why—lack of time, lack of interest, getting off to a bad start . . . .

Since no one will have all gain or all loss in any course, you may want to include in your introduction or conclusion a sentence about the other side.

Answers

Answers

Words Often Confused (p. 10)

EXERCISE 1

1. new, already
2. doesn't, it's
3. know, effect
4. advice, compliment
5. except, here
6. choose, are
7. course, know
8. conscious, our
9. affect, an
10. have, or

EXERCISE 2

1. an, due
2. chose, know
3. It's, effect
4. know, have
5. it's, all ready
6. does, accept
7. course, an
8. it's, effect
9. Our, are
10. hear, doesn't

EXERCISE 3

1. clothes, an
2. Here, advise
3. conscious, know
4. effect, forth
5. already, choose
6. know, it's
7. course, know
8. no, advice
9. have, it's
10. an

EXERCISE 4

1. Here, are, our
2. new, desert
3. know, it's
4. no, do
5. already, our
6. accept, advice
7. an, break
8. chose, fourth
9. course, effect, its
10. know, it's, an

EXERCISE 5

1. course, clothes
2. know, compliments
3. doesn't, choose
4. conscious, it's
5. New, or
6. already, an
7. fourth, clothes
8. are, do
9. hear, it's, accept
10. have, advice

EXERCISE 6

1. are, choose
2. advise, choose, or
3. know, it's, or
4. course, here
5. conscious, effect

6. course, conscience
7. accept, except
8. already
9. knew, break
10. An, does

EXERCISE 7

1. It's, here, already
2. course, have
3. knew, clothes
4. no, know
5. hear, break

6. doesn't, do
7. choose, our
8. accept
9. advice, an, effect
10. conscious

EXERCISE 8

1. an, course, a
2. It's, fourth, already
3. advise, accept
4. advice, effect
5. desert

6. dose, effect
7. conscious, compliment
8. have, choose, clothes
9. know, here, our
10. An, does, break

EXERCISE 9

1. have, fourth
2. forth, choose
3. an, dessert
4. have, conscience
5. It's, break

6. advice, no, effect
7. course, already
8. course, due
9. Doesn't, compliment
10. are, accept, our

EXERCISE 10

1. conscious, our, break
2. accept, advice
3. coarse, desert
4. have, an
5. all ready, an

6. compliments, new
7. chose, desert
8. It's, an
9. knew, effect
10. know, already

Words Often Confused (continued) (p. 18)

EXERCISE 1

1. piece, quite
2. have, than
3. You're, dessert
4. Here, choose
5. know, advice

6. course, doesn't
7. It's, too
8. break, your
9. Who's, woman
10. knew, past

EXERCISE 2

1. Where, threw
2. loose, lose
3. It's, already
4. knew, quite
5. know, write

6. fourth, it's
7. It's, does
8. principal, too
9. have, past
10. course, effect

EXERCISE 3

1. They're, than
2. weather, too, to
3. past, already
4. you're, through
5. Where, women

6. Who's, write
7. whether, principal
8. quiet, peace
9. personal, than
10. knew, lose

EXERCISE 4

1. You're, quiet, you're
2. personal, doesn't
3. You're, lose, write
4. led, its
5. an, passed

6. moral, principles
7. Where, lose
8. whether, peace
9. woman, Women's
10. Who's, than

EXERCISE 5

1. know, quite, advice
2. led, its
3. piece, loose
4. You're, all ready
5. loose, led

6. Your, conscience, advice
7. personnel, their
8. principal, passed
9. quite, too, to
10. piece, write

EXERCISE 6

1. led, then
2. lead, their
3. piece, advice
4. through, it's, due
5. Whose, your

6. new, an, effect, personnel
7. morale, than
8. Does, they're
9. There, they're
10. piece, coarse

EXERCISE 7

1. whether, weather
2. Where, your
3. their, than
4. choose, than
5. Whose, advice

6. principal, too
7. threw, right
8. women, passed
9. Where, write
10. you're, too

EXERCISE 8

1. advice
2. its, than
3. Where, does
4. are, your
5. Write, you're, too

6. all ready, dessert
7. They're, personnel
8. know, whether, passed, course
9. Whose, principles
10. does, loose

EXERCISE 9

1. There, too, their
2. effect, advice, than
3. quite, weather
4. too, to
5. morale, personnel

6. Where, piece
7. quite, there
8. You're, right, it's
9. principal, does
10. know, woman

EXERCISE 10

1. Who's, write
2. past, then
3. does, whether, you're
4. It's, too, who's
5. principal, does

6. course, than
7. quite, they're
8. whether, or
9. new, their
10. through, know

Contractions (p. 23)

EXERCISE 1

1. I'm, didn't
2. I'd, I'd
3. I'm, didn't
4. I'd, didn't
5. didn't, I've

6. It's, it's
7. It's, I'll
8. can't, isn't
9. can't, they've
10. I'm, I'll, I've

EXERCISE 2

1. I'm, I've
2. isn't, it's
3. I've, there's
4. hasn't, we've
5. who's, can't

6. It's, who's
7. I'm, who's, I'll
8. I'm, they're
9. I've, there's
10. I've, wouldn't

EXERCISE 3

1. can't, didn't
2. You'd, you'd
3. I've, haven't
4. Don't, it's
5. Let's, what's

6. I'm, it's
7. I'd, it's
8. I've
9. it's (first one)
10. I've, can't

EXERCISE 4

1. Didn't, she's
2. She's, she's
3. You've, she's
4. couldn't, I'd
5. she's, Don't

6. doesn't, isn't
7. won't, don't
8. You're, aren't
9. That's, isn't
10. It's, we're

EXERCISE 5

1. I've
2. didn't, they've
3. they'd, they've
4. They'd
5. Isn't, didn't

6. We've
7. It's, isn't
8. What's
9. haven't, that's
10. It'll, they've

EXERCISE 6

1. Haven't
2. I've
3. aren't, they're
4. aren't, they're
5. There's

6. you've, you'll
7. they're
8. It's
9. It's
10. it's, they're

EXERCISE 7

1. I've
2. They're, can't
3. They've
4.
5. it's

6. they're
7. can't, aren't
8. it's
9. aren't
10. They're

EXERCISE 8

1. I've, it's
2. I'd, I'd
3. I'd
4. you've, it's
5. it's

6. you'll
7. you're, you'll
8. you're
9. It's, you're, don't
10. you'll

EXERCISE 9

1. It's, there's
2. can't, he's
3. What's, doesn't
4. can't, I'm
5. Don't, I'm

6. I'm, won't
7. wouldn't, didn't
8. I'd, can't
9. It's, I'm
10. I'm, it's

EXERCISE 10

1. doesn't, hasn't
2. She's, who's
3. It's, they're
4. He's, I've
5. He's, isn't

6. You're, aren't
7. I'm, you're, it's
8. Two's, three's
9. We'd, couldn't
10. haven't, we're

Possessives (p. 30)

EXERCISE 1

1. girl's
2. husband's
3. Ned's, Dennis'
4. men's, boys'
5. brother-in-law's

6. team's
7. Norma's
8. audience's
9.
10. Johnsons'

EXERCISE 2

1. chairperson's
2. Terry's
3. senator's
4. Jeffrey's
5. Someone's

6.
7. Yesterday's
8.
9. George's
10. night's

EXERCISE 3

1. Women's
2. world's
3. Mom's
4. Haley's
5. Rebecca's

6. Dad's
7. else's
8. brother's
9. Tom's
10. Charles'

EXERCISE 4

1. girls'
2.
3. wife's
4.
5. Martha's, Sarah's

6. anyone's
7. Girls'
8. father's
9. Michael's
10. Gerald's

EXERCISE 5

1. Chicago's, New York's
2. club's
3. Dylan's
4. college's
5. judge's

6.
7. Mr. Jones'
8.
9. Diana's
10. Cheryl's

EXERCISE 6

1. Children's
2. Harry's
3.
4. anybody's
5.

6. dean's
7. day's
8. Saturday's
9. governor's
10.

EXERCISE 7

1. president's
2. Jerry's
3. Paul's
4. twins'
5.
6. dad's, mother's
7. Peter's
8. child's
9.
10. Ralph's

EXERCISE 8

1. settlers'
2. Ruth's
3. bartender's
4. Beethoven's
5. people's
6. Lincoln's
7. mother's
8.
9.
10. else's

EXERCISE 9

1. Ted's, Leroy's
2.
3.
4. students'
5. anybody's
6. everybody's
7. professor's
8. Someone's
9. person's
10. students'

EXERCISE 10

1. day's
2. Tony's, Sue's
3. Sue's
4. Scouts', orthodontist's
5. day's
6. mother's
7. week's
8. Chicago's, Miami's
9. family's
10. people's

Review of Contractions and Possessives (p. 34)

EXERCISE 1

1. I've
2. I'd, don't
3. doesn't
4. it's
5. plant's

6.
7. plant's
8. That's, I'd, don't
9. they're, they're
10. they're

EXERCISE 2

1. I'd, we'd
2. Doug's
3.
4. we'd, we've
5. We'd, it's, country's

6. world's
7. It's, they've
8. visitors'
9. we'd
10. earth's

EXERCISE 3

1. can't
2. she's, family's
3. She's
4. She's
5. it's

6. everything's
7. I've
8.
9. They've
10. snake's

EXERCISE 4

It's going to be a summer of traveling for my brothers. They're going to the West Coast in Mark's car. They had thought of taking Miles' van, but it's a gas guzzler. Mark's VW won't be so expensive to run. They've not planned their route yet, but they'll no doubt hit Arizona because Mark's best friend lives there, and a few nights' lodging and a few free meals won't be unwelcome. The boys will be gone a month or maybe longer if they're lucky enough to find jobs. Their objective is to see whether they'd like to settle in the West and also simply to see some country they've not seen before.

Doubling the Final Consonant (p. 38)

EXERCISE 1

1. putting
2. controlling
3. admitting
4. mopping
5. planning
6. hopping
7. jumping
8. knitting
9. marking
10. creeping

EXERCISE 2

1. returning
2. swimming
3. singing
4. benefiting
5. loafing
6. nailing
7. omitting
8. occurring
9. shopping
10. interrupting

EXERCISE 3

1. beginning
2. spelling
3. preferring
4. fishing
5. hunting
6. excelling
7. wrapping
8. stopping
9. wedding
10. screaming

EXERCISE 4

1. feeling
2. motoring
3. turning
4. adding
5. subtracting
6. streaming
7. expelling
8. missing
9. getting
10. stressing

EXERCISE 5

1. forgetting
2. misspelling
3. fitting
4. planting
5. pinning
6. trusting
7. sipping
8. flopping
9. reaping
10. carting

Subjects and Verbs (p. 52)

EXERCISE 1

1. trees are
2. They grow
3. They are
4. Redwoods grow
5. They resist
6. bark resists
7. trees live
8. Many were
9. many are
10. wood varies

EXERCISE 2

1. we saw
2. fire swept
3. smoke was
4. flames were
5. flames rose
6. motorist saw
7. he alerted
8. fighters spread
9. They had
10. cabin burned

EXERCISE 3

1. instructor stresses
2. attitude is
3. I keep
4. I worked
5. paper has
6. I typed
7. papers make
8. paper satisfies
9. I enjoyed
10. work brings

EXERCISE 4

1. koala is
2. It is
3. koala looks
4. animal has
5. food consists
6. it eats
7. Leaves are
8. koala is
9. It crawls
10. koala rides

EXERCISE 5

1. cloud was
2. lizard darted
3. Locusts swarmed
4. sound grew
5. we saw
6. wind shifted
7. mountains were
8. sun sank
9. prairie became
10. We were

EXERCISE 6

1. skiers wanted
2. deer was
3. Juncos came
4. I made
5. child stood
6. house contained
7. I exceeded
8. exhibits were
9. exhibits were
10. letter is

EXERCISE 7

1. (You) stand
2. Swimming is
3. He dived
4. he swam
5. (You) do
6. She seems
7. excuse was
8. crowds moved
9. It was
10. team made

EXERCISE 8

1. Persians built
2. windmills meet
3. windpower provides
4. future looks
5. government supports
6. It encourages
7. It gives
8. windmills are
9. they provide
10. windpower has

EXERCISE 9

1. Picasso burned
2. Van Gogh applied
3. Seurat used
4. picture is
5. we saw
6. Shakespeare used
7. United Nations receives
8. it remains
9. person knows
10. amoeba is

EXERCISE 10

1. state has
2. cardinal is
3. states chose
4. states are
5. bird is
6. It belongs
7. nene is
8. bird is
9. wren was
10. bird is

Prepositional Phrases (p. 57)

EXERCISE 1

1. All are
2. Most require
3. Many prefer
4. book is
5. Much goes

6. ability helps
7. third studied
8. Most passed
9. One passed
10. end is

EXERCISE 2

1. Many left
2. we won
3. Three were
4. atmosphere was
5. we made

6. result was
7. Most goes
8. All went
9. she won
10. All cheered

EXERCISE 3

1. Two went
2. All wanted
3. we wanted
4. road is
5. all were

6. quietness was
7. All learned
8. place was
9. it kept
10. three had

EXERCISE 4

1. Hibernation differs
2. animals relax
3. life stops
4. breathing becomes
5. beating becomes

6. body is
7. kinds freeze
8. Animals prepare
9. They store
10. Groundhogs become

EXERCISE 5

1. bird is
2. it is
3. eagles are
4. Cedar Glenn is
5. they gather

6. they stay
7. area is
8. eagles perch
9. eagles spend
10. Havens ensure

EXERCISE 6

1. poppies grew
2. mountain rose
3. garden was
4. we found
5. we spent

6. sandpiper scuttled
7. we saw
8. we hiked
9. trip was
10. forms survive

EXERCISE 7

1. maples are
2. sap rises
3. farmers tap
4. they make
5. One is

6. arch spans
7. Rainbow Bridge is
8. it is
9. Great Pyramid exists
10. temples stand

EXERCISE 8

1. composition is
2. Hundreds speculate
3. flight is
4. blackbird builds
5. monument stands

6. Egyptians used
7. faces grinned
8. Artists produced
9. glass has
10. America uses

EXERCISE 9

1. One is
2. I pursue
3. rung was
4. I made
5. rung was

6. coat finished
7. One was
8. metal was
9. I cleaned
10. coat made

EXERCISE 10

1. Neither owns
2. Each drives
3. advantages are
4. Both are
5. someone pays

6. she found
7. Many were
8. Most helped
9. One became
10. feeling was

More About Verbs and Subjects (p. 61)

EXERCISE 1

1. fires have been
2. fires were started
3. Conditions must be
4. Vegetation contains, will burn
5. fires start, burn
6. Fire can race
7. land can change
8. rain will put
9. number has increased
10. vigilance is

EXERCISE 2

1. she had been collecting
2. She would identify
3. she would place
4. Limpets had been
5. shells could be found
6. Others could be found
7. she awoke, looked
8. She went, wandered
9. She picked, took
10. she, friends went, had

EXERCISE 3

1. Yellow has been
2. Pencils have sold
3. pencils are sold
4. pencil can draw
5. America could conserve
6. cans can be separated, can be put
7. cities are recovering
8. farmers had been hoping
9. heat had been
10. rain came, flooded

EXERCISE 4

1. Dr. Salk discovered, freed
2. House, Senate passed
3. incumbent, opponent engaged
4. We visited, listened
5. Lincoln has been called
6. books have been written
7. He rose, steadied, launched
8. education broadens, deepens
9. tragedy sobers, uplifts
10. music echoed, reechoed

EXERCISE 5

1. Miriam has been
2. I confide, take
3. We have spent
4. We walk, identify
5. we came, wondered
6. It did look
7. we saw
8. heron was teetering
9. sun sank, disappeared
10. Darkness did come

EXERCISE 6

1. Library is
2. items are included
3. items are added
4. forms are included
5. It was established
6. it has become
7. Libraries can borrow
8. people can go, use
9. manuscripts, photographs, recordings, reels are
10. It houses

EXERCISE 7

1. papers are stored
2. pieces may be found
3. collection is included
4. Two-thirds are
5. book is
6. copy is
7. collections are housed
8. building is
9. sculptures, paintings, murals were produced
10. Visitors are given

EXERCISE 8

1. I have been reading
2. explosion was
3. It buried, killed
4. blast was, was
5. It was
6. blast blew, caused
7. miles were buried
8. eruption occurred
9. blast had, caused
10. volcanoes are

EXERCISE 9

1. days were
2. Night came, lasted
3. mountains, cliffs appeared
4. cars could climb
5. Bears, deer roamed
6. man opened, looked
7. tracks could be seen
8. Van Allen is known
9. lights are caused
10. Year was planned

EXERCISE 10

1. Astronomers have been
2. atmosphere has interfered
3. telescopes can get
4. plans are being made
5. It will orbit, get
6. It will provide
7. It will operate, circle
8. Galileo made
9. Improvements have been made
10. telescope will open

Getting Rid of Run-together Sentences (p. 68)

EXERCISE 1

1. Pronunciations change, words are being added
2. (You) read, you can look
3. (You) note, they will help
4. Keeping is, you can review
5. (You) use. It's
6. (You) use, you'll forget
7. handguns circulate, million are sold
8. Half are committed
9. people believe, resent
10. others complain, they are working

EXERCISE 2

1. I am writing, he is
2. He has designed, he won
3. He has designed, achievement has restored
4. complex consists, it has
5. building, courthouse are included
6. courthouse is, roof is
7. Robson Square is, it is
8. Robson Square has
9. tank is heated, cooled; buildings are heated, cooled
10. I've learned, I hope

EXERCISE 3

1. team;
2. park. It's
3. bus.
4. States,
5. clear;
6.
7. trout. We
8.
9. country,
10. them. We

EXERCISE 4

1. tonight.
2. go,
3. morning?
4. class,
5. day;
6. untidy;
7. phone. It's
8. limit. It's
9. while;
10. 55,

EXERCISE 5

1. blowing. Our
2. torrents;
3. shore. We
4.
5. quiet. Only
6.
7. cold;
8. cracks,
9.
10. downstream. It

EXERCISE 6

1. farm;
2. TV. He
3. books;
4. succeed. He
5. way;
6. off. He
7. work,
8. back,
9. years,
10. them,

EXERCISE 7

1. violent. They
2. hour. Some . . . higher,
3.
4. long;
5. small, and . . . short,

6. knowing. They
7. walls. Shield
8. floor. Closets
9. shelter,
10. season,

EXERCISE 8

1.
2. fence,
3. tunneling;
4. West,
5. West. More

6. fence,
7. night,
8. country. Only
9. side,
10. barrier,

EXERCISE 9

1. Museum. It
2. *Louis.* Here
3. vehicles. They
4.
5. Workshop. Here

6. ceiling,
7.
8. sensational;
9.
10. Institution. It

EXERCISE 10

1. Last spring we were driving through Arizona and decided to see the Petrified Forest. Therefore we took the 27-mile drive through that strange landscape. Trees have turned to stone, and thousands of great stone logs lie on the ground. We learned a great deal about petrified wood and were glad for the experience. We had seen a new part of our country. The National Park Service is preserving the area for future generations.

2. The most striking feature of the oceans is their vast size. The next most striking feature is the constant motion of their surfaces. One cause of the motion is the wind. It may make waves from an inch to over 60 feet in height. Another cause of waves is geologic disturbances such as earthquakes and volcanic eruptions below the surface of the oceans. Waves from geologic disturbances are sometimes incorrectly called tidal waves, but they have no relationship to the tides.

Getting Rid of Fragments (p. 75)

EXERCISE 1

1. I refused to go because I had homework to do.
2. I could make good grades if I studied.
3. After I finish college, I'll get a job.
4. They were out playing Frisbee while he was studying.
5. Her essay would have been better if she had rewritten it.
6. Unless you return your library book today, you'll have to pay a fine.
7. A large vocabulary is the characteristic that most often accompanies outstanding success.
8. He was searching for the money that he had dropped in the snow.
9. Although he looked a long time, he couldn't find it.
10. Until you understand subjects and verbs, you cannot understand clauses.

EXERCISE 2

1. when you are tired
2. if you hadn't called
3. when one of the Navy players came onto the field
4. as he raced down to the goal line
5. that I could someday go to the Super Bowl
6. although he really preferred his motorcycle
7. If it's nice tomorrow
8. While the leaves are still on the trees
9. that you were coming with me
10. While she is away

EXERCISE 3

1. If you are too busy for a vacation
2. Although I studied
3. If you want to learn to write
4. After I rewrite
5. When the sun went down
6. As it became dark
7. that may be the largest object in the universe
8. Whereas the earth's diameter is about 8,000 miles
9. If you stood on the moon and looked back toward Earth
10. which was built in the third century B.C.

EXERCISE 4

1. As he ran to catch the ball, he missed it.
2.
3.
4. Because no one had told me about the new ruling, I was late with my report.
5. When I make up my mind to really work, I can accomplish a lot.
6.
7. If I can just spend a couple of hours on my math, I can pass that test.
8.
9. When I'm finished with both of them, I can relax.
10.

EXERCISE 5

1.
2. As the ambulance came racing down the street, a crowd gathered.
3. When a book is really interesting, I read it rapidly.
4.
5. As we learned more about the problem, we sympathized with him.
6. Because I had so much homework for that evening, I stayed at home.
7. Unless something goes wrong, we're going to win.
8. While everyone else was studying, he was watching TV.
9.
10.

EXERCISE 6

1.
2. When he had drunk his fill from the cool spring, he continued on his way.
3. After the sun sank behind the hills, it got cold.
4.
5. Even though she is my best friend, I don't tell her everything.
6.
7. As he jumped into the air to catch the Frisbee, she ran away.
8.
9.
10. Since I had had nothing for lunch but an apple, I was hungry.

More About Fragments (p. 80)

EXERCISE 1

1. After answering the telephone and taking the message, she left.
2.
3. After falling on the ice and breaking his leg, he could no longer compete.
4. The announcement that there would be no classes on Friday was welcome.
5.
6. I don't know whether . . . .
7. My parents want . . . .
8. Not wanting to disappoint them, I made the effort to go.
9. My father is . . . .
10. Having always done his best in school, he graduated with honors.

EXERCISE 2

1. We had walked . . . .
2. We walked where . . . .
3. Trying to keep the fire burning, we gathered more wood.
4.
5. Having traveled almost 200 miles, we were weary.
6. It was a boring . . . .
7. I had nothing to do . . . .
8. Her family enjoyed the gracious . . . .
9. She needed a place . . . .
10. She finished the day . . . .

EXERCISE 3

1. They were facts . . . .
2. My hobby is not expensive.
3. She came at a time . . . .
4. Although neither of us was eager to undertake the job, we did it.
5. Each of us hoped . . . .
6. He was a fellow . . . .
7. Even though we were told that the game might be postponed, we went anyway.
8. I was sure . . . .
9.
10. The audience applauded . . . .

EXERCISE 4

Individuals can help save our forests. Americans waste vast amounts of paper because they don't think of paper as forests. They think nothing of wasting an envelope because an envelope is only a tiny piece of paper, but it takes two million trees to make the yearly supply of 112 billion envelopes. Even small savings can encourage others to save until finally the concerted efforts of enough individuals can make a difference.

EXERCISE 5

Future historians will probably call our age the time when humans began the exploration of space. Some historians say that space exploration marks a turning point in the history of the world. Some people criticize space exploration saying that the money should have been spent on the poor here on earth. Others say, however, that we wouldn't have spent the money on anything of greater human value. The annual space budget is less than one percent of federal spending whereas the bulk of federal spending goes to defense and to health, education, and welfare. There have been practical payoffs from space exploration. One is the trans-oceanic television broadcasts that can be relayed by communications satellites. Another payoff is the daily weather picture that appears on television screens. Still another payoff is the earth-resources satellites that circle the earth and help map remote regions, search for water and minerals, and monitor crops and timber. And the final payoff is military reconnaissance that helps make possible arms limitation agreements among nations.

EXERCISE 6

When curiosity flourishes, worlds can be changed. Why? How? What if? Young people ask these questions and take joy in the search for solutions. Their worlds abound with endless possibilities. So, too, it is with scientists whose laboratories are as limitless as the universe and whose ideas shape worlds. To interest young minds in the wonders of science, Phillips Petroleum has made possible a film series called "The Search for Solutions." These stimulating films are aired on PBS and seen by over two million students per month. They capture the excitement of discovery and the discoverer. They teach and encourage, but most of all they interest because childlike curiosity in the right hands can help turn darkness into light.

—Phillips 66

Review of Run-together Sentences and Fragments (p. 84)

1. In the 1960s Lake Erie was so polluted that experts feared there wouldn't be a single living organism in it within 20 years. Strict anti-pollution laws in the United States and Canada, however, have eliminated much of the industrial pollution. Also better sewage-treatment methods have reduced the flow of phosphorus into the lake. Now the waters are alive with fish again, and the beaches are crowded with swimmers.

2. How to dispose of hazardous chemical wastes is one of the greatest environmental problems. Society has benefited from the chemicals that control pain and disease and those that create new industrial products, but almost 35,000 chemicals used in the United States are classified as possibly hazardous to human health. The Environmental Protection Agency estimates that the United States is generating more than 77 billion pounds of hazardous chemical wastes a year and that only 10 percent are being handled safely. At least half of the wastes are being dumped indiscriminately, poisoning the earth and the underground water supplies. Toxic chemicals are adding to disease according to the Surgeon General, and virtually the entire population is carrying some body burden of these chemicals.

3. The science of medicine has had a long history. It began with superstitions, and illness was attributed to evil spirits. The ancient Egyptians were among the first to practice surgery. Anesthesia was, of course, unknown. Therefore the patient was made unconscious by a blow on the head with a mallet. Surgery was also practiced in early Babylonia, and the Code of Hammurabi lists the penalties that an unsuccessful surgeon had to pay. For example, if a patient lost an eye through poor surgery, the surgeon's eye was put out.

4. In 1598 the famous Globe Theater was built across the Thames from London. Shakespeare became a shareholder, and his plays were produced there. The theater was octagonal and held about 1,200 people. The "groundlings" stood on the floor and watched the play, but the wealthier patrons sat in the two galleries. Those paying the highest fees could sit upon the stage. The stage jutted out into the audience; thus the players and the audience had a close relationship.

Using Standard English Verbs (p. 88)

EXERCISE 1

1. walk, walked
2. am, was
3. has, had
4. do, did
5. needs, needed

6. helps, helped
7. want, wanted
8. attends, attended
9. talks, talked
10. suppose, supposed

EXERCISE 2

1. am, was
2. do. did
3. has, had
4. ask, asked
5. enjoy, enjoyed

6. finishes, finished
7. learns, learned
8. works, worked
9. listen, listened
10. play, played

EXERCISE 3

1. doesn't, do
2. expect, changed
3. suggest, watch
4. bothers, missed
5. did, wanted

6. were, are
7. did, did
8. asked, wasn't
9. were, weren't
10. were, returned

EXERCISE 4

1. joined, like
2. played, play
3. needs, hopes
4. doesn't, are
5. work, learn

6. expects, insists
7. practice, have
8. enjoys, benefits
9. watch, do
10. were, praised

EXERCISE 5

1. liked, work
2. learned, discussed
3. explained, did
4. do, hope
5. liked, dropped

6. checked, decided
7. picked, did
8. encouraged, listened
9. is, is
10. advises, treats

EXERCISE 6

1. started, was
2. collect, have
3. asked, were
4. wanted, decided
5. want

6. disposed, received
7. are, have
8. are, measure
9. help, impress
10. intend

EXERCISE 7

1. finished, returned
2. asked, had
3. occurred, was
4. happened, reported
5. expected, appeared
6. did, happened
7. were, weren't
8. was, wasn't
9. arrived, rested
10. enjoy, am

EXERCISE 8

1. listened, did, pleased
2. volunteered
3. are, need
4. contained, listed
5. attended, benefited
6. helps, listens
7. celebrated, enjoyed
8. discussed, offered
9. changed, surprised
10. plan, hope

EXERCISE 9

1. impressed, changed
2. bores, do
3. needs, intend
4. asked, did
5. sealed, dropped
6. discovered, are
7. happened, was
8. asked, walked
9. occurs, complained
10. expect

EXERCISE 10

1. pleased, wanted
2. ordered, finished
3. handed, finished
4. loaned, want
5. complained, disliked
6. dropped, had
7. occurs, need
8. observed, started
9. wants, doesn't
10. hopes, does

Standard English Verbs (compound forms) (p. 96)

EXERCISE 1

1. finish, finished
2. finish
3. finished, finish
4. finishing
5. finished
6. finished
7. finish
8. finished
9. finish
10. finished

EXERCISE 2

1. were, changed
2. saw, asked
3. broken, eaten
4. looked, saw
5. decided, gone
6. eaten, begun
7. spoken, learned
8. intend, began
9. were, realized
10. helped, were, beginning

EXERCISE 3

1. saw, eaten
2. need, take
3. jog, play
4. were, impressed
5. speak, begun
6. seems, want
7. know, become
8. imitating, use
9. teach, beginning
10. like

EXERCISE 4

1. were, saw
2. seen, begun
3. driven, eaten
4. asked, did
5. ate, asked
6. written, asked, received
7. come, begun
8. saw, suggested
9. gone, washed, prepared
10. saw, were, ran

EXERCISE 5

1. wanted, gave
2. made, done
3. become, appreciated, done
4. watching, say
5. spending, are
6. have, continues
7. makes, are
8. taken, sung
9. chosen, learned
10. asked, did

EXERCISE 6

1. decided, seen
2. frozen, reached
3. was, gone
4. observed, saw
5. announced, won
6. smiled, received
7. were, done
8. Were, accepted
9. discussed, impressed
10. analyzed, gave

EXERCISE 7

1. said, visit
2. hoping, come
3. were, drove
4. seen, grown
5. taken, taking
6. was, stay
7. occupied, took
8. seen, were
9. asked, like
10. were, collected

Making Subjects, Verbs, and Pronouns Agree (p. 107)

EXERCISE 1

1. is
2. is
3. is
4. doesn't
5. is, his
6. were
7. doesn't
8. has
9. think
10. intend

EXERCISE 2

1. is
2. has
3. has
4. hopes
5. likes
6. were
7. live
8. were
9. were
10. Doesn't

EXERCISE 3

1. is
2. helps
3. are
4. has
5. were, were
6. depends
7. doesn't
8. work
9. requires
10. is

EXERCISE 4

1. has her
2. like
3. lives
4. doesn't
5. has
6. has her
7. doesn't
8. were
9. were
10. spend

EXERCISE 5

1. are
2. has, her
3. have, their
4. doesn't
5. expect
6. hope, intend
7. enjoy
8. spend
9. go
10. takes

EXERCISE 6

1. are
2. exhibits
3. was
4. is
5. come
6. like
7. were, weren't
8. were, were
9. were
10. feels

EXERCISE 7

1. watch
2. are
3. was
4. were
5. is

6. doesn't
7. were
8. expects
9. were
10. is

EXERCISE 8

1. was, its
2. enjoys
3. doesn't
4. contain
5. remain

6. Weren't
7. doesn't
8. is
9. Doesn't
10. have

EXERCISE 9

1. is, his
2. are, their
3. intend
4. presents
5. are

6. Doesn't
7. plan
8. doesn't
9. are
10. doesn't

EXERCISE 10

1. insist
2. fulfills, contains
3. were
4. has, his
5. doesn't

6. are
7. doesn't
8. has
9. sleep
10. were

Choosing the Right Pronoun (p. 112)

EXERCISE 1

1. me
2. me
3. I
4. she
5. he

6. her
7. her
8. she
9. I
10. me

EXERCISE 2

1. him
2. me
3. me
4. I
5. me

6. I
7. us
8. us
9. me
10. My sister and I

EXERCISE 3

1. us
2. We
3. us
4. me
5. him

6. he
7. him
8. me
9. Lou and I
10. I

EXERCISE 4

1. He and I
2. he and I
3. us
4. he
5. me

6. me
7. me
8. I
9. I
10. us

EXERCISE 5

1. me
2. me
3. me
4. me
5. they

6. me
7. My wife and I
8. David and I
9. me
10. I

Making the Pronoun Refer to the Right Word (p. 115)

EXERCISE 1

1. I put the omelet on the table, took off my apron, and began to eat.
2. I was pleased that they offered me a job.
3. Trying to decide what trip to take isn't easy.
4. She said to her sister, "My room is a mess."
5. I have a pair of glasses, but my eyes are so good that I don't use the glasses except for reading.
6. The president said to the dean, "You have been too lenient."
7. The child was pleased when I praised the finger painting.
8. I thought he would phone, and I waited all evening for the phone to ring.
9. The teachers established a play center where the children can spend their leisure.
10. Ray said to the professor, "Your watch is wrong."

EXERCISE 2

1. When I picked up the dog's dish, the dog began to bark.
2. Because I have always been interested in coaching football ever since I was in high school, I have decided to become a coach.
3. My family was annoyed because I decided not to get a summer job.
4. She asked her sister, "Why wasn't I invited to the party?"
5. His father said to Jay, "You can take my new tennis racket to school."
6. I have always liked French Provincial furniture and have finally decided to buy a French Provincial dresser.
7. She said to her instructor, "You don't understand what I'm saying."
8. She likes to swim; in fact she spends most of her summer swimming.
9. She was chosen student body president because she is good in her studies even though she is not very good in sports.
10. The boss was really despondent when he talked with Ed.

EXERCISE 3

1. His motorcycle swerved into the side of a house, but the house was not damaged.
2. As I approached the playpen, the baby began to cry.
3. As soon as the fender was repaired, I drove the car home.
4.
5. The instructor said, "Your typewriter needs a new ribbon."
6. He said to his father, "I ought to wash the car."
7. I walked into the room, climbed on the ladder, and began to paint the ceiling.
8.
9. She said to her mother, "You need to be positive before making such a big decision."
10. We couldn't find a single bottle and blamed Rudy for drinking all the cokes.

EXERCISE 4

1. Andy said to his brother, "Your car has a flat tire."
2. It would be cold in New England at this time of year, and I don't like the cold.
3. He asked the mechanic, "Why am I having trouble?"
4. Her sister came in crying at 4 a.m.
5. As I tried to attach the leash, the dog jumped away.
6.
7. The cars whizzed past, but no one even looked my way.
8. As soon as I approached the robin's nest, the robin flew away.
9. I've decided to save all my money for a trip although saving that much won't be easy.
10. She said to her daughter, "I missed my appointment."

EXERCISE 5

1. He said, "Dad, I need a new suit."
2. Since we couldn't find the cake plate, we realized the children must have eaten the cake.
3.
4. The child screamed when I moved the tricycle.
5. I have adjusted the steering wheel, and you can take your car home any time.
6. After I had read the story of Lindbergh's life, I decided I want to be an airline pilot.
7. He said to the man, "Won't you come back when I have time to talk?"
8. Jerome was very angry when he talked to his father.
9. Ben said, "Dad, you ought to get a refund for the faulty tire."
10. When I opened the door of the kennel, the puppy ran away.

Getting Rid of Misplaced or Dangling Modifiers (p. 119)

EXERCISE 1

1. Years later you will . . . .
2. I came across my grandfather sound . . . .
3. I saw a furry little caterpillar crawling . . . .
4. As he took her in his arms, the moon . . . .
5. While I talked on the phone, the cake . . . .
6.
7. Lincoln Park is the most interesting park I have seen in the city.
8. She was engaged to a man named Smith, who had a . . . .
9. When I was fourteen, my . . . .
10. We gave all the food we didn't want to . . . .

EXERCISE 2

1. After I had cleaned my room, my dog . . . .
2. A son weighing eight pounds was . . . .
3. I don't enjoy his company because he's . . . .
4. I don't care for cucumbers unless they are pickled.
5. I tried to quiet the screaming and kicking child.
6. The car I bought from a used car dealer had a . . . .
7. I saw the broken ladder leaning . . . .
8. After watching TV all evening, I found the dirty dishes . . . .
9. When I was six, my . . . .
10.

EXERCISE 3

1. I brought the dog, badly in need of a bath, into . . . .
2. I watched the horses in the pasture quietly . . . .
3. Having been born and raised in the country, I naturally find the old cookstove appealing.
4. Excited and eager to go, we saw the bus waiting for us in . . . .
5. The house where I was born is . . . .
6. I stopped and talked to the child who was . . . .
7. As we unwrapped gift after gift, the puppy . . . .
8. I decided to give the clothes I had no use for to . . . .
9. Although his car was almost eight years old, he refused to turn it . . . .
10. She put the sandwiches that she had not eaten back . . . .

EXERCISE 4

1. When I was ten, my . . . .
2. We could see little white pieces of paper falling . . . .
3. While she was on a two-week vacation, the office . . . .
4. I saw in the evening paper that . . . .

5. Because I played Frisbee all evening, I did not get my English paper finished.
6. Consulting the Lost and Found section of the paper, we soon had the dog safe . . . .
7. Just as we arrived, the youngster went careening down the driveway on . . . .
8. After eating lunch hurriedly, we started in two taxis . . . .
9. We saw the parade moving . . . .
10.

EXERCISE 5

1. While tobogganing down the hill, we saw a huge bear come into view.
2. The class made me aware of some little speech habits, which I got rid of very soon.
3.
4. The monkey watched us as it peeled . . . .
5.
6. Dressed in a long blue evening gown, she seemed to him prettier than ever.
7. Living in a small town, one . . . .
8. We watched the first spring warblers darting . . . .
9. Because I had gone to too many parties, my . . . .
10. The series of lectures we are having on religions of the world will . . . .

Using Parallel Construction (p. 124)

EXERCISE 1

1. and sleeping late . . . .
2. and by taking him . . . .
3. or making an oral report.
4. and with modern . . . .
5. and studied for . . . .
6. and packed the car . . . .
7. the pleasant boss . . . .
8. and camping out.
9. and to get along . . . .
10. and bubble gum.

EXERCISE 2

1. and to perform . . . .
2. and took pictures . . . .
3. and scratching . . . .
4. and to value cooperation.
5. and an old popcorn . . . .
6. than to have a great . . . .
7. and entertaining.
8. and to read better books.
9. and concluded . . . .
10. and often rainy.

EXERCISE 3

1. and understanding . . . .
2.
3. and security.
4. and all kinds . . . .
5. sometimes even sat and . . . .
6. and to come when called.
7. then went to bed.
8. inches wide.
9.
10. and can't even smell.

EXERCISE 4

1. and judo lessons.
2.
3. and unhappy.
4. and friendly children . . . .
5. and his fear.
6. and interested in . . . .
7. and then placed it . . . .
8. and unselfish.
9. and finally how to add the fertilizer.
10.

EXERCISE 5

1.
2. and a bank teller.
3. and making . . . .
4. keep the display counters neat and of course wait . . . .
5. demanding, satisfying, and challenging.
6. meets people, can help people, and has . . . .
7. and gets along . . . .
8. and to have a vacation.
9. and an Indian blanket.
10. and by train.

EXERCISE 6

1. and cold weather . . . .
2.
3. and the sounds of insects.
4. and entertaining.
5. and the anemone blossoms waving in the wind.
6. and a redheaded woodpecker tapping . . . .
7. and watching for birds . . . .
8. or swim without . . . .
9.
10. and educational.

EXERCISE 7

1. in one corner her bulging . . . .
2. waited for Sue . . . .
3. and the increase in crime.
4. and by air.
5.
6. and by cooking economy . . . .
7. and rewriting all . . . .
8. charm and tact.
9. and how to change . . . .
10.

EXERCISE 8

1. Every college student should know how to type because
   1. some instructors require typed papers
   2. typing, if one is good at it, saves time
   3. a typed paper often gets a higher grade
2. Going home every weekend is unwise because
   1. I spend too much time on the bus
   2. I get behind in my college work
   3. it is too expensive
   4. I miss out on weekend activities at college
3. Commercial billboards along highways should be prohibited because
   1. they often cause accidents
   2. they mar the scenery
4. Learning to sew is valuable because
   1. sewing your own clothes saves money
   2. sewing teaches you to be creative
5. My chief objectives in this course are
   1. to learn to spell
   2. to learn to write well-constructed sentences
   3. to learn to write a clear composition

Avoiding Shift in Time (p. 130)

EXERCISE 1

1. saw, looked
2. came
3. came
4. becomes
5. thinks, becomes
6. came
7. remembered
8. turned
9. writes
10. tells

EXERCISE 2

1. went
2. surprised
3. escapes
4. gets
5. gave, had
6. crawled
7. have
8. went
9. ran
10. didn't

EXERCISE 3

As I traveled down the highway, I signaled to turn left. I started the turn . . . . I pulled off the road. . . . I stopped the truck and got out . . . .

EXERCISE 4

My mother stood . . . because she was afraid I was going to fall off the roof. In spite of her I finally got it up . . . . I was listening . . . . Eventually I decided I wanted . . . . Mostly I just listened and worked . . . .

EXERCISE 5

He says . . . . He says . . . .

EXERCISE 6

. . . trees provided . . . . and they lived . . . . Several families lived . . .

EXERCISE 7

. . . he decided that the routine of study was . . . . he tramped, taught school, made shoes, and edited . . . . he was writing poetry . . . . he found himself famous.

EXERCISE 8

thorny bush catches . . . fence is difficult . . . scarecrow frightens . . . dog makes her . . . . where she is given . . . which she plans . . . . that she is able to overcome . . . .

Avoiding Shift in Person (p. 136)

EXERCISE 1

1. you should
2. when I
3. you won't
4. I really have
5. one spends

6. my brain
7. I couldn't take it easy the way I
8. if one wants
9. sugar and stick to
10. we could see

EXERCISE 2

1. we could see
2. we couldn't see
3. to help me
4. you should read
5. they have to set

6. when I have to
7. your car
8. as we grew up we became
9. get their equipment
10.

EXERCISE 3

1. I made a piece . . . . I did this on my own
2. give us two work sheets . . . if we didn't do them . . . keep after us until we did . . . . we could tell our problems to.
3. made us feel we were getting . . . prepared us . . . .

EXERCISE 4

It was my sign of independence. It was my ticket to freedom. I didn't have to ask to borrow the family car, and I didn't have to explain where I was going or when I'd be back . . . . every accessory imaginable . . . . Funny how it costs freedom to support freedom.

EXERCISE 5

we could see the people below . . . . as close to floating on a cloud as it's possible to get. We couldn't feel the wind, of course, because we were drifting with it, but we could see the ground moving along beneath us . . . . when we went high, we could see for miles . . . . Few experiences can compare with floating on a cloud.

Getting Rid of Wordiness (p. 142)

EXERCISE 1

1. I woke up at four this morning.
2. We were considering whether to charge admission.
3. Many people never read a book.
4. After our eight-hour hike, we were hungry.
5. He had tried football, basketball, and hockey.
6. He can be depended upon to do what he says he will.
7. I was surprised yesterday when my college roommate stopped to see me.
8. I think she's planning to go.
9. I had no money by the end of the year.
10. The three kinds of stones we found were unique.

EXERCISE 2

1. No doubt our team will win.
2. They carried him home drunk.
3. There is more permissiveness today than formerly.
4. Justice is too slow in our country.
5. Justice should be swift and sure.
6. He has worked hard all his life.
7. His height makes him a good basketball player.
8. The melons were large and sweet.
9. Most students don't leave campus on weekends.
10. Finally one should learn more at college than what is learned in courses.

EXERCISE 3

1. Many people were there.
2. At present thousands of acres along the river are under water.
3. Something should be done to prevent flooding.
4. No one seems to be working on the problem.
5. Finally the doctor arrived but could do nothing for her.
6. The plane circled the airport for half an hour and then disappeared.
7. I was unaware that she had arrived.
8. He left college because he wanted some business experience.
9. The wealthier countries should aid the developing countries.
10. In 1981 my brother accepted a job with Bell and Howell of Chicago.

EXERCISE 4

1. Most people spend too much time watching TV.
2. I forgot about last night's meeting.
3. Most writers use too many words.
4. A new car should not be driven too fast for the first 500 miles.
5. I'm happy to accept your invitation.
6. I intend to finish my year here and then look for a job.

7. Most people want a clear, concise business form.
8. The president should bring the motion to a vote.
9. I thought she was just pretending to be ill.
10. I'm trying to get rid of wordiness in my papers.

EXERCISE 5

To help new students find their way around the Library, the staff offers orientation programs. Many faculty members also bring their classes to particular subject areas for orientation. And printed handouts, such as special subject bibliographies and instructions for using periodical indexes and psychological abstracts, are available.

Review of Sentence Structure and Agreement (p. 146)

1. B	6. B	11. B	16. B	21. A
2. A	7. A	12. A	17. B	22. A
3. A	8. B	13. A	18. A	23. B
4. B	9. B	14. B	19. A	24. A
5. B	10. B	15. A	20. B	25. B

Punctuation (p. 151)

EXERCISE 1

1. Hurry!
2.
3. late;
4. Toronto. We'd
5. crusty. It

6. week.
7. best:
8. trips. It
9. parks:
10.

EXERCISE 2

1. health. Some
2. morning:
3. tickets;
4. mistakes;
5. eggs. She

6. lessons?
7. trotted;
8. galloped.
9. Help!
10. Tommy? Where's he?

EXERCISE 3

1. years. He
2. places:
3. countryside;
4. rock. He's
5. animals;

6. rocks;
7. fern;
8. leaf;
9.
10. park. It

EXERCISE 4

1. moved. They
2. theirs. It's
3. garden. All
4. tame;
5. down. All

6.
7. ready.
8.
9. order:
10. decision. The

EXERCISE 5

1. president;
2. attended college;
3. following:
4.
5. oldest elected president;

6. at 42. He
7. 1914. It
8.
9. students:
10.

EXERCISE 6

1. farms?
2. energy. Now
3. jobs:
4. soil;
5. morning. Tractors

6. years. The
7. itself. Other
8. food;
9. can;
10. farms. They

EXERCISE 7

1. Michigan?
2. village;
3. past;
4. Dearborn;
5. carriage;

6. great;
7.
8. buildings. He
9. museum. One
10. old way of life. Ford

EXERCISE 8

1. clocks;
2.
3. hourglass;
4. 1354;
5. pendulum;

6. popular;
7. parts;
8. too;
9. short;
10. parts;

EXERCISE 9

1. party;
2. following:
3. things:
4. morning;
5.

6. subjects:
7. school;
8. gallon. Now
9. errand. Now
10. difference.

EXERCISE 10

1. player. Then
2. up. He
3. 1980. His
4. leg. Some
5. weather:

6. perseverance;
7. him. He
8. up;
9. miles;
10. point.

Commas (p. 157)

EXERCISE 1

1. trip,
2. brochures,
3. time,
4. newspapers, encyclopedias,
5. Yes,
6. away,
7. planning,
8. college,
9. Hawaii, Tahiti,
10. far,

EXERCISE 2

1. lately,
2. years,
3. dull,
4. lecture,
5. me,
6. daydreaming,
7. off,
8.
9. marks,
10. all,

EXERCISE 3

1.
2. sentences,
3. answer,
4. exercises,
5. statement,
6.
7. finish,
8. finished,
9. writing,
10. writing,

EXERCISE 4

1. winter,
2. ice,
3. water,
4. snakes,
5. radar,
6. Conway, South Carolina,
7.
8. trails,
9.
10. Province, China, on January 23, 1556,

EXERCISE 5

1. eager,
2. English, American,
3. England, Robert . . . San Francisco, California, March 26,
4. surprised, hurt,
5.
6. century,
7. September 6, 1665,
8. entered,
9. colors, oils,
10. sentence,

EXERCISE 6

1. animal,
2. 1800s,
3. West,
4. settlers, by sportsmen,
5. supply,
6. States,
7. management, the . . . comeback,
8. Yellowstone National Park, National Bison Range in Montana,
9. free,
10. heritage,

EXERCISE 7

1. States,
2. Maine, Shenandoah in Virginia, Mammoth Cave in Kentucky, Everglades in Florida,
3.
4. summer,
5. stalagmites,
6. cave,
7. water,
8. purple, brown,
9. cave,
10. levels,

EXERCISE 8

1. River, Frozen Niagara,
2. left,
3. parks,
4. acres,
5. created,
6. geysers, hot springs, lakes, rivers,
7. Yellowstone,
8. 1870,
9. nature,
10. prohibited,

EXERCISE 9

1. hour,
2. "swift creature,"
3. delicate,
4. today,
5. measured,
6. head,
7. trees, and . . . leaves, twigs,
8. branch, draws . . . lips,
9. acacia,
10.

EXERCISE 10

1. harm,
2. anyone,
3. eat,
4. animals,
5. world,
6. ignored, and . . . chips, bread, cheese,
7. animals,
8.
9. laws,
10. thoughtlessness,

Commas (continued) (p. 163)

EXERCISE 1

1. Bill, who . . . asleep,
2.
3.
4. hoping, Marge,
5. car, it seems,

6. have, of course,
7.
8. wife, who . . . kindergarten,
9. odd, Ellen,
10. tried, nevertheless,

EXERCISE 2

1. Yes, Warren,
2. imagined, moreover,
3.
4.
5.

6. was, beyond a doubt,
7. should, I think,
8.
9. Minnesota,
10. Kilauea, which . . . Hawaii,

EXERCISE 3

1.
2. Amazon, flowing . . . Atlantic, and the Nile,
3.
4.
5. country, of course,

6. need, many think,
7. punishment, they say,
8.
9.
10. Atchison, where . . . born,

EXERCISE 4

1.
2.
3.
4. Mel,
5. positive, however,

6.
7. gardening, it seems,
8. spot,
9. Place, thirty acres . . . timber,
10.

EXERCISE 5

1. was, on the whole,
2. better, I think,
3. writing, I find,
4.
5.

6. suit, which . . . Easter,
7. ago, Hanson Gregory, captain . . . art,
8. dad, who . . . football,
9.
10. Dickens, a 19th-century author,

EXERCISE 6

1.
2. Greenland, the . . . world,
3. car,
4. here, Debra,
5.

6. had, in spite of his inexperience,
7. said, furthermore,
8.
9.
10. examination, which . . . anyone,

EXERCISE 7

1. contest, which . . . students,
2. think, Michael,
3. Conductor,
4. Providence,
5.

6. Williamsburg, which . . . Virginia,
7. area, which . . . acres,
8. place, certainly,
9.
10. decided, however,

EXERCISE 8

1. garden, it has been said,
2. you, Jon,
3.
4. vote, we have found,
5.

6.
7. collection, which . . . years,
8. world, and . . . existed,
9. Hippocrates, who . . . medicine, set . . . oath,
10. Shaw, who . . . writers,

Review of the Comma (p. 167)

1. Many Americans do not know about Highway 1,
2.
3. The Keys, which go southwestward from the mainland of Florida,
4. The Keys are great places for shell collecting, bird watching,
5. Shell collectors, who say the Keys beaches are the best places in the United States for shells,
6. Bird watchers are interested in the herons, pelicans,
7. Various kinds of coral abound,
8.
9. On Grassy Key is the Flipper Sea School,
10. On some of the smaller Keys are found Key deer,
11. Almost extinct 20 years ago, they are now, however,
12. Key West, which is the end of the Overseas Highway,
13. With its freewheeling life-style and its marvelous weather,
14. Walking is a good way to see Key West,
15. Among the famous artists and writers who have found inspiration at Key West over the years are James Audubon, Hart Crane,

Quotation Marks (p. 169)
EXERCISE 1

1. "Let's get something to eat,"
2. "Do you want to go now or after the movie?"
3. "Why not both times?"
4. "Snow and adolescence are the only problems that disappear if you ignore them long enough,"
5. "Some people stay longer in an hour than others can in a week,"
6.
7. "Doing work I like is more important to me than making a lot of money,"
8. "With all its sham, drudgery, and broken dreams," said Adlai Stevenson, "it is still a beautiful world."
9. We went to see *The Wild Duck,*
10. "Our future as a nation is going to depend not so much on what happens in outer space as on what happens in inner space—the space between our ears,"

EXERCISE 2

1. "The actions of some children," said Will Rogers, "suggest that their parents embarked on the sea of matrimony without a paddle."
2. "The best time to tackle a small problem," said my father, "is before he grows up."
3. "When Mom goes shopping," says Kip, "she leaves no store unturned."
4. I agree with the Spanish proverb, "How beautiful it is to do nothing and then rest afterward."
5. He found her munching chocolates and reading a book entitled *Eat, Drink, and Be Buried.*
6. Mark Twain said, "When I was a boy of 14, my father was so ignorant I could hardly stand to have the old man around. But when I got to be 21, I was astonished at how much the old man had learned in seven years."
7. Mark Twain said, "The parts of the Bible which give me the most trouble are those I understand the best."
8. "Work consists of whatever a body is obliged to do, and play consists of whatever a body is not obliged to do,"
9. On observing the great number of civic statues, Cato, the Roman, remarked, "I would rather people would ask why there is not a statue of Cato than why there is."
10. "One does not complain about water because it is wet," said Abraham Maslow, "nor about rocks because they are hard."

EXERCISE 3

1. I've just read "Barn Burning,"
2. "The construction of an airplane," wrote Charles Lindbergh, "is simple compared to the evolutionary achievement of a bird."

3. "If I had the choice," Lindbergh continued, "I would rather have birds than airplanes."

4.

5.

6. Pablo Casals, the great cellist, spent hours on a single phrase. He said, "People say I play as easily as a bird sings. If they only knew how much effort their bird has put into his song."

7. "As it is the mark of great minds to say many things in a few words," wrote La Rochefoucauld, "so it is the mark of little minds to use many words to say nothing."

8.

9. "Whatever you have you must either use or lose,"

10. "A span of time either leaves you better off or worse off," wrote John Gardner. "There is no neutral time."

EXERCISE 4

1. "Finish every day and be done with it," said Ralph Waldo Emerson. "Tomorrow is a new day."

2. "Life can only be understood backward," said Kierkegaard, "but it must be lived forward."

3. "A friend is a person with whom I may be sincere. Before him I may think aloud,"

4. "The only conquests which are permanent and leave no regrets," Napoleon said, "are our conquests over ourselves."

5. "Nearly all men can stand adversity, but if you want to test a man's character, give him power,"

6.

7. In the novel *Fathers and Sons*

8. "Nobody can carry three watermelons under one arm,"

9. "The taller the bamboo grows the lower it bends,"

10. "The man who does not do more work than he's paid for," said Abraham Lincoln, "isn't worth what he gets."

EXERCISE 5

1. "The cost of a thing is the amount of what I call life which is required to be exchanged for it, immediately or in the long run,"

2. "A man is rich," said Thoreau, "in proportion to the number of things he can afford to let alone."

3. Viewing the multitude of articles exposed for sale in the marketplace, Socrates remarked, "How many things there are that I do not want."

4. I have been reading *Comfortable Words,*

5. "Perhaps the most valuable result of all education," said Thomas Huxley, "is the ability to make yourself do the thing you have to do, when it ought to be done, whether you like it or not."

6.

7. "Education does not mean teaching people to know what they do not know," said John Ruskin. "It means teaching them to behave as they do not behave."

8. "Sometimes when fate kicks us and we finally land and look around, we find we have been kicked upstairs,"

9. "At the end," said Richard E. Byrd, "only two things really matter to a man, regardless of who he is; and they are the affection and understanding of his family."

10. "There are at least as many stars," wrote Sir James Jeans, "as there are grains of sand upon all the seashores of the earth."

Capital Letters (p. 173)

EXERCISE 1

1.
2. "The Death of the Hired Man"
3. English
4. Labor Day
5. Dad

6.
7. Wednesday
8. Community College.
9.
10. Rink

EXERCISE 2

1. Institute of Technology
2. East
3.
4. "Tougher Meat Laws Needed in Ontario"
5. West Coast, Yukon

6. Yosemite National Park
7. University of Southwestern
8.
9. Aunt
10.

EXERCISE 3

1. Latin America
2. Mexico, Central and South America
3. French, English
4. Professor, French
5. Community College

6.
7. Aquarium, Grant Park
8. "A Worn Path"
9. "What's
10.

EXERCISE 4

1. High School
2. Community College, Community College
3. Dad, Mother
4. Thursday, Women's Club
5. the East

6. Sunday
7. Main Street, Saturday
8. South, East
9. Canal, River
10.

EXERCISE 5

1. Canada
2. Southern Vocational College, University
3. Dad
4. Black Hills
5. Park

6. World War
7.
8. Psychology, History
9. State College
10.

EXERCISE 6

1.
2. River
3. Granddad
4.
5. Institute of Technology

6. Lake
7. Granddad
8. English
9. Professor
10.

EXERCISE 7

1. United Kingdom
2. Britain, France
3. "The Fall of the House of Usher"
4. Spanish
5. African
6. Fourth
7.
8. Dad
9.
10. University of Calcutta

Review of Punctuation and Capital Letters (p. 176)

EXERCISE 1

1. The Taj Mahal, which is in Agra,
2. Do you read *Time* or *Newsweek*?
3. I'm glad it's snowing;
4. Skiing, skating,
5. Figure skating, which I'm just learning,
6. His knapsack contained the following items: food, matches,
7. As we put the horses in their stalls, we could hear Dad
8. There is much inferior paint on the market,
9. A little old lady from Boston refused to travel saying, "Why should I travel? I'm already here."
10. The doctor at the clinic said, however,

EXERCISE 2

1. No, he didn't come. We'll
2. You'll find them where you left them, Son.
3. The boy fought, bit, kicked, and screamed,
4. When I was in high school, I memorized Robert Frost's poem "The Road Not Taken."
5. An Arabian proverb says, "I had no shoes and complained until I met a man who had no feet."
6. You can get the document by writing to the Superintendent of Documents, Government Printing Office, Washington,
7. My mother, who is not a writer herself,
8. The bus driver had been late in starting;
9. The gutters were full of water;
10. Have you read Alvin Toffler's book *The Third Wave*?

EXERCISE 3

1. I've been reading about insects,
2. Adult insects have six legs,
3. Although they are often destructive,
4. Some destroy crops,
5. We followed the trail into the clearing;
6. In 1973 humans made their deepest penetration into the earth— 11,391 feet—in Transvaal, South Africa.
7. Although I've not read *Ghosts*,
8.
9. "The trouble with the average family," said Bill Vaughn, "is that it has too much month left at the end of the money."
10. Coming out of the Capitol, the senator said, "You save a billion here and a billion there, and it soon mounts up."

EXERCISE 4

1. I've been trying to teach my small son to ride a bike,
2. He rides a few feet;
3. He's just not coordinated;
4. He keeps trying,
5. It's harder on me than on him,
6. Since I have learned to write a thesis statement with supporting reasons,
7. I still need to do the following things: improve my spelling, get rid of wordiness,
8. Can the story be true, then, that we read in the paper?
9. The *Christian Science Monitor* and the *Wall Street Journal*
10. "Life," said Samuel Butler, "is like playing a violin solo in public and learning the instrument as one goes on."

EXERCISE 5

1. Water is the only absolutely essential substance for all life. Some organisms can live without oxygen,
2. I finished high school two years ago and now am attending Passaic County Community College.
3. Some people are affected by gloomy weather. It
4. The highest speed ever achieved on land is 631 mph at Bonneville Salt Flats, Utah, on October 23, 1970.
5. The sign in the dentist's office read, "Support your dentist. Eat candy."
6. Who are you going with? Will there be room in the car for me?
7. Have you seen the play *The Glass Menagerie* by Tennessee Williams?
8. He tried to improve his vocabulary by looking up new words, by keeping word lists,
9.
10. Reading improves your understanding of human nature;

Proofreading Exercise 1 (p. 179)

THOSE FAULTY PARTS

I was only ten years old, but I had all the confidence of a great scientist. I had already built a little electric motor and fixed the electric parts in all the toys anyone would bring me. And now I had a magazine article that told how to build a simple battery-powered radio. The directions looked straightforward, *all* I needed was the parts.

My world extended only as far as my bicycle could take me, so the only place I knew of that sold radio parts was the TV repair shop five blocks away. I don't know what the men there first thought of a ten-year-old kid trying to build a radio, but I persisted until one of them gathered up the parts and sold them to me. It cost a few weeks' allowance money, but I *knew* it was going to be worth it.

Well, after a few days of work, I had it *finished*. Admittedly my wiring *didn't* look as neat as that in the picture. As a matter of fact, those people had used a few more wires than I had, but I didn't feel that all of them were really necessary.

But my radio didn't work! And my ten-year-old mind concluded that it must be that the TV repair shop had sold me faulty parts. I bicycled back with my new radio under my arm and demanded an explanation I was upset. After a long discussion, one of the men finally took my radio and started working on it. I think he was afraid I might cry or something.

In about half an hour, and after many changes, he got it working.

"No charge, kid," he said.

"Thank you," I said in my most polite voice, thrilled at the sound of music coming from my radio.

What a feeling of accomplishment! It was as if I'd invented something great. I guess the TV repairman must have had a bit of feeling of accomplishment too as a beaming ten-year-old rode away with a little radio that worked under his arm.

Proofreading Exercise 2 (p. 180)
I DON'T WANT TO

I must have tried to give up smoking a dozen times. Sometimes I'd last

a month/ ~~And~~ *and* sometimes only a day or two. Always I'd start again. Then

it hit me. The trouble was I didn't really want to stop. I was one of those

who say they want to stop but really don't. If people truly wanted to stop,

I reasoned, they would. What I really needed, then, was simply to not

want to smoke.

One day I added up all the negative aspects of smoking—the cost,

the yellow stains on my fingers, the nervousness, the bad breath, the

rotten taste in my mouth every morning, the smoker's cough, the danger

to my health. Then, too, I told myself that smoking was a sign of weak-

ness. I was unable to control myself. I was caught in a habit that big

tobacco companies were continuously promoting. That bothered me. I

was, against my will, doing exactly what some big companies wanted me

to do. *It* ~~it~~ was then I decided that I really didn't want to smoke.

The day I decided I didn't want to smoke, I simply stopped. Oh, it took

a couple of weeks of effort to break the habit, but it's been three years

now, and I haven't had another cigarette. All it took was just not to

want to.

Proofreading Exercise 3 (p. 181)
CURB THAT ENTHUSIASM

There we were, the two of us, in an eight-foot rubber raft, approaching Three Forks Rapids. Neither of us had ever tried river rafting before, and it was scary. We had our life jackets strapped on tight and were bracing ourselves for what might come.

As we were swept along in the incredibly swift current, I held the two oars and tried to direct the raft. Nick, in the front, was ~~suppose~~ *supposed* to watch for rocks and yell out which direction to head, but already the thunder of the water hurtling through the rapids had drowned out his voice. Anyway I was really rowing as hard as I could just to keep the raft pointing downstream, let alone directing it more specifically.

Then came the first big drop! ~~Its~~ *It's* an amazing feeling riding over a sudden four-foot drop in a river. But somehow we stayed upright and landed below in the white foaming water. We cheered and congratulated each other for a moment but then braced ourselves for the next big drop coming right up.

Amazingly we did it. We managed to keep the raft afloat again with both of us still in it.

"Great!" I yelled. "We made 'em both."

"We're good!" Nick shouted.

Laughing and yelling, he turned around, but then as we yelled and laughed, we both ~~happen~~ *happened* to lean the same way, and sure enough, after running the rapids unscathed, we now found the raft ~~tiping~~ *tipping* sideways, and over we went into the calm water . . . .

The *next* time, we told each other as we righted the raft and climbed back on board, we're going to curb our enthusiasm.

Comprehensive Test on Entire Text (p. 183)

1. ~~Its~~ *It's* useless to wait~~,~~*;* ~~hes~~ *he's* probably not coming.

2. If one wants a larger vocabulary, ~~you~~ *one* should study word roots.

3. ~~Spending~~ *I spent* entirely too much time on that one ~~coarse~~ *course* last semester.

4. Dad ~~ask~~ *asked* my sister and me to water the lawn, ~~we was~~ *We were* glad to do it.

5. While they were waiting for ~~there~~ *their* daughter, ~~they're~~ *their* motor stalled.

6. I ~~cant~~ *can't* decide whether to finish my math, study my history, or ~~whether~~

   ~~I should~~ take it easy for a change.

7. If you're going to be ~~hear~~ *here*, Alice, you can answer the phone for me.

8. ~~Your~~ *You're* going with me, aren't you~~.~~*?*

9. We freshmen helped ~~a~~ *an* upperclass student with registration. ~~he~~ *He* really

   appreciated it.

10. I was ~~quiet~~ *quite* sure that ~~Rons~~ *Ron's* car was in the driveway.

11. When we were on our trip, we visited some cities in the ~~south~~ *South*.

12. ~~Which~~ *The cities* had many beautiful old homes and lovely gardens.

13. ~~Its~~ *It's* Mr. ~~Petersons~~ *Peterson's* car, but ~~hes~~ *he's* not driving it.

14. Each of the students ~~are~~ *is* planning ~~a~~ *an* individual report.

15. Looking under the car, *we found* the missing baseball ~~was found~~.

16. ~~Marks~~ *Mark's* grades are always higher than ~~Dougs~~ *Doug's*.

17. "~~Ill~~ *I'll* be ready in a minute," Jeanne said.

18. This semester I'm taking ~~french~~ *French*, history, and ~~english~~ *English*.

19. *The Doll's House*, which I read last year, is a play by Ibsen.

20. She ~~told~~ *said to* her sister, "~~she needed~~ *I need* a new purse."

21. They ~~didnt~~ *didn't* think, however, that they would have time to come back.

22. She was ~~suppose~~ *supposed* to read the short story "The Elephant's Child" from

Rudyard Kipling's book <u>Just So Stories</u>.

23. Whether you agree with me or whether you follow your own ideas *is up to you.*

24. We waited as long as we could. ~~than~~ *Then* we went on without her.

25. ~~Whats~~ "*What's* done to children, they will do to society," wrote Karl Menninger.

Summary of "Can It!" (p. 196)

An antilitter campaign is speading across the country and reducing litter levels as much as 70 or 80 percent in many cities. The CLEAN COMMUNITY SYSTEM, sponsored by nonprofit Keep America Beautiful, Inc., is trying to change people's attitudes through education programs starting in kindergarten and continuing through the schools and in public forums. When a new litter-measuring technique shows people that they have made a difference, they then want to continue. Strict enforcement of new antilitter laws also has helped. The campaign, which depends more on public support than on money, is succeeding in 181 cities across the land.

Summary of "Digging for Roots" (p. 198)

Learning word roots can reveal some interesting stories. Also it's the quickest way to improve your vocabulary. First, looking up the roots of a word will help you remember its meaning. Second, learning the roots of one word will help you learn other words containing the same roots. And finally, learning word roots will give more meaning to words you already know. You can find word roots in your dictionary in square brackets either just before or just after the definition.

Summary of "Simplicity" (p. 200)

Clutter is the disease of American writing. Business letters, reports, brochures, and instructions are not understandable. People are afraid to say things simply. But the secret of good writing is to strip every sentence of unnecessary words and of long words where short ones will do. Clear thinking is necessary for clear writing. If a writer writes carelessly, he'll lose his reader. The writer must constantly ask himself: What am I trying to say? Writing clearly is hard work. Few sentences come out right the first time, or the third. Keep rewriting until you say what you want to say.

Summary of "The Nature of the Universe" (p. 207)

The Universe contains billions of galaxies. Each galaxy contains billions of stars like our sun. Distances in the universe are so great that they're measured in light years. A light year is the distance light travels in one year at the speed of 186,000 miles a second. That is, light travels almost eight times around the earth in one second. Our Milky Way galaxy is about 100,000 light years in diameter, and the faint Andromeda galaxy, one of the closest to us, is so far away that light we now see started coming toward us over two million years ago.